Battle of Britain
Target London

Battle of Britain
Target London

7 September 1940–17 September 1940

Dilip Sarkar MBE FRHistS FRAeS

AIR WORLD

First published in Great Britain in 2024 by
Air World
An imprint of Pen & Sword Books Limited
Yorkshire – Philadelphia

ISBN 978 1 39905 801 8

A CIP catalogue record for this book is
available from the British Library.

Typeset by Mac Style
Printed in the UK by CPI Group (UK) Ltd, Croydon, CR0 4YY.

MIX
Paper | Supporting responsible forestry
FSC® C013604

Pen & Sword Books Limited incorporates the imprints of After the Battle, Atlas, Archaeology, Aviation, Discovery, Family History, Fiction, History, Maritime, Military, Military Classics, Politics, Select, Transport, True Crime, Air World, Frontline Publishing, Leo Cooper, Remember When, Seaforth Publishing, The Praetorian Press, Wharncliffe Local History, Wharncliffe Transport, Wharncliffe True Crime and White Owl.

For a complete list of Pen & Sword titles please contact:

PEN & SWORD BOOKS LIMITED
47 Church Street, Barnsley, South Yorkshire, S70 2AS, England
E-mail: enquiries@pen-and-sword.co.uk
Website: www.pen-and-sword.co.uk
or
PEN AND SWORD BOOKS
1950 Lawrence Road, Havertown, PA 19083, USA
E-mail: uspen-and-sword@casematepublishers.com
Website: www.penandswordbooks.com

Contents

Author's Note and Glossary

The aviation-minded reader will notice that I have referred to German *Messerschmitt* fighters by the abbreviation 'Me' (not 'Bf', which is more technically correct), or simply by their numeric designation, such as '109' or '110'. This not only reads better but is authentic: during the Battle of Britain, Keith Lawrence, a New Zealander, flew Spitfires and once said to me 'To us they were just "Me's", "109s" or "110s", simple, never "Bf".'

In another attempt to preserve accuracy, I have also used the original German, wherever possible, regarding terms associated with the *Luftwaffe*, such as:

Adlerangriff: 'Attack of the Eagles'
Adlertag: 'Eagle Day'
Eichenlaub: The Oak Leaves, essentially being a bar to the Ritterkreuz.
Erprobungsgruppe: Experimental group, in the case of *Erprobungsgruppe* 210, a skilled precision bombing unit.
Experte: A fighter 'ace'. Ace status, on both sides, was achieved by destroying five enemy aircraft.
Fähnrich: Officer cadet.
Fallschirmjäger: Paratroopers.
Freie Hunt: A fighter sweep.
Gefechstand: Operations headquarters.
General der Jagdflieger: General of Fighter Pilots.
Geschwader: The whole group, usually of three *gruppen*.
Geschwaderkommodore: The group leader.
Gruppe: A wing, usually of three squadrons.
Gruppenkeil: A wedge formation of bombers, usually made up of vics of three.
Gruppenkommandeur: The wing commander.
Jagdbomber ('*Jabo*'): Fighter-bomber.
Jagdflieger: Fighter pilot.

Jagdgeschwader: Fighter group, abbreviated JG.
Jagdwaffe: The fighter force.
Jäger: Hunter, in this context a fighter pilot or aircraft.
Kampfflieger: Bomber aircrew.
Kampfgeschwader: Bomber group, abbreviated KG.
Kanal: English Channel.
Katchmarek: Wingman.
Kriegsmarine: German war navy.
Lehrgeschwader: Literally a training group, but actually a precision bombing unit, abbreviated LG.
Luftflotte: Air Fleet.
Oberkannone: Literally the 'Top Gun', or leading fighter ace.
Oberkommando der Heer (OKH): German army high command.
Oberkommando der Luftwaffe (OKL): German air force high command.
Oberkommando der Marine (OKM): German naval high command.
Oberkommando der Wehrmacht (OKW): German armed forces high command.
Ritterkreuz: The Knight's Cross of the Iron Cross.
Rotte: A pair of fighters, comprising leader and wingman, into which the *Schwarm* broke once battle was joined.
Rottenführer: Leader of a fighting pair.
Rottenfleiger: Wingman.
Schwarm: A section of four fighters.
Schwarmführer: Section leader.
Seelöwe: *Sealion*, the codename for Hitler's proposed seaborne invasion of England.
Seenotflugkommando: Luftwaffe air sea rescue organisation.
Stab: Staff.
Staffel: A squadron.
Staffelkapitän: The squadron leader.
Störflug: Harassing attacks, usually by lone Ju 88s.
Stuka: The Ju 87 dive-bomber.
Sturkampfgeschwader: Dive-bomber group, abbreviated StG.
Vermisst: Missing.
Wehrmacht: Armed forces.
Zerstörer: Literally 'destroyer', the term used for the Me 110.
Zerstörergeschwader: Destroyer group, abbreviated ZG.

Each *geschwader* generally comprised three *gruppen*, each of three *staffeln*. Each *gruppe* is designated by Roman numerals, i.e. III/JG 26 refers to the third *gruppe* of Fighter Group (abbreviated 'JG') 26. *Staffeln* are identified by numbers, so 7/JG 26 is the 7th *staffel* and belongs to III/JG 26.

Rank comparisons may also be useful:

Gefreiter:	Private 1st Class
Unteroffizier:	Corporal, no aircrew equivalent in Fighter Command.
Feldwebel:	Sergeant
Oberfeldwebel:	Flight Sergeant
Leutnant:	Pilot Officer
Oberleutnant:	Flight Lieutenant
Hauptmann:	Squadron Leader
Major:	Wing Commander
Oberst:	Group Captain

RAF Abbreviations:

AAF:	Auxiliary Air Force
AASF:	Advance Air Striking Force
A&AEE	Aeroplane and Armament Experimental Establishment
AC1:	Aircraftman 1st Class
AC2:	Aircraftman 2nd Class
ACW1:	Aircraftwoman 1st Class
ACW2:	Aircraftwoman 2nd Class
AFC:	Air Force Cross
AFDU:	Air Fighting Development Unit
AFS:	Auxiliary Fire Service
AHB:	Air Historical Branch
AI:	Airborne Interception radar
AOC:	Air Officer Commanding
AOC-in-C:	Air Officer Commanding-in-Chief
ASR:	Air Sea Rescue
ATA:	Air Transport Auxiliary
ATS:	Armament Training School
BEF:	British Expeditionary Force
CAS:	Chief of the Air Staff

CFS:	Central Flying School
CGS:	Central Gunnery School
CO:	Commanding Officer
DAF:	Desert Air Force
DES:	Direct Entry Scheme
DFC:	Distinguished Flying Cross
DFM:	Distinguished Flying Medal
DSO:	Distinguished Service Order
E/A:	Enemy Aircraft
EFTS:	Elementary Flying Training School
ENSA:	Entertainments National Service Association
FAA:	Fleet Air Arm
FIU:	Fighter Interception Unit
FTS:	Flying Training School
GPC:	Guinea Pig Club
HE:	High Explosive
HF:	High Frequency
HQ:	Headquarters
ITW:	Initial Training Wing
LAC:	Leading Aircraftman
LFB:	London Fire Brigade
LFS:	London Fire Service
MC:	Military Cross
MO:	Medical Officer
MOD:	Ministry of Defence
MRAF:	Marshal of the Royal Air Force
MSFU:	Merchant Ship Fighter Unit
MT:	Motor Transport
MTB:	Motor Torpedo Boat
NCO:	Non-Commissioned Officer
OR:	Other Ranks
ORB:	Operations Record Book
OTC:	Officer Training Corps
OTU:	Operational Training Unit
PDC:	Personnel Distribution Centre
POW:	Prisoner of War

RAE:	Royal Aircraft Establishment
RAFVR:	Royal Air Force Volunteer Reserve
RFS:	Reserve Flying School
RN:	Royal Navy
RNAS:	Royal Navy Air Service
R/T:	Radio Telephone
SASO:	Senior Air Staff Officer
SHAEF:	Supreme Headquarters Allied Expeditionary Force
SMO:	Station Medical Officer
SOO:	Senior Operations Officer
SSC:	Short Service Commission
SSQ:	Station Sick Quarters
TAF:	Tactical Air Force
VHF:	Very High Frequency
UAS:	University Air Squadron
U/S:	Unserviceable
WAAF:	Women's Auxiliary Air Force
WDAF:	Western Desert Air Force

Also:

'Angels' refers to height measured in thousands of feet, hence 'Angles One-Five' means 15,000ft. A 'vector' is a compass course, measured in degrees, a 'Bandit' is a confirmed enemy aircraft while a 'Bogey' and an 'X-Raid' are as yet unidentified but potentially hostile radar plots. 'Tally Ho!' was shouted when the enemy were sighted and the leader was ordering an attack. To the Germans, hostile aircraft were 'Indians' and the German fighter pilot's victory cry was 'Horrido'.

Foreword

As the incoming 696th Right Honourable The Lord Mayor of the City of London, it is with great honour and profound respect that I introduce this compelling account of one of the most critical periods in our city's great history: the Battle of Britain. More specifically, it covers the struggle that played out over the skies of London. This book brings to life the harrowing months of 1940 when our capital faced an existential threat from above, and it is a tribute to the resilience and courage that defined London during its darkest hours.

I was born in 1968, a generation removed from the terror of those times, yet the legacy of the Battle of Britain loomed large over those of us born around that time. Further, although my career has taken me around the globe, London has been the unifying theme. London – the host of the network of networks which constantly refreshes the commercial life of the country – has given me the opportunity to prosper.

During my tenure as the Aldermanic Sheriff of London, I had the unique privilege of residing in the Old Bailey for a year in 2022/23. From this vantage point, I could walk my beloved Italian greyhound around the majestic St Paul's Cathedral – Sir Christopher Wren's remarkable masterpiece – whose survival during the Blitz has become a symbol of London's endurance. The dome of St Paul's stood tall amidst the inferno, a beacon of hope and defiance against the Luftwaffe's relentless onslaught.

This survival was not a mere stroke of fortune but the result of the extraordinary efforts of the Royal Air Force. Without the RAF's tenacity and sacrifice, we might have lost St Paul's and countless other architectural treasures that define the character and history of London. The RAF pilots, often referred to as 'The Few' by Winston Churchill, performed feats of aerial bravery that turned the tide of war and safeguarded the soul of our city.

This book offers a poignant reminder of those perilous days when the skies above London were a battleground. It paints vivid portraits of the young pilots who soared into the fray, knowing that the fate of their country rested on their shoulders. Their heroism, along with the indomitable spirit of London's citizens, forged a legacy of resilience that continues to inspire us today.

Through meticulous research and gripping narrative, this volume not only chronicles the strategic and military aspects of the Battle of Britain but also brings to light the human stories that unfolded beneath the barrage of bombs.

The author and historian Dilip Sarkar captures the essence of a city under siege, where ordinary men and women stood steadfast amidst the ruins, determined to preserve their freedoms and their way of life.

Through these pages, you will gain a deeper appreciation for the sacrifices made to defend London. You will come to understand how close we came to humiliating defeat – which would have meant much worse than losing the architectural marvels that now stand as testaments to our heritage and resilience. The RAF's victory in the skies ensured that London could rise from the ashes, phoenix-like, to rebuild and renew.

In reading this book, may we all be reminded of the enduring spirit of London and the incredible courage of those who fought to protect it. It is their story of valour, resilience, and unwavering determination – qualities that continue to define this great city. May we honour their legacy by cherishing and safeguarding the London they fought so valiantly to save.

Alderman Alastair King DL, November 2024
696th Right Honourable The Lord Mayor of London

Introduction

Target *Loge*

Fighter Command's unsustainable losses of the past few days, coupled with the knowledge that the Germans had now assembled hundreds of invasion barges at the Channel ports, gravely concerned Air Chief Marshal Sir Hugh Dowding, Chief of Fighter Command. Moreover, moon and tide predictions meant that if the Germans were to mount their threatened seaborne invasion, Operation *Seelöwe* would have to set sail over the next few days – before unfavourable autumn weather made such an ambitious sea crossing impossible. Beyond doubt, then, this was now a decisive time for both sides: Britain's survival hung in the balance, and the Germans needed to force a decision, quickly – or lose what was an unexpected and unique opportunity in history to invade and conquer Britain.

In the previous volume, *Airfields Under Attack: 19 August 1940–6 September 1940*, we explored what is generally accepted by the Battle of Britain's popular narrative to have been the most critical phase. In that narrative we are told that 11 Group's airfields were so battered by German bombing that their future as operational bases was hanging by a thread. Our investigation revealed that the period was critical – but not because the airfields were on their knees.

Had the Germans concentrated their efforts on, and not deviated from, airfield targets, however, the story could have been very different – as Air Vice-Marshal Sir Keith Park said himself: 'had he carried on for another week or ten days hammering my fighter aerodromes, I think he might have had them right out of action'. The critical factor by the dawn of 7 September 1940, then, was not that 11 Group's airfields were a shambles – but that Fighter Command was losing pilots, including those with irreplaceable combat experience, at an unsustainable rate. Again, as Park said,

> during the first week in September, I was a very worried man because I was short of pilots; that was the only thing that worried me … I was

> never really grounded through lack of aircraft although we were nearly grounded through lack of pilots on many occasions. We were short of pilots from early in the battle owing to bad planning on the part of the Air Ministry's training department. After the battle was over, truly won, I was sent to Flying Training Command for a year to take over the training of our fighter pilots and the first thing I learned, to my amazement, was that Fighter Command … that Flying Training Command, had never heard throughout 1940, they'd never been told by anybody, that we were desperately short of pilots.
>
> Well, that was my main problem and the reason that I spent every afternoon from after I thought the main attacks were over … 4 or 5 o'clock … I went up to the Northolt aerodrome every afternoon in the week and climbed into my old Hurricane and flew around some of the aerodromes every day, seven days a week in order to talk to the pilots, the flight commanders, the squadron commanders, to see how they were standing the strain – because I was caning them. I was working them to the limits of their physical and mental capacity and we had no relief.

That was the problem especially vexing Air Chief Marshal Dowding as we now forensically investigate the events of 7 September 1940–17 September 1940 – *the* crucial phase in the fighting.

After lunch on the afternoon of 7 September 1940, Dowding held an urgent meeting at Fighter Command HQ to decide measures for 'going downhill' in an economical manner – while providing for a rapid climb back. When losses decreed, depleted squadrons in 11 Group were replaced by those from other groups, which were at full-strength. Freshly trained replacement pilots lacked combat experience, however – and that was an acute problem. The DCAS, Air Vice-Marshal Sholto Douglas, felt that Dowding was being overly 'pessimistic'. Dowding, conversely, was bemused by Douglas's apparent inability to grasp the difference between a trained and a combat-ready pilot – and in any case, there were insufficient trained replacement pilots, combat-experienced or otherwise.

Dowding's SASO, the Australian Air Vice-Marshal Strath Evill, provided figures confirming that in the four weeks ending 4 September 1940, casualties totalled 338, whereas during that period the Operational Training Units had only converted 280 pilots. Air Vice-Marshal Keith Park, a New Zealander, pointed out that his 11 Group was suffering nearly 100 casualties a week. Losing patience, Dowding apparently snapped at the DCAS: 'You *must* realise that we *are* going downhill'.

Douglas's response was to suggest creation of a fourth OTU, but Evill interjected, pointing out the impracticality of this suggestion because it would take too long, Dowding adding that another training unit would be a further drain on precious resources. The solution – arrived at by the ever-able Dowding and his faithful lieutenant, Park – was the 'Stabilising Scheme'.

This categorised fighter squadrons as 'A', 'B' or 'C' units. 'A' were those in the frontline, maintained with a minimum strength of sixteen operational pilots; 'B' were those being rested, with up to six combat-ready pilots, who could be called upon if necessary; 'C' were those currently rebuilding, in quieter northern sectors, having previously suffered heavy losses over southern England, and unlikely, therefore, to be brought to battle. This, then, provided an opportunity for OTU-fresh pilots to receive further operational training on these 'C' squadrons before either rotating south or being posted to 'A' or 'B' units.

When the minutes of the 'Going Downhill' conference were later provided to the DCAS, he objected, claiming that the minutes misrepresented him, casting him in the role of 'Mutt', a foolish music-hall comedian who asked stupid questions. Fighter Command's SASO, Evill, replied that the minutes were virtually verbatim.

Dowding and Park stood firm in the belief that their use of resources was sound, and – especially at such a time of crisis – had no time for Air Ministry incompetence or politics. Unfortunately, they failed to appreciate that their open contempt for the DCAS at this conference had placed them in grave danger from the enemy within – which will become evident in due course. Nonetheless, Dowding's 'going downhill' strategy would now hold the line. What no one in Britain knew, however, was that 7 September 1940 would, regardless of what state the airfields were actually in, prove to be the major turning point in the Battle of Britain.

On the night of 24/25 August 1940, German bombers, intending to attack Rochester and Thameshaven, unintentionally bombed central London – contrary to Hitler's express orders that attacks on the British capital were prohibited without his personal permission (see Volume 4). *Reichsmarschall* Hermann Göring, Hitler's deputy and chief of the Luftwaffe, had also overstepped the mark on 19 August 1940 in his Karinhall memorandum, declaring that he had reserved the personal right to exclusively order raids on London and Liverpool.

The *Reichsmarschall* was furious when he learned that bombs had then been dropped on the British capital without his authority, immediately requiring reports identifying the crews responsible – promising that each aircraft captain involved would be punished and 'posted to infantry regiments'. Churchill was determined to 'return the compliment … upon Berlin', and so that next night saw Bomber Command send Hampdens and Wellingtons to Berlin. The target, however, was covered in cloud; bombs largely fell harmlessly in countryside south of the German capital, although two people were injured in a Berlin suburb and a chalet was destroyed. The effect on German morale, though, was shocking: Göring had assured the German Volk that such a thing would never happen, that it was just not possible for the RAF to bomb Germany; the people believed him. Now, they were left stunned and disillusioned.

Hitler too was furious. On 4 September 1940, he addressed a gathering at the launch of the *Winterhilfe* campaign at the Sportspalast in Berlin-Schöneberg. RAF airmen, he said, had not the courage or skill required to fly across the North Sea and bomb Germany by daylight, but instead did so by night, protected by a cloak of darkness, their bombs dropped indiscriminately on residential areas, farmhouses and villages.

The *Führer* continued:

> You will understand that we must now reply, night for night and with increasing force. And if the British air force drops two, three or four thousand kilos of bombs, then we will drop 150,000, 180,000, 230,000, 300,000 or 400,000 kilos, or more, in one night. If they declare that they will attack our cities on a large-scale, we will erase theirs! We will put a stop to the game of these night-pirates, as God is our witness.

At a stage in the Battle of Britain when the Luftwaffe was actually making significant progress in terms of wearing down Fighter Command, owing to the bombing of Berlin and the loss of prestige for Hitler that entailed, the *Führer*, as Churchill had rightly anticipated, now ordered Göring to retaliate and attack London itself.

Soon after the war, at the Nuremburg Trials, Göring explained:

> I considered the attacks on London useless, and I told the *Führer* again and again that inasmuch as I knew the English people as well as I did my own people, I could never force them to their knees by attacking London. We might have been able to subdue the Dutch people by such measures, but never the British.

The *Luftwaffe War Diaries*, however, do not support Göring's claim, and he, in fact, took personal – and enthusiastic – control of the battle's direction from this point onwards. On 3 September 1940, he had met with his Luftflotten commanders, *Generalfeldmarschalls* Albert Kesselring and Hugo Sperrle, and, according to Kesselring, 'pressed the view that the current tactical policy should now be abandoned in favour of a large-scale assault on the most important target – the English capital'. Sperrle, however, did not accept Göring's view that the enemy fighter force had become too weak to resist such an attack, and argued that the current pressure on Fighter Command's airfields should be maintained.

Kesselring could not understand why Air Chief Marshal Dowding had not withdrawn his fighters north, beyond German fighter range, but believed that Fighter Command must have surely reached this point by now. However, it was clear that the RAF would not be destroyed on the ground, and so the enemy chiefs agreed that the only option was to 'force their last reserves of Spitfires and Hurricanes into the air'. London, it was felt, was the only target likely to provoke this required reaction.

Göring also remained frustrated with his fighter pilots, blaming them, and them alone, for the fact that Fighter Command remained undefeated. In fact, so inaccurate was Luftwaffe intelligence regarding the disposition of Fighter Command, that Göring was even beginning to doubt his fighter pilots' combat claims (which were, in fact, infinitely more accurate, overall, than Fighter Command's). Shortly after the arrival of the *Reichsmarschall*'s personal train, 'Asia', in the Pas-de-Calais, the Luftwaffe Chief sent for *Oberst* Werner Mölders, *Kommodore* of JG 51, and *Major* Adolf Galland, *Kommodore* of JG 26, haranguing and blaming them personally for the Jagdwaffe's perceived failure to date. This is hard to understand – because the fact of the matter was that by operating over south-east England in strength, through a combination of close escort and free-hunting fighter sweeps, the German fighters had well-protected the bombers and inflicted substantial losses on Fighter Command in the process.

Upon conclusion of this forty-minute tirade, Göring asked his two favourite *Kommodoren* what he could do to improve their units' efficiency. Mölders asked for the new DB 601N engine, which performed better at high altitude than the powerplant currently fitted to the Me 109E-4. Galland, however, asked for JG 26 to be re-equipped with Spitfires! Göring was beside himself with rage, missing the point completely: because of a lower wing loading, the Spitfire could easily slow down and turn tightly at low speed, whereas the Me 109's advantage was flying straight and level, climbing and diving at speed – meaning that if tied to a close escort role, the Me 109's flying characteristics were such that German fighter pilots were unable to turn tightly and slowly enough to always see their more ponderous charges.

Galland's point, therefore, was that the Spitfire was much better suited to bomber escort work than the Me 109. From this point onwards, in fact, relations between the Luftwaffe Commander-in-Chief and his fighter arm deteriorated, not least because Göring now insisted that the fighters would remain closely shackled to the bombers at all times. Gone, so far as the *Jagdfliegern* were concerned, was the advantage of initiative and surprise afforded by *Freie Jagd* fighter sweeps, and they were now being forced to undertake a role alien to their psyche as hunters and contrary to the intended function of their machines.

Like the Spitfire and Hurricane, the Me 109 had been designed and intended as a single-engine, short-range, defensive interceptor – not a long-range offensive or escort fighter. That was supposed to be the job of the twin-engine, two-man Me 110 – which, it must be said, performed well during the early phases of the Battle of Britain, especially during the heavy fighting over Portland and Weymouth Bay. The type had since, though, suffered heavy losses – and had demonstrably failed to protect Luftflotte 5's bombers raiding north-east England from bases in Norway on 15 August 1940.

This meant that the enemy's radius of operations was restricted to the range of the Me 109. After the war, General Galland (as he became) commented that German bombers, therefore, could be escorted only to attack targets in less than a tenth of the British Isles – leaving Fighter Command free to rest and rebuild its squadrons in the remaining nine-tenths, concentrating resources on making good losses instead of fighting and being worn down in a wider battle. And, as Galland wrote, that one-tenth was 'extraordinarily well defended'. This, though, included London, which was a crucially important target as a port, an administrative and political hub, and population centre.

Although the Luftwaffe in 1940 lacked the strategic heavy bomber required to destroy London, according to Galland:

> We fighter pilots, discouraged by a task which was beyond our strength, were therefore looking forward impatiently and excitedly to the start of bomber attacks. We believed that only then would the British fighters leave their dens and be forced to give us open battle.

What, though, of Operation *Seelöwe*, the proposed seaborne invasion of southern England?

According to *Generalfeldmarschall* Albert Kesselring, chief of Luftflotte 2, which was to bear the brunt of this latest assault, this new phase saw:

> the scrapping of the invasion idea. Our main assignments were now the disturbance of production and incoming supplies with their underlying purpose of slowing down British armament production and initiating a full-scale economic war. The 'reprisal raids' were also started.
>
> From the new nature of our missions those who could read the signs knew that sentence had been passed on Operation *Seelöwe*, and with it the opportunity missed to exploit a unique chance ... When Hitler ordered a reprisal raid on London this was only an apparent infringement of the new directive, as the targets selected fell under the heading 'Economic War'.

Kesselring's post-war memoir, however, frequently down-plays events, and this is one such example: Operation *Seelöwe* was actually still very much alive. Certainly the clock was ticking towards autumn, when, after mid-September 1940, the uncertain British weather alone would make such a complex sea crossing impossible – but this forthcoming attack on London was fully intended to achieve the aerial superiority Operation *Seelöwe* required. Indeed, it was Hitler's last hope to force the decision, because, as Kesselring wrote, the 'unique chance' arising after the Fall of France would indeed be lost.

According to *Grossadmiral* Erich Raeder, chief of the German navy, on 6 September 1940 Hitler remained undecided regarding a landing in Britain, and still hoped victory could be achieved by other means. Nonetheless, Hitler, still regarded Operation *Seelöwe* as

> the means by which the end of the war can in all probability be achieved at one stroke. The *Führer*, however, is not thinking of carrying out this operation if the risk involved is too great. Its failure ... is on no account to lead to a decisive gain of prestige for Britain.

Beyond doubt, then, the new phase ahead was critical to the future and survival of Operation *Seelöwe*. The Luftwaffe now had to achieve aerial supremacy over southern England – and quickly, if Britain was to be defeated in 1940. As an anonymous German airman wrote, 'I think I can speak for my comrades when I assert that every one of them drops his bombs not because he wants to kill Britons, but because he feels somehow that it's the best way to end the war quickly' – and Hitler's strategy had always been a swift victory over Britain.

From Fighter Command's perspective, an attack on London meant that German bombers had further to fly over south-east England to reach their targets, providing Fighter Command more opportunities for successful interceptions – especially as the Me 109s would only have ten minutes fuel for combat over the capital, thereby stemming Fighter Command's current rate of pilot casualties. Air Vice-Marshal Park was under no illusion as to London's importance as a target, because the capital, which he was charged with defending, contained 'all the main naval docks and a great many of the aircraft factories and all my vital aerodromes ... which were vital to the whole battle'.

The outcome of the phase ahead, then, was equally crucial for Fighter Command and the defence of Britain.

As a target, London, being within range of Me 109 escorting fighters, was vulnerable to air attack – and at the time was perhaps, as the diplomat and historian Philip Ziegler wrote in his superlative *London at War 1939–45*, 'the greatest city in the world'. It was certainly the largest, with a population of 8.3 million compared to New York's 6.93 million. The port of London handled 25 per cent of Britain's imports, nearly 50 per cent more than the country's second port, Liverpool, and more than any other port anywhere in the world.

The City of London, between the poor East End and wealthy West End, was the epicentre of Britain's financial industry, the famous 'Square Mile' handling over 50 per cent of the world's international trade. Furthermore, London was not simply the seat of British government – it was also capital of the British Empire and the focal point of road and rail networks connecting the whole country. Most importantly, London was Britain's royal capital, including the residences of Windsor Castle and Buckingham Palace, while the crown jewels were secured at that ancient fortress and prison, the incomparable Tower of London.

The capital was also Britain's most diverse city, with substantial immigrant populations, although, again as Ziegler wrote, in those days 'Black and brown faces were comparatively rare but not freakish, especially in the East End, and there was a lively Chinese community around the docks'. Nearly a quarter of Britain's 430,000 Jews lived in London, and the migrant population had also been increased by 50,000 refugees, mainly Jewish, fleeing Nazi persecution in Europe. London was also prosperous owing to rearmament, the capital generating 25 per cent of Britain's wealth. London, then, was undoubtedly also the greatest target and prize.

According to Professor Richard Titmuss in *Problems of Social Policy*, London 'was expected to be the target of massed assault by enemy bombers. The theory of a "knock-out blow" which the enemy would aim at the country's nerve centre influenced many of the early plans, and explained much of the birth and development of the wartime emergency services.'

London had already suffered aerial bombardment during the First World War: on 31 May 1915, a German Zeppelin had dropped a ton of bombs on the city, killing seven Londoners and injuring thirty-five more. These nocturnal raids continued for eighteen months, but the German airships themselves were slow and vulnerable, and over time Britain's aerial defences improved until losses inflicted upon the raiders became unsustainable. Consequently the Germans decided on daylight raids using conventional aircraft, the worst being on 13 June 1917 when the East End was attacked by a force of Gotha bombers which killed 162 and injured 426 people.

In total, London suffered 670 fatalities from air attack throughout the First World War – but the fear of air attack had been cemented. Indeed, this was bolstered further still between the wars, when the Spanish city of Barcelona and Basque town of Guernica were savagely bombed by the Luftwaffe, causing substantial damage and loss of life – and, of course, the belief between the wars was that 'The bomber will always get through', as the British Prime Minister Stanley Baldwin famously told the House of Commons in 1931. This was hardly reassuring for British civilians, especially Londoners in what was Britain's prime target.

In 1924, Sir John Anderson had become chair of an Imperial Defence Committee sub-committee researching what precautions could be taken against air raids. An assumption was that London would be attacked immediately in the event of any future war, it being anticipated that 2,000 tons of bombs would be dropped in the initial 24 hours, 150 on day 2 and 100 every day for weeks on end thereafter. After the Spanish Civil War, however, the Air Staff increased the first day's figure to 3,500 tons, causing 58,000 deaths.

The fear of bombing between the wars, especially after Guernica, was almost hysterical on occasion, as former British Prime Minister Harold MacMillan wrote in his 1967 memoir *The Blast of War 1939–1945*, 'We thought of air warfare in 1938 rather as people think of nuclear power today.' The effect of bombing, the British philosopher Bertrand Russell ominously predicted, would turn London into 'one vast raving bedlam, the hospitals would be stormed, traffic will cease, the homeless will shriek for peace, the city will be a pandemonium'. That may well have been an exaggeration, but nonetheless Uri Bialer, in his masterful study *The Shadow of the Bomber: The Fear of Air Attack and British Politics 1932–39* considered that 'the fear of aerial bombardment in inter-war Britain was unprecedented and unique'.

Scaremongering films like *Things to Come*, written by H.G. Wells and brought to cinema screens in 1936 by Alexander Korda, did little to alleviate public concerns: telling the story of 'Everytown' – which deliberately resembled London – flattened by hordes of bombers in a futuristic war beginning in December 1940, the film was considered frightening and realistic. A year later, *The Gap*, written by veteran news broadcaster E.V.H. Emmett, was no more reassuring: an Air Ministry-backed film aimed at encouraging volunteers for Territorial Army anti-aircraft units, the film showed an enemy raid succeeding because such units were deficient in manpower – serving only to emphasise the terrifying paradigm that the bomber always got through.

Similarly, on 6 June 1939, *The Warning* was released, aimed at recruiting Air Raid Precaution volunteers, which tracked the development and successful execution of an enemy raid. From a question of public confidence and morale, an antidote was required to all this doom and gloom – which, ironically, would be delivered by Korda, with support from Churchill and both the ministries of air and information. The result was the first British film of the Second World War, *The Lion Has Wings*, directed by Brian-Desmond Hurst, Michael Powell and Adrian Brunel, and staring Ralph Richardson (who was training to become a FAA pilot), and, again ironically, Ronald Adam – a wing commander and sector controller at Biggin Hill during the Battle of Britain – who played the enemy bomber chief.

For the first time, the Spitfire, which had already won hearts and minds, was star of the show, and those of 74 Squadron specifically were featured, along with Wellingtons of 149 Squadron, assuring the public that, according to Powell, the RAF was perfectly equipped, able and ready to 'blow the Luftwaffe out of the sky'.

At 11.27 hrs on 3 September 1939, minutes after Neville Chamberlain's historic broadcast announcing that Britain and France had declared war on Nazi Germany, air raid sirens wailed across London – sending Londoners scurrying for shelter and fearing that this long-predicted aerial armageddon had arrived. Fortunately, it was a false alarm, the first of many – although as London fireman Vic Flint recorded in his diary (as recorded in Neil Wallington's *Firemen at War*, see Bibliography), the siren had 'put the fear of God into us'.

There was, though, no attempt by either side to administrator a 'knockout blow', not least because neither air force was equipped to do so, both lacking, at the time, four-engine heavy bombers. Moreover, despite certain unhappy rumblings regarding air raid warning policies and often inadequate length of warnings, Daily Home Intelligence Reports and mass observation studies evidence that, on the whole, British civilians had withstood air attacks to date with resilience and fortitude (see Volume 4). In fact, the anticipated turning of a population against its own leaders through bombing had actually generated the bipolar emotion of hatred for the enemy – especially toward the German airmen responsible. Certainly, British cities, especially Liverpool, had suffered heavy bombardment so far, and that Russell's predictions had not come to pass were doubtless encouraging to the War Cabinet. No city, anywhere in the world, however, had yet been subjected to the unprecedented scale of attack that the Luftwaffe now planned for London.

In Greater London, primary buildings were bolstered with sandbags; sticky tape criss-crossed windows in the hope of arresting flying shards of shattered glass and preventing injury; certain premises wore camouflage; anti-invasion obstructions and trenches covered the city's famous parks and open spaces; air raid shelters had sprung up hither and thither, along with concealed strongpoints; men and women in uniform could be seen everywhere; everyone, from children to the elderly, carried a gasmask, and the silver barrage balloons of the 'Great London Barrage' swayed in numbers over the capital. According to *Roof Over Britain: The Official Story of The AA Defences 1939–1942*, though:

> London at this time was not adequately defended. All over England there was still a shortage of anti-aircraft guns, and as we might be attacked anywhere, it was essential to give cover to all our large cities. In the Thames Estuary a considerable concentration of anti-aircraft guns had built up, because many of the German daylight attacks had been made via the Thames Estuary.

It would imminently become evident that London's defences needed doubling urgently. Re-siting gun batteries, however, was complicated and took time, requiring the levelling of positions, telephone lines laying and coordinating into the System.

The official account makes clear, though, that the guns' primary function was not necessarily the destruction of enemy aircraft but more the disruption of bombing attacks or, preferably, preventing the enemy reaching its intended targets, all achieved by forcing the enemy to fly at high altitude, thereby making accurate bombing difficult or impossible, and render enemy formations unable to fly the straight and level course required to achieve results.

The guns involved were the 4.5-inch heavy gun, which hurled a high explosive shell to a height of eight miles in fifty seconds, and the 3.7-inch, which could fire almost as high, with a smaller shell and higher rate of fire. There were even some 3-inch relics from the First World War, also with a high rate of fire, sending up high explosive or shrapnel shells every three seconds. Then there was the lighter Bofors, firing 120 two-pound shells per minute up to 6,000ft. Each heavy battery comprised two, four, six or eight guns, the battery normally being of four guns divided into two sites – which could be several miles apart. The noise of the guns, regardless of their effectiveness, also contributed to morale, this violent cacophony giving civilians hope and heart that the defences were hitting back at their tormentors.

For the London Fire Brigade, the greatest test of all was imminent. In 1939, professional firemen formed the service's core, supplemented by 23,000 auxiliary volunteers, men and women from all walks of life – including conscientious objectors. Most of the volunteers, however, were inexperienced in fire-fighting by the time the outbreak of hostilities saw them called up – and no one had experience of the huge conflagrations the LFB would soon be dealing with. Since 1933, the LFB and Home Office had planned for war, a greater priority being placed on this work after the bombing of Madrid and Guernica in the Spanish Civil War.

With its great docks and wharves, London was particularly vulnerable to the magnesium burning incendiary bomb, sparks easily being carried by wind and blast to ignite nearby properties – including warehouses packed with highly inflammable exports such as fat and oil products. The LFB's red Leyland, Merryweather and Albion fire appliances were accommodated at its fifty-nine fire stations, their pumps capable of 1,000 gallons per minute, and turntable ladders reaching 100ft high. Much smaller trailer pumps also existed, capable of being towed by an ordinary car, and all such emergency equipment had been issued directly by the Home Office and in increasing quantities since 1938. That year also saw the first Auxiliary Fire Service substations commissioned, three subsequently opening in the City of London, the remainder in the primary docklands target area.

When war broke out, the fire service changed to a regional structure, Greater London comprising the LFB and sixty-six smaller brigades, all within the London Fire Service, with a mutual aid system in place so that in the event of a huge fire, a regional fire officer could expect assistance from neighbouring regions. London's regional fire officer was Aylmer Firebrace, whose responsibility was enormous, although the region was sub-dived into five districts, each controlled by assistant regional fire officers.

These men had many serious concerns, not least the vulnerability to bombing of London's water supplies – leading to an investment of £500,000 by the government in 1938 to provide additional steel mains exclusively for fire-fighting. Short-spur mains were also installed in anticipation of the flammability of the dwellings surrounding the heart of the city. Fireboats, able to pump 4 tons of water per minute, saw to using the natural water resource provided by the great River Thames, the boats piping this water inland for further sharing. The LFB operated three such boats from the same number of floating fire stations on the Thames, and by the beginning of 1940 the AFS were operating ten more fireboats at six more stations, and eight barges, towed by tugs, enabled the use of further pumps.

By April 1940, however, the lack of action saw an exodus of auxiliaries leaving the AFS – nearly 50 per cent by June 1940. Morale was low. Like everyone else in Britain, what the fireman did not know when 7 September 1940 dawned was that their finest hour – and with it infernos of inconceivable proportions – was just hours away.

Across the Channel, the OKL's plan for the surprise attack on London, starting on 7 September 1940, was as follows:

> While Luftflotte 3 operates at night, during the day Luftflotte 2, using single and twin-engine fighter formations at the same time, will carry out attacks until the dock installations and the city's power and other supplies are destroyed. The city is divided into two target areas: Target Area A comprises East London with its extensive dock installations, while Target Area B covers West London with the city's power supply plants and supply installations.

Although blissfully unaware of it, Londoners were about to endure the capital's worst ordeal since the Black Death (1346–1353) and Great Fire (1666). The Battle of London was about to begin, a contest between the resolve of unarmed civilians against high explosive and incendiary bombs, and air mines, a battle propelling the fire, police, ambulance and medical services into the van of the Home Front – and many an unlikely hero would emerge from the impending carnage.

Appropriately, the Luftwaffe codeword for London was *Loge* – the fire God of Norse legend. Hitler was a great admirer of the composer Richard Wagner, whose work included *Der Ring des Nibelungen* (The Ring of the Nibelungen). At the end of the fourth act, *Das Rheingold*, *Loge*, having decided that the other Gods are corrupt, decides to destroy Valhalla by fire.

In the final scene, *Loge* is killed by Wotan, the chief God, but flames still rear up from his corpse, destroying the other Gods and Valhalla. Considering the ultimate consequences for the Nazi regime of the new phase's outcome, some may recognise some ironic parallels there.

Arguably, the bombing of London was the start of Germany losing the Second World War – a Wagnerian *Twilight of the Gods* indeed …

Target London

A Diary
7 September 1940– 17 September 1940

Saturday, 7 September 1940

The morning was surprisingly quiet, Eastender Violet Regan remembering it as: 'Beautiful. The warm sun shone from a clear blue sky onto the little streets of Cubitt Town, Isle of Dogs. No premonition of the terrible ordeal that was to be endured for the rest of the day and night occurred to me as I went about my usual chores.'

It was ominously quiet in Air Vice-Marshal Park's underground Operations Room at 11 Group HQ, Uxbridge. Joan Fanshawe (née Moxon) had been a WAAF 'Ops "B"' plotter – straight from school – there since July, who remembered the airfield attacks as a 'very hectic time'. This particular morning was different:

> Sometimes, if it was quiet, we were doing absolutely nothing … just reading books or drinking tea. If the weather was bad, there was nothing you could do, so you were just sitting doing nothing – chatting. As soon as a raid came up, everything dropped – you went straight to work. There were always floor supervisors around – usually two. And they were making certain we behaved. I think we knew that we were doing something important. When we were really busy, when these big German raids came over, there was no time to think of anything, you were just thinking of putting the next plot on. You didn't have time to think of who was up in the air, or what was going on or anything, we were just merely putting plots on. We were just little minions putting the plots on – the big decisions were being made up above us [reproduced with kind permission of The Battle of Britain Bunker].

And 'big decisions' would certainly be made this day, regardless of the slow start – which gave no inkling of what lay ahead.

That morning, Air Vice-Marshal Park took advantage of the lack of enemy activity to issue his twelfth instruction to Group and Sector Controllers regarding the 'Interception of enemy bomber formations':

1. From reports by RAF personnel at aerodromes, also from AA gun stations, and lastly from our own fighter formations, it is evident that during the past week some enemy bomber formations have proceeded uninterrupted to their inland objectives. This has happened on numerous occasions when we have had from twelve to twenty squadrons despatched to intercept and to cover aerodromes. The reason is mainly that our fighters are patrolling so high that they are normally becoming heavily engaged with the enemy fighter screen, flying above 20,000ft.
2. On one occasion yesterday, only seven out of eighteen squadrons despatched, engaged the enemy. On another occasion on the same day, seven out of seventeen squadrons engaged the enemy.
3. It is obvious that some of our controllers are ordering squadrons intended to engage bombers to patrol too high. When Group order a squadron to 16,000ft, Sector Controller in his superior knowledge, adds on one or two thousand, and the squadron adds on another two thousand in the vain hope that they will not have any enemy fighters above them. The net result has been that daily some of the enemy bomber formations slip in under 15,000ft, frequently without any fighter escort, and bomb their objectives, doing serious damage as at Brooklands. In fact, the majority of the enemy bomber formations have only been intercepted after they have dropped their bombs on the way out.

This was a barely concealed rebuke to sector controllers. As the 11 Group Controller, Wing Commander Lord Willoughby de Broke, said, Park 'would leave it to us to set the stage, then review the situation and make the necessary changes'. Nonetheless, it was now clear that in future sector controllers were to follow, to the letter, orders issued by the Group Controller – enabling the leader in the air to then decide the best response once the enemy was sighted. Park's orders also meant that in future, the main German thrust would be intercepted by a strong defensive force between the coast and target, which, it was assumed, would be one of the sector stations around London.

Ideally, squadrons would give battle in pairs, and Spitfires, with their superior high-altitude performance, were to engage the enemy fighter screen, which frequently operated at 20,000ft or more. Hurricane squadrons were to focus on attacking the enemy bombers, which operated lower down, at around 15,000ft and a few thousand feet above, thus better suiting that fighter's medium altitude performance. Two squadrons were to defend the close-by aerodromes of Kenley, Biggin Hill and Croydon, while those airfields to the west and south-west would be 10 Group's responsibility. North of the Thames, the plan was that 12 Group would provide cover, allowing the 11 Group squadrons holding the fort there to go forward and join the fighting further south. If necessary, should 12 Group's airfields be threatened (as indeed they had been), assistance could be requested from 11 Group via Fighter Command HQ Operations Room.

Air Vice-Marshal Park was not yet to know it, but his airfields would not be the enemy's target this day.

Across the Channel, *Generalfeldmarschall* Kesselring's staff officers had been busy – and the detailed operational orders decided for this first major attack on *Loge* by I and II *Fliegerkorps* was about to become reality. At 17.00 hrs (BST) the initial attack was to be made by one *Kampfgeschwader* of II *Fliegerkorps*, the purpose being to 'force English fighters into the air so that they will have reached end of their endurance at time of main attack'.

That main bombardment, by II *Fliegerkorps* was to begin forty minutes later, and five minutes afterwards elements of I *Fliegerkorps*, reinforced by II *Fliegerkorps*' KG 30, would continue the destruction. For the main attack, the Ju 88s of KG 30 and II/KG 76 would be positioned on the right, KG 1's He 111s in the centre, and Do 17s of I and III/KG 76 on the left.

Determined to keep his bomber losses to a minimum, *Reichsmarschall* Göring deployed 648 fighters, shackling one *Jagdgeschwader* to each *Kampfgeschwader*: JG 26 for KG 30, JG 54 for KG 1 and KG 27 for KG 76; somewhat optimistically, the Me 110s of ZG 76 were tasked with clearing 'the air of enemy fighters of I *Fliegerkorps*' targets, thereby covering the attack and retreat of bomber formations'.

The fighters and bombers were to rendezvous over the French coast. Because the Me 109s were operating at the extremity of their range, there was no time to waste and the bombers were to fly directly to their targets, KG 30's formation staggered between 15,000–17,000ft, KG 1 18,000–20,000ft, and KG 76 15,000–17,000ft, this intended to 'provide maximum concentration of the attacking force'. The Operational Order made the intention clear, which was: 'to complete the operation by a single attack. In the event of units failing to arrive directly over target, other suitable objectives in *Loge* may be bombed from altitude of approach'.

No clue, however, is given as to what was considered a 'suitable' alternative target.

Having bombed, the enemy crews were briefed to make a starboard turn before returning to the Kentish coast via Maidstone and Dymchurch, returning to France across the Channel, only leaving the fighters over the Pas-de-Calais.

The 'main objective of the operation', the Order concluded, was 'to prove that the Luftwaffe can achieve this' – evidencing that doubt existed in certain quarters of the OKW.

After dark, the Germans planned no respite for the defenders or beleaguered Londoners: night-bombers, mainly from Luftflotte 3, guided to their targets by *Loge*'s fires, were to continue the assault.

The Daily Home Intelligence Report, 7 September 1940:

> Morale is unchanged ... There is evidence to show that night raids cause far more upset to people than daylight raids ... Regional complaints that London receives excessive publicity for its raids, both in the press and on the wireless, while important provincial towns have to hide their identity even from themselves.

Generaloberst Ulrich Grauert, chief of I *Fliegerkorps*, however, was heartily recommending 'ruthless terror attacks as reprisals against big cities' – and London was Britain's biggest city. It is unlikely that anyone, anywhere, would envy London for the publicity this day would generate all over the world.

Having been depressed by the Luftwaffe's failure to date, *Reichsmarschall* Göring was now inspired by the new plan, arriving in the Pas-de-Calais on his personal, luxurious train, 'Asia', to enthusiastically take personal command of the attack on London. 'Asia' was preceded by another train of ordinary coaches and flatbeds of road vehicles. The command train had anti-aircraft guns at either end; Göring's coach comprised two bedrooms, an office, comparatively luxurious toilet facilities; a second coach served as a sitting and projection room, while a third served as his command post and operations room, and the fourth a diner. Guests and staff officers were accommodated in subsequent carriages – the entourage including the drug-addicted *Reichsmarschall*'s devoted nurse, Christina Gormanns, and his physician, Dr Robert Kropp.

This was the first time, in fact, that Göring had personally visited the Channel coast – and did so now to fulfil his prophecy of two years previously to General Hellmuth Felmy, at that time commander of Luftflotte 2, that one day so many German aircraft would attack London that the sky would darken. That day had come. Upon arrival, Göring's cavalcade visited various units before descending with his entourage on *Generalfeldmarschall* Kesselring's forward command post on the cliffs at Cap Gris-Nez to await events.

That morning, only the odd German reconnaissance bomber was active over Britain. At 08.40 hrs, a section of 12 Group's 266 Squadron's Spitfires, New Zealanders Pilot Officers Wycliff Williams and Richard Trousdale, and Pilot Officer Robert Roach, were:

> Ordered from Coltishall to patrol Yarmouth at 25,000ft and subsequently vectored towards enemy aircraft first sighted at 09.00 hrs West of Norwich at 30,000ft. Tally Ho given but due to dazzle E/A twice lost sight of. When next seen was at 23,000ft approx. twenty miles NW of Walcheran Island. Chase continued eastwards until nearly over the Island when Section made a surprise attack. E/A made no evasive tactics but one of our aircraft experienced cannon fire from rear. After further attacks, black smoke poured from starboard engine of E/A which was seen to go into a vertical dive and crash in flames. No casualties to pilots or aircraft of this Squadron. [ORB]

It had been a long chase over the North Sea, the interception occurring at 09.37 hrs (no record of which Do 17 this was, however, has been found). Next into action were Spitfires of 10 Group's 152 Squadron: at 10.30 hrs, 20,000ft over Lyme Regis, ten miles out to sea and heading South, Green Section, Pilot Officer Walter Beaumont and Sergeant John Christie, reportedly sighted a Do 215 and gave chase, catching and attacking the bomber which was last seen flying out of sight, towards the Channel Islands, emitting smoke from its starboard engine.

The first actual attack came in soon after 11.00 hrs: some seventy enemy aircraft crossed the coast at Folkestone and separated, one formation flying west to Hastings, the remainder fanning out over east Kent. Two waves of bomb-carrying Me 109s were bound for the coastal airfield at Hawkinge; the Station ORB describes what happened next:

> The Station was today attacked by Me 109s, six to twelve in number, flying at about 1,500ft, at 11.25 hrs. Eighteen bombs, the largest being 250lbs were dropped in line straddling the Officers' Mess, the one undamaged Hangar, the Camp and old HQ office buildings and across the North side of the aerodrome, the last falling in Hawkinge village.
>
> Casualties were: one soldier killed, six soldiers, three civilians, two airmen and one officer slightly wounded. Four cases only to Hospital. A number of civilians, probably six, were killed by a direct hit on a civilian shelter in Hawkinge Village.
>
> The aerodrome defences came into immediate action. No damage was sustained by defence equipment. A direct hit demolished part of the hutted accommodation called 'Hostel', and another hit destroyed the Station HQ office building. One small crater in the centre of the aerodrome and several craters around the northern perimeter.
>
> The aerodrome remained serviceable if care taken. No aircraft on the ground were damaged. No GPO 'Red' warning was received in time [referring to the air raid warning given, or lack thereof], but the Camp siren was sounded on receipt of AA 'Red' warning and direct observation of enemy aircraft approaching – a little less than one minute before the attack. A certain amount of machine gunning of the aerodrome accompanied the bombing.

Killed in the shelter hit at Mill Lane, Elham, were War Reserve Constable Henry Kettle, and his wife, Helen, both aged 30, and Henry's mother, Annie Kettle, aged 60, and 21-year-old PC Ronald Parker.

Hawkinge was the closest airfield to the Germans and so was vulnerable for that reason, making it difficult to defend from surprise attacks such as this.

Flight Lieutenant Peter Brothers:

> I flew Hurricanes with 32 Squadron, and during our time at the coastal aerodromes at Hawkinge and Manston, or even further inland at Biggin Hill, we were often scrambled late. The Controller obviously had to ensure that it was the real thing and not a 'spoof' to get us airborne and catch us whilst refuelling. This was frustrating at forward bases as there was so little time anyway.

There was also a little action over mid-Wales, when at 12.30 hrs Sergeant Lionel Pilkington, a trainee fighter pilot converting to Spitfires at 7 OTU, Hawarden, near Chester, intercepted and attacked a Ju 88 of 3(F)/123 which was on a reconnaissance of Bristol and Liverpool. With a disabled engine, at 12.30 hrs the bomber force-landed at Hafotty-y-Bulch, Mallwyd, Machynlleth, on the southern edge of what is now the Snowdonia National Park; the crew were captured.

Afterwards, the RDF screens and plotting tables went strangely blank for some hours. What was happening? The weather was good and heavy attacks on airfields were anticipated. To quote Trevor Howard, playing Air Vice-Marshal Park in the 1969 film *Battle of Britain*, 'The bastards are up to something.' But what?

At 15.30 hrs, RDF began reporting the assembly of German formations over the Pas-de-Calais. Fifteen minutes later a small German force, which had been patrolling the Dover Strait, swept over New Romney. By 15.55 hrs, one enemy formation was over Cap Gris-Nez, a second was ten miles off Dunkirk and heading for the Thames Estuary, and a third was flying west, between St Omer and Boulogne. The estimated total of aircraft involved suggested that this was the biggest challenge Fighter Command had faced so far.

On the cliffs at Cap Gris-Nez, Göring, Kesselring, General Bruno Loerzer, commander of II *Fliegerkorps*, and various high-ranking staff officers watched excitedly as 348 bombers escorted by 617 fighters passed overhead. This massive formation of nearly 1,000 aircraft occupied a staggering twenty-mile wide front, stepped up a mile-and-a-half high and spread out over 800 square miles. The sky had indeed darkened, the noise deafening – and, as the illustrious *Reichsmarschall* said: 'If we lose now, we deserve to have our arses kicked.' Looking up at the Luftwaffe's might roaring towards London, wave after wave, it was no doubt difficult to comprehend that Germany could lose. Göring was in his element; ecstatic in what he believed would be recorded by history as his triumphal hour.

At 16.20 hrs, 253 Squadron was scrambled from Kenley to patrol Thameshaven; 504 went up from Hendon with orders to patrol Canterbury, and 249 took-off from North Weald to cover Maidstone, all at 15,000ft. A wing of two Northolt squadrons, 1 and 303, were ordered to patrol north-east London at 20,000ft. Between 16.30 and 16.37 hrs, four more German formations were detected, two of just six aircraft or less off Beachy Head, an even lesser number off Dover, twenty plus off Dungeness, and the fourth, of unspecified size, crossed the coast over New Romney at 16.37 hrs.

This represented a broad front – but what was the main target and which of these multiple formations would attack it? As ever, the 11 Group Sector Controller did not know the answer, and could only guess, based upon experience, the enemy's intention – which also meant trying not to be drawn into reacting in strength to what may be a diversionary raid. Nonetheless, with four enemy formations detected, between 16.35 and 16.40 hrs, 43 Squadron was scrambled from Tangmere and sent to Beachy Head; 111 from Croydon to Maidstone; 79 Squadron from Biggin Hill to patrol base, and 501 Squadron from Gravesend, also to patrol base. At 16.40 hrs, an enemy formation of twenty plus crossed in over Folkestone, and the Observer Corps reported fifty plus over Hythe, flying north-west, and five minutes later another force came in between Dover and Deal, steering north-west.

At the same time, 603 Squadron was scrambled from Hornchurch to patrol base, and 'A' Flight of 66 Squadron was ordered up from Kenley to patrol base.

At 16.30 hrs, rightly anticipating that this was an attack of unprecedented scale, 11 Group requested, via Fighter Command HQ Operations Room, assistance from 12 Group – which was exactly the opportunity Air Vice-Marshal Trafford Leigh-Mallory and Squadron Leader Douglas Bader were waiting for to deploy the new 'Duxford Wing'. At 16.45 hrs the wing, comprising the Duxford-based Hurricanes of 242 and 310 Squadrons, and the Fowlmere Spitfires of 19, was scrambled to patrol North Weald at 10,000ft.

Bader, however, climbed the wing higher – arriving over the allocated patrol line at 15,000ft. No.12 Group's arrival then permitted certain 11 Group detachments patrolling north of the Thames to head south – and more 11 Group squadrons were scrambled at 17.00 hrs: 1(RCAF) Squadron went up to patrol its Northolt base; a Flight of 72 Squadron from Croydon to patrol the Thames Estuary, and 46 Squadron from Stapleford Tawney also headed for North Weald. Assistance was also requested from 10 Group, sending the Spitfires of 234 and 609 squadrons hurrying towards London. Twenty-one squadrons, or elements thereof, were scrambled, therefore, to patrol the airfields surrounding London.

At 17.00 hrs, three waves of bombers – eighty in total – escorted by fighters were over Rochester, heading west. The barrage loosed off by the Medway AA gunners signalled the start of what would be an epic air battle. Although detail is scant, the first defending squadron in action was possibly 501 Squadron, which engaged 'the largest formation of the war [ORB]', at 17.00 hrs over Maidstone, Flight Lieutenant John Gibson subsequently claiming a damaged Me 110.

Also at 17.00 hrs, 1 Squadron, which had taken off to patrol with the Poles of 303 Squadron, engaged the incoming raiders over the Thames Estuary and Essex, Flight Lieutenant John Holderness claiming a 'Do 215 [*sic*]' destroyed and Sergeant Arthur Clowes an Me 110. The 303 Squadron ORB details events:

> Combat over Essex about 17.00 hrs. About forty Do 215 [*sic*] with Me 109s behind … Patrol eastwards at 15,000ft, then 20,000ft. Flight Lieutenant Forbes took the Squadron to 24,000ft and got into position above and partially up-sun. Enemy was travelling northwards and when 1 Squadron attacked his tail turned eastwards. Flight Lieutenant Forbes led Squadron in formation to attack the bombers on quarter, out of the sun. Protecting fighters only came into action after the first attack was finished. After bringing down one Dornier, Flight Lieutenant Forbes was wounded slightly and damage to aircraft caused him to return, landing safely …
>
> The following officers scored: Pilot Officer Zumbach two Do's. Flying Officer Henneberg one Me 109 and one probable. Flight Lieutenant Forbes one Do destroyed and one probable. Flight Lieutenant Paskiewicz two Do's destroyed. Pilot Officer Lokuciewski one Do destroyed and one probable. Flying Officer Pisarek one Me 109. Flying Officer Urbanowicz one Do destroyed and one Me 109 probable. Pilot Officer Daszewski one Do destroyed and one probable. Sergeant Szaposznikow

> one Do destroyed and one Me 109 destroyed. Sergeant Wojtowicz two Do's destroyed. Squadron returned independently having expended their ammunition.

The Poles had benefited from 1 Squadron attacking simultaneously and the Spitfires of 41 and 72 squadrons entering the battle over action around the same time. Most important, having climbed much higher, 303 Squadron had the advantage of height and sun. Nonetheless, the claims arising, it must be said, bear little resemblance to reality: only two Do 17s (no 215s were actually involved) were lost over England, and there were various claims by other squadrons for Dorniers destroyed.

As frequently demonstrated in this narrative, aircraft identification, however, was frequently inaccurate, and it is possible that certain of 303's claims actually concerned Me 110s of ZG2, which lost seven aircraft that afternoon, although some of these are attributed to the Duxford Wing. With over 1,000 aircraft involved, it is often pointless to try and ascertain who shot down who, which is really the case here – and the times and locations recorded in pilots' personal combat reports and other official records are also frequently unreliable. That 303 Squadron, though, substantially overclaimed, like, in due course, the Duxford Wing, is demonstrable.

Whatever the truth of it, the Poles' bravery and tenacity is, of course, indisputable – and some execution had undoubtedly occurred. This, however, was not entirely without loss: Pilot Officer Jan Daszewski – who had scored combat victories during the Polish campaign – was shot down by Me 109s and baled out, badly wounded. Pilot Officer Marian Pisarek – soon to become a fighter ace and highly successful fighter leader – was also shot down, baling out, unhurt. Unfortunately, his Hurricane crashed into the back garden of 40 Roding Road, Loughton, demolishing an air raid shelter and killing the three civilian occupants. Like Forbes, Flying Officer Henneberg was also shot-up by 109s, and returned safely to Northolt.

Shortly after 1 and 303 Squadrons left Northolt, 1(RCAF) Squadron followed them into the air with orders to patrol base. The Canadians sighted part of the huge German formation bombing London were but forbidden to engage by the Northolt Sector Controller, who was mindful of the need to maintain defence of base.

Like Northolt's other two squadrons, however, the seven Spitfires of Croydon's 72 Squadron entered the fray over the Thames shortly after 17.00 hrs, Flying Officer John Villa and Sergeant John White both claiming He 111 'probables' east of Rochester. Sergeant White, however, was hit by return fire and forced-landed at Eynsham – watched by Flying Officer Villa, who 'circled round him in case enemy fighters should attack him'; White was safe but wounded in the leg and forehead. Flight Lieutenant Thomas Elsdon, a Cranwellian and on this occasion 'Tennis Leader', claimed an Me 109 'probable', but was also shot-up and severely wounded in a knee and shoulder. Unable to bale out, the pilot made it to Biggin Hill where, unable to lower his undercarriage, he made a wheels-up crash-landing.

No.41 Squadron, up from Hornchurch, also engaged at 17.00 hrs and in the same area, claiming a Do 17 destroyed, one probably destroyed and another damaged, and a 'Do 215 [*sic*]' damaged in addition to one Me 109 destroyed, another claimed as a probable and one damaged. Again, these successes were not without loss: Sergeant Robert Ford was shot down and safely forced-landed, unhurt, at West Hanningfield; similarly, Sergeant John McAdam was shot-up and crash-landed near Rayleigh, where his Spitfire burned out, and Pilot Officer Oliver Morragh-Ryan's Spitfire was damaged in the action, his undercarriage collapsing when he forced-landed near Basildon, although the pilot was unhurt.

The Hurricanes of 249 Squadron also intercepted 'Raid 22' before it bombed, as the unit's Intelligence Patrol Report detailed:

> About thirty He 111s and Do 17s were seen heading for London at 19,000ft, escorted by at least 100 fighters, mostly Me 109s, stepped-up behind to 25,000ft. Enemy bombers were in three parallel lines each of three vics in line-astern. Our fighters attacked broadside on and one vic of bombers was seen to be left straggling behind, smoking, but it was impossible to say which of our pilots were responsible. Enemy formation turned aside from London and went East, just South of North Weald aerodrome.

Pilot Officer Tom Neil 'destroyed an Me 109 which broke up and turned over and went down smoking near Maidstone, although he did not see it crash'. Pilot Officer George Barclay 'destroyed an Me 109 which emitted brilliant flames and black smoke from the cockpit. It dived steeply and pieces fell off, but he did not see it crash; this was South of Maidstone.' Barclay also damaged by a Do 17 and a He 111 but was hit by return fire from the latter, consequently crash-landing at Harlow, fortunately unhurt. Sergeants Richard Smithson and Fred Killingback were both shot down by Me 109s, baling out wounded over Maidstone, and Flying Officer Patrick Wells was hit by a He 111's return fire and baled out over Faversham. Pilot Officer Robert Fleming, a former member of the London University Air Squadron, was shot down by an Me 109 and killed, crashing at Hollingbourne.

That afternoon, 7-year-old Eastender Ken James had been out playing with the Harding twins before being called in by his mother for tea when the sirens sounded, sending the family hurrying to the Anderson shelter in their garden:

> Soon the sound of aircraft could be heard and my dad called me up to see a great mass of planes flying up the Thames. They seemed to darken the sky. Then the bombs started to fall. We crouched in the shelter, which shook with each explosion. Suddenly a tremendous bang was heard … it was a direct hit on the Hardings' shelter, killing them and their whole family excepting the elder brother who was attending a wedding.

When the preliminary warning sirens wailed over London at 16.33 hrs, Violet Regan, for whom the day had begun so beautifully, was about to sit down and eat with her husband, a member of the Poplar Heavy Rescue Service. After so many alerts the couple were complacent and did not take cover. The sound of heavy gunfire, though, sent them out to watch proceedings from outside their Anderson shelter:

> Very soon we heard the ominous drone of distant aeroplanes – German aeroplanes. I remember the rising excitement of our neighbours as they anxiously called to each other. The frantic barking of the dogs … Suddenly, there they were, silhouetted clearly against the blue sky. They consisted of three separate flights and headed in our direction … altogether … over one hundred planes.

> I watched in horror as bombs fell from the planes. My husband yelled at me to take cover, then he was gone, to join his colleagues at the Heavy Rescue Depot in neighbouring Millwall. I helped calm my terrified neighbour and her three children who were screaming with fright and stayed with them until their parents arrived. Then I went into my own shelter.
>
> For a long time I sat listening to the awful bedlam going on outside: bombs exploding, clanging fire bells, and during lulls the crying of terrified children and voices of adults trying to soothe them. The barking of hysterical dogs went on and on. There seemed to be no let-up or respite from the awful din. I thanked God that my two little girls were safe in the Oxfordshire countryside; although sadly missed, they were spared this horror.
>
> Later on I heard someone calling my name. It was our Air-Raid Warden, who informed me that time bombs had fallen in the vicinity of a nearby oil-storage facility and the tanks were liable to explode at any minute. Everyone must leave their homes and take refuge at nearby Glengall Road School.

The Reverend Maurice Wood, watching events from the safer distance of Westminster, remembered the German formations as 'majestic'. The first bombs fell on West and East Ham, Canning Town, Silver Town, the Royal Docks and the Woolwich Arsenal. Then, further upstream, the Surrey Commercial Docks was hit – where 1.5 tons of imported, highly flammable, timber were stored. High explosives blew buildings apart, and incendiaries wickedly set light to factories, dockyard installations and domestic dwellings without prejudice. Immediately, fire stations became inundated with calls for help, and, such was the scale of the conflagrations – fireman's parlance for an out of control and spreading blaze – that just thirty minutes after the first bombs crashed down the fire control centre at West Ham was urgently requesting 500 more pumps from London Regional Control.

As the docklands burned, the initial local fire response made little impression on the flames; within hours, hundreds more pumps would be deployed and shared between the London, West India and St Katharine's Docks on the north bank of the Thames below iconic Tower Bridge. To

Peter Blackmore, an AFS fireman among the first responders, 'Everything seemed to be on fire in every direction, even some barrage balloons in the sky were exploding. The cinder-laden smoke which drifted all around us made one think of the destruction of Pompei. [reproduced with kind permission of Neil Wallington, see Bibliography].'

As Hackney became wreathed in smoke, flame and death, Ted Harrison thought, 'Blimey! We've lost the war.' Strangely, the guns were silent, though; Violet Regan: 'Somebody screamed "What's the matter with our guns? They haven't fired a shot!" It was true. Apart from the salvo loosed off at the beginning of the raid, no gun had fired a shot in our defence.' Moreover, up defending airfields and outwitted by the enemy's change of direction and surprise attack, Fighter Command had failed to prevent or disrupt the attack – although certain defending squadrons had engaged.

High above the flames, Squadron Leader Bader and the Duxford Wing's attention to the enemy was alerted by the Medway gunners' initial volley, the enemy then sighted to the wing's east at 20,000–5,000ft higher than the wing, even though Bader had ignored the Controller's orders to patrol at 10,000ft and instead climbed to 15,000ft. Bader requested permission from the Duxford Sector Controller to engage – which was granted. Immediately, this highlights the problem of communication, and why the system simply did not provide for tactical control of 12 Group's wing by 11 Group – over whose area the Duxford Wing now operated.

The 11 Group Controller had no means of communicating directly with the 12 Group formation leader – and it is highly unlikely that Duxford referred to 11 Group before giving Bader permission to leave his allocated patrol line over North Weald and engage. Certain previous commentators have charged that Bader failed to comply with instructions, left his patrol line in search of the enemy, thereby failing to protect North Weald – but clearly this is not the case: any fault lay with the 12 Group Controller, who we assume to have been the Station Commander and 'Big Wing' supporter, Wing Commander Woodhall.

Although the main German formation was at 20,000ft, typically the Me 109s were another 5,000ft higher – giving the enemy escorts a 10,000ft height advantage on the Duxford Wing. Bader later wrote that his wing had been 'alerted late' – hence why the Duxford Wing was now in a tactically disadvantaged position. More accurately, the wing had been poorly positioned height-wise – and had Bader not used his own initiative and climbed that extra 5,000ft, that disadvantage would have been greater still. These two immediate problems of height and control emphasise from the outset the difficulties involved for both 11 and 12 Groups where operating the Duxford Wing was concerned – the system, or communications, had simply not provided for this unexpected scenario.

Climbing at full throttle to at least get level with the Germans, the element of surprise was lost. Unsurprisingly, given the difference in performance between the Spitfires and slower Hurricanes, the wing became 'straggled out so that full weight could not be pressed home'. The wing had certainly lost 'cohesion' – but the reason for that was not the fault of either Duxford's Controller or Squadron Leader Bader.

Inevitably, the German fighter escort fell on the thirty-six Duxford fighters; Bader: 'To be attacked by an enemy fighter when you are climbing is fatal if your opponent is experienced. You are flying slowly and are thus virtually unmanoeuvrable, as well as being a sitting target for an opponent flying above you and flying faster.' Bader climbed flat-out and turned left to cut off the enemy.

Confirming how 'straggled out' his formation was, the only other fighter to reach the enemy with Bader was his Red 2, FAA pilot Sub-Lieutenant Dickie Cork:

> Squadron Leader Bader gave a very short beam burst at about 100 yards at E/A which were then flying section of three line astern in a large rectangle. Then, accompanied by Red Two, gave short bursts at the middle E/A of back section. The E/A started smoking preparatory to catching fire. Squadron Leader Bader did not notice result which was later confirmed by Pilot Officer Turner as diving down in flames from the back of the bomber formation. At the time of Squadron Leader Bader's attack on the Me 110, a yellow-nosed Me 109 was noticed reflected in his mirror, and he turn to avoid the E/A.
>
> Big bang was heard by him in the cockpit of his Hurricane. An explosive bullet came through the right-hand side of the fuselage, touching map case and knocking off corner of the undercarriage selector quadrant and finished up against the petrol priming pump. Squadron Leader Bader executed a steep diving turn and found a lone Me 110

> below him, which he attacked from straight astern and above him, and saw E/A go into a steepish straight dive finishing up in flames in a field just north of railway line turning approximately East (West of Wickford, due North of Thameshaven).

According to the 242 Squadron Intelligence Report:

> Red Two, sighted E/A to East and above. He climbed to meet E/A and carried out beam attack on the leading section of bombers, firing at a Do 215 on the tail-end of the formation. Port engine burst into flames after two short bursts and crashed vertically. Red Two was then attacked by E/A from rear and hit in starboard mainplane. He broke away downwards and backwards, nearly colliding head-on with an Me 110.
>
> Red Two gave short burst before pulling away and saw front cabin of 110 break up and machine go into vertical dive. Two of the crew baled out. While Red Two was following E/A down, E/A was stalling and diving. An Me 109 attacked Red Two from the rear, one shot from the E/A going through the side of Red Two's hood, hitting bottom of reflector sight and bullet-proof windscreen. Red Two received a number of glass splinters in his eyes so broke away downwards with half roll and lost sight of E/A.

Red 3, Pilot Officer Denis Crowley-Milling, attacked an Me 110, setting its port engine ablaze before being attacked by an Me 109. One cannon shell smashed into the Hurricane's radiator, and others hit the aileron and pilot's seat; years later, Air Marshal Crowley-Milling remembered:

> What the official report doesn't mention is that my windscreen was also shattered by a cannon shell. Fortunately we had armoured glass, which was laminated, a couple of inches thick, which saved my life. I managed to put the Hurricane down at Stow Maries. It was all pretty traumatic but at least I was personally unscathed!

AC1 David Evans, 242 Squadron groundcrew: 'The "Crow" was lucky. When we got the Hurricane back home we found a 7.9 mm round jammed in the windscreen. The armoured glass, and armour plate, was something else "Stuffy" Dowding had argued for – many pilots must owe him their lives for this foresight.'

The Me 110 that Pilot Officer Crowley-Milling accounted for, jointly with Green 4, Sub-Lieutenant Richard Gardner, crashed at Little Burstead. Again, the Squadron Intelligence Report continues:

> Blue 1 (F/Lt Powell-Sheddon) climbed to 22,000ft to engage E/A but did not engage for some 10 minutes. He finally chased an Me 109 which was itself chasing a Hurricane. Both swerved in front of Blue One, about 100 yards away. Blue 1 gave a quick deflection burst at E/A as it passed. E/A turned left and again crossed Blue 1's path at same range. Blue 1 gave another burst and hit E/A's tail.
>
> Blue 1 then got a third burst from above and behind at a range of fifty yards, bullets hitting E/A from which pieces came off. Blue 1 got into E/A's slipstream, ceased fire and got out slightly to one side and fired again at E/A which then hung in the air for a few seconds and then fell forward in a vertical dive, smoke pouring from the starboard wing and fuselage. E/A disappeared into black smoke over Thameshaven.

Meanwhile, as Squadron Leader Brian Lane DFC climbed 19 Squadron's Spitfires, an Me 110, which was being attacked by two Hurricanes of 310 Squadron, flashed in front of 'A' Flight, which, with Lane leading, sped off in pursuit. All five pilots subsequently fired at the hapless 110, which crashed near a railway line, one mile east of Hornchurch. This aircraft belonged to *Stab* II/ZG 2, which was escorting He 111s of KG 53; one crew member was killed when his parachute failed, the other landed safely in a field only to be captured by two elderly women from a nearby house. After the combat, 'A' Flight was split up so Squadron Leader Lane, Flight Lieutenant Walter 'Farmer' Lawson and Sergeant Bernard 'Blondy' Jennings, having lost contact with the ongoing air battle, returned to Fowlmere.

The other pilots of 19 Squadron, however, were still engaged. Red 3, Pilot Officer Wallace 'Jock' Cunningham, blacked out after breaking off the pursuit of the Me 110 destroyed by 'A' Flight, came to and joined up with a squadron of Hurricanes heading south-east. At 17.20 hrs, these fighters executed a front-quarter attack on twenty He 111s at 20,000ft. Pilot Officer

Cunningham's Spitfire hurtled through the bombers, in an attempt to break their formation, before singling out a particular Heinkel which caught fire and lost height. After a further attack, Cunningham last saw the raider ten miles inland from Deal, but after only a short burst at another vic of He 111s his ammunition was expended.

After attacking the Me 110 with the rest of 'A' Flight, Flight Sergeant George 'Grumpy' Unwin found himself alone at 4,000ft. Climbing under full boost to 25,000ft he saw 'a Hurricane squadron going somewhere in a hurry' and followed them. Suddenly, the three separate enemy waves of thirty bombers each appeared, with their inevitable close fighter escort.

Flight Sergeant Unwin:

> I was surrounded by Me 109s and ended up fighting a running battle between Ramsgate and west London. The usual fight ensued, during which I definitely hit at least five of them but only two were shot down, both in flames. I then climbed for a breather and shadowed the third enemy formation when I saw a fourth arriving. By this time two of the other three formations had turned north and the other went straight in a westerly direction.
>
> The leading formation turned east and I was at 25,000ft and above them. As there did not appear to be any of their escorts left, I dived on the rear vic and gave them the rest of my ammunition, about 50 rounds in each gun, and from 450, closing to fifty yards range. The bomber at which I fired wobbled a bit but otherwise carried on. Without ammunition I returned to Fowlmere.

When Squadron Leader Bader Tally Ho'd and led 242 Squadron to attack the bombers, Squadron Leader Douglas Blackwood led the Czechs of his 310 Squadron in a charge at the enemy fighters. After the initial squadron attack in line astern, the Czechs were split up, acting independently or in pairs. Over Canterbury, Sergeant Bohumir Furst attacked a 1/LG 2 Me 109, which, although the pilot managed to bale out, exploded in mid-air; the Czech then struck against an Me 110 of 6/ZG 2 which ditched in the Channel off Birchington. The exchange was far from one-sided, however: Sergeant Josef Koukal was shot down and baled out over Sheppey, grievously burned, and Pilot Officer Vilem Goth, who claimed two Me 109s destroyed over Southend, was shot-up and forced-landed at Purleigh.

No.242 Squadron's Pilot Officer John Benzie was missing, later confirmed to have been killed. Bader: 'it was windy work, let there be no mistake. On landing I rang the Operations Room in a fury, to be told that we had been sent off as soon as 11 Group had called for us at Duxford.'

The allegation that the Duxford Wing were always called for late by 11 Group, however, was already a vexing issue; Wing Commander Douglas Blackwood:

> I think that we should have been requested earlier as that would have enabled us to climb out to sea and then attack high over the Thames Estuary. But I think that *everyone* was doing their best, we were all learning. 11 Group felt it was their responsibility to defend London, without 12 Group interfering.

Clearly, though, that was not the case, because 11 Group had no hesitation in calling upon Air Vice-Marshal Brand's 10 Group.

The limitations of RDF and the system, however, meant that it was not just squadrons in 12 Group which complained about being scrambled late; Air Commodore Peter Brothers was then an experienced flight commander serving in 11 Group:

> Until 9 September 1940 I flew with 32 Squadron. During our time at coastal aerodromes at Hawkinge and Manston, or even Biggin Hill, which was further inland, we were often scrambled late. The Controller obviously had to ensure that it was the real thing and not a 'spoof' to get us airborne and catch us while refuelling. This was frustrating as at such forward bases there was so little time anyway.

For reasons beyond the control of those directing the battle, this would remain an irresolvable difficulty. Bader himself once expressed his own thoughts on the time factor:

> Some ignorant people have stated in print that the wing took a long time to get off the ground. Not so. As the two Hurricane squadrons

got off the ground from Duxford, the Spitfires did so from Fowlmere. There was no time wasted in forming up. I just set course and kept going, and everyone else just formatted [*sic*] on my lead. We took off in sections of three, in line abreast, and as soon as the first three were getting towards the far hedge then the next three would be taxying into position and so on. There was no orbit. I used to get off the ground and get absolutely right on course.

The chaps then joined me, the Spitfires staying 5,000ft above us. I usually set the pace to climb at 140 mph. We reckoned to be at the Thames Estuary at about 20,000ft, which was forty-eight miles away. There was no time lost through us getting off.

Once we were off, we were off, there was no milling about, all this was done on the climb and en route. No time lost. The leader is the fellow who sets the pace, to give the blokes at the back time to settle down and so on. Obviously, a squadron in a hurry was faster than a wing because the leader has less blokes to worry about. I used to go on at Leigh-Mallory about why we couldn't get off early and be down there, but he said, 'Look, we can't go until Air Vice-Marshal Park requests us. Do please remember, Bader, that they've got plenty of problems down there without us adding to them.

Wing Commander Woodhall also supported Bader's view that information from the controller should be provided to assist – not restrict – the leader in the air:

Douglas had made an intimate study of the fighter tactics developed by famous pilots like McCudden, Ball and Bishop in the First World War and was a great believer in the advantages of making the correct use of the sun, and first gaining superior height. As I saw it my job as Sector Controller was to vector the fighter leader on a course and to a height which would place him above and up-sun of the enemy, and keep him informed of the enemy's position, course and speed as accurately as possible from the information we had on the operations table. As soon as our fighter leader sighted the enemy, it was over to him.

Although the Duxford Wing's first action on 7 September 1940 had been 'windy work' provoking Bader's 'fury', the squadrons involved made the following combat claims:

> 242 Squadron: 10 destroyed, 2 probables, 5 damaged.
> 310 Squadron: 5/3/3.
> 19 Squadron: 5 destroyed.
>
> Wing Total: 20/3/6.

The wing's losses:

> 242 Squadron: 1 pilot killed, 2 Hurricanes damaged.
> 310 Squadron: 1 pilot badly burned and Hurricane destroyed, another damaged.
> 19 Squadron: 0.

From the evidence available, however, it is difficult to confirm more than six kills by 242 Squadron – suggesting an over-claiming ratio of 3:1. Once more, though, the claims of Bader and his pilots appear to have been accepted without question. Inevitably, the Duxford Wing's tally on 7 September 1940 generated further congratulatory signals from both Leigh-Mallory and the Secretary of State for Air, Sir Archibald Sinclair. Woodhall was certainly convinced that the wing's claims were accurate: 'Bader and the intelligence officers checked these figures very carefully – with me.' They were wrong.

Returning to that first raid on London, Kenley's 253 Squadron also intercepted after the first wave of bombers had hit their targets. Led by the newly promoted Flight Lieutenant Gerry Edge (who had joined the squadron from 605 and was now de facto CO), at 17.15 hrs 253 Squadron sighted the second wave, thirty He 111s escorted by fifty Me 109s and 110s, approaching Thames Haven at 20,000ft. North of London the Germans turned SSE, so Edge, having already turned east, led the Hurricanes in a diving attack from abeam:

> successfully breaking up their formation and forcing some to dive for cover of thick smoke over the Thames Estuary. Red Leader, [Flight

> Lieutenant Edge] … delivered a quarter attack on a He 111 from port and then starboard, stopping E/A's port engine and observing starboard engine streaming oil. Red 2 [Pilot Officer Murch] attacked a He 111 from dead astern, giving E/A five-second burst and observed both starboard and port engines on fire. Several other bombers were attacked but no results observed. [ORB]

The Hurricanes had managed to intercept without interference from the enemy fighter escort, and all 253 Squadron's pilots returned safely to Kenley at 17.45 hrs.

No.602 Squadron's Spitfires had been ordered to patrol Mayfield and, at 17.30 hrs and 18,000ft:

> sighted twenty-six Do 17s escorted by 100 Me 109s. The Do 17s were attacked. After breaking away, the CO [Squadron Leader Sandy Johnston] flew to Staines where from 5,000ft he saw ten waves of enemy bombers, four of which he attacked … Enemy casualties were one Me 110, one Me 109 and one Do 17 destroyed, two Me 109s probable, and one Ju 88, two Do 17s and one He 111 damaged. [ORB]

Two Spitfires, however, were missing: Pilot Officer Hugh Coverley was shot down and baled out badly burned over Tonbridge – unfortunately, his parachute descent went unnoticed. Without help, the pilot died; his body lying undiscovered for nine days. Pilot Officer Henry Moody, who at 30 was considered old by fighter pilot standards, was also shot down but was never seen again. Pilot Officer Osgood 'Pedro' Hanbury was shot-up and made it safely back to base, but Pilot Officer Ellis Aries, hit by a Do 17's return fire, crash-landed near Wrotham with a damaged glycol tank; fortunately he was unscathed.

Squadron Leader Bill Harkness, Yellow 1, had led 257 Squadron up from Martlesham Heath to first patrol Chelmsford before being sent to Rochester at 15,000ft. At 17.30 hrs, Harkness sighted another wave of German bombers flying west up the Thames Estuary, towards London, which he reported to Sector Operations. Harkness then climbed the squadron, turning north, but were seen by the high-flying Me 109 escorts circling above the bombers.

Harkness led the Hurricanes in a head-on attack on the port section of three bombers.

Pilot Officer Kenneth Gundry, Yellow 2, followed his leader but without firing, and Sergeant Peter Robinson, Yellow 3, following Gundry in line-astern while doing a steep turn to the right, was suddenly hit by AA fire; his Hurricane was blown onto its back and dropped like a stone to 8,000–10,000ft. Recovering, Robinson climbed to 21,000ft where he found thirty bombers heading east and for home.

Diving out of the sun, he attacked the nearest Do 17, one of the rearmost of the formation, which was in line-astern, delivering a four-second burst from above and astern. Breaking left and intending to attack again, Robinson was hit from above by an Me 109, an exploding cannon shell ripping a hole in his starboard wing and radiator; the pilot was unhurt, however, and returned his damaged but robust Hurricane to base.

Flight Lieutenant Hugh Beresford, the commander of 'A' Flight, was leading Red Section and followed Harkness into the head-on attack, but was unable to fire because the Hurricanes of Yellow Section were ahead and obstructed Red Section's field of fire. Instead, Red 1 climbed 500ft in a clockwise circle, above the bombers, intending to engage them from astern. Red 2, Sergeant Robert Fraser, then shouted an urgent warning over the R/T of four yellow-nosed 'Snappers' (Me 109s) diving on Red Section from astern. Fraser broke, turning tightly, as the 109s opened fire with their 20mm cannon from 500 yards – and blacked out, descending to 10,000ft before recovering.

No enemy aircraft were about, so he climbed up to 21,000ft, keeping up-sun, and attacked a formation of thirty bombers, also withdrawing to the east with their fighter escort. Having expended his ammunition without any noticeable effect, Fraser was obliged to break off and return to base. Sergeant Reg Nutter, Red 3, had become separated from Red 2 during this violent evasive action and lost height, finding himself at 8,000ft above the Thames Estuary and the focus of AA fire. Diving towards the south bank, Nutter orbited Gravesend to avoid the gunfire, then returned to base.

Of their leader, Flight Lieutenant Beresford, shot down when Red Section was ambushed by the Me 109s, nothing was heard of again until 1979, when a Hurricane crash-site at Elmley, Spitend Point, on the bleak Isle of Sheppey, was excavated by aviation archaeology enthusiasts and his remains recovered

(Flight Lieutenant Beresford was subsequently interred at Brookwood Military Cemetery with full military honours).

The commander of 'B' Flight, Flying Officer Lancelot Mitchell, Green 1, was followed by Green 2, Pilot Officer Charles Frizzell, a Canadian, as Green Section followed Yellow and Red in their initial head-on attack. Having fired a one-second burst at a bomber, Frizzell found himself at just 2,000ft, so climbed to get behind the bombers when an Me 109 dived on him; Frizzell managed a short burst at the fleeting enemy fighter but then also found himself in the midst of the AA barrage at 15,000ft, so broke away northwards, formating with Yellow 1 and 2. Sergeant Donald Hulbert, Green 3, climbed after Flying Officer Mitchell and Red Section to attack the bombers but was shot-up by an Me 109, a cannon shells hitting his wing and puncturing his petrol tank. Hulbert dived, turning, making a safe landing in a stubble field festooned with various obstructions at Bashford, near Sittingbourne.

Towards the action's conclusion, Pilot Officer Arthur Cochrane, a Canadian, Blue 1, heard Flying Officer Mitchell on the R/T, talking to Sector Control – but the commander of 'B' Flight was never heard of or seen again.

Shortly after 257 Squadron's sections went into line-astern for their head-on charge, Pilot Officer Cochrane's engine cut-out, forcing him to glide away from the action – escorted by Blue 2, Pilot Officer Carl Capon. At 10,000ft, his motor coughed back into life, so Cochrane climbed, Capon lagging a mile behind. Following an inconclusive chase with a 109, Cochrane dived on and attacked a retreating Do 17 from up-sun, causing white smoke to pour from the enemy aircraft before three parachutists jumped from their doomed machine which dived into the sea (possibly an aircraft of 4/KG 2 recorded as lost over London, the crew of which were missing). Separated from Cochrane, Capon had been unable to rejoin the action and returned to base alone, as did Sergeant Arthur Page, who, on what was his first operational sortie, passed out as the engagement began, recovering several thousand feet below and headed back to Martlesham Heath.

Pilot Officer Cochrane's claim was the only one recorded by 257 Squadron in this combat – which had cost the squadron both flight commanders killed. Afterwards, 'Morale', according to Reg Nutter, 'was not good'.

The previous day, 504 'City of Nottingham' Squadron had arrived in 11 Group to operate from Hendon, as Sergeant Basil 'Mike' Bush recalled:

'We of 504 Squadron had flown our Hurricanes South from Catterick to Hendon. I recall that whenever we were at readiness, awaiting the call to scramble, our favourite number was, appropriately, Vera Lynn singing *In Room Five-hundred-and-four*!'

At 16.20 hrs on 7 September 1940, the gramophone was set aside when Squadron Leader John Sample DFC scrambled with his Hurricanes with orders to head for Canterbury and intercept the London-bound raiders. Like most other squadrons, they missed the Germans, but engaged the withdrawing enemy.

At 17.00 hrs, Pilot Officer John Hardacre lost the squadron in the sun but sighted, near either Billericay or Wickford, twenty He 111s at 12,000ft, in six vics of three, escorted by Me 110s. Two Me 110s dived to attack him and another Hurricane, reportedly coded 'US-X' (US was 56 Squadron's code letters, the squadron having been withdrawn a week before, this machine remaining behind and taken on charge by 249 Squadron). Hardacre emptied all his ammunition into one of the Me 110s, which fell in flames after the pilot baled out. The pilot of Hurricane US-X, possibly Pilot Officer Hugh Beazley of 249 Squadron, was seen to set the other Me 110's port engine ablaze.

At 17.20 hrs, the remainder of 504 Squadron was bounced over Eastchurch by six Me 109s which ambushed the Hurricanes from out of the sun. Sergeant Bush, flying Hurricane P3021, TM-N, was hit – a cannon shell smashing through his instrument panel and into the petrol tank beyond:

> I was damned lucky not to catch fire as when hit petrol splashed all over me. Fortunately it did not ignite and I managed a safe forced-landing at Eastchurch on the Isle of Sheppey. It was a bit hairy for a moment or two, though! Due to repairs being carried out I was unable to return to Hendon with my aircraft until 9 September 1940. They gave me a week off to recover.

According to the ORB, Bush had a 'shell through his windscreen and petrol. Great credit to him for saving his aircraft.'

Pilot Officer Kenneth Wendel, a New Zealander from Auckland and veteran of the Fall of France, was less fortunate, however: eyewitnesses on the ground reported having seen his Hurricane falling completely out of control, having been hit by the Me 109s, the aircraft crashing near Faversham, killing the 24-year-old pilot. None of his fellow pilots even saw him go down.

At 17.35 hrs, seven of Sample's men were near Manston and found a formation of Dorniers and their fighter escort withdrawing eastwards, which they attacked from the sun, the CO damaging one of the bombers while Pilot Officer Blair 'Crasher' White claimed a 109 probable. Five minutes later, Sergeant Denis Helcke, who had become separated in the confusion, was over Ramsgate when he sighted a straggling He 111 and attacked the bomber in company with a Hurricane of 310 Squadron; according to the squadron's after-action report, the enemy aircraft was hit and ditched in the sea – at which point, in frustration, the rear-gunner fired off a parting salvo at his tormentors.

Considering how roughly some squadrons fresh to 11 Group were treated by the enemy, 504 Squadron could have fared worse.

At 17.40 hrs, six Hurricanes of 46 Squadron were patrolling North Weald at 10,000ft when another wave of enemy bombers and their escorts were sighted flying NNW 'in one big wedge' (46 Squadron Intelligence Patrol Report refers) at 15,000ft, their escorting Me 109s stepped up to 20,000ft. The Hurricanes managed to briefly attack the bombers from the east before the Me 109s engaged and a dogfight developed over the Thames Estuary.

Flight Lieutenant Alexander Rabagliati was flying the experimental Hurricane armed with four hard-hitting 20mm Hispano cannons – but opening fire at a bomber from 300 yards, only 130 rounds belched forth before all four weapons frustratingly jammed, although the 'Do 215 [*sic*]' was damaged, as was another by Sergeant Edward Tyrer, who also claimed a 109 damaged, while Pilot Officer Peter Gunning claimed a probable. The squadron suffered no casualties and all six Hurricane pilots returned safely to Stapleford Tawney, although one aircraft was slightly damaged.

The twelve Spitfires of 603 Squadron were also patrolling north of the Thames, over their Hornchurch base, when, at 17.40 hrs, four waves of German bombers 'very well protected by fighters', according to the squadron's Fighter Command Combat Report, were seen between 15,000–18,000ft and approaching from the east. Immediately, Squadron Leader George Denholm turned into the enemy, opening fire at long-range.

In the ensuing combat over Tilbury, the New Zealander Flying Officer Brian Carbury destroyed an Me 109 and a 'He 113 [*sic*]', both of which 'crashed in flames', and also hit another 'He 113' which was last seen diving, streaming glycol. Flying Officer Brian MacNamara shot down a He 111 of 5/KG 53, which forced-landed at Old Marsh, Isle of Grain; one of the crew was killed, the others were captured after setting fire to their machine. Flying Officer James Morton hit the 6/JG 26 Me 109 of *Unteroffizier* Ernst Braun in both radiators, claiming the enemy fighter as a probable – although Braun actually abandoned his aircraft off Dover and was captured. Morton also hit another 109, leaving that too streaming glycol, and a He 111, which poured smoke from both engines.

Squadron Leader Denholm, however, returned to base with a wing damaged by a cannon shell, and similarly Flying Officer Peter Pease crash-landed at Hornchurch with damaged undercarriage and a ruptured fuel tank. The South African Pilot Officer Basil 'Stapme' Stapleton was also shot-up, making a forced-landing at Sutton Valence from which he walked away unscathed. Sergeant Alfred Sarre was shot down over the Thames, though, and baled out, wounded; he survived but would never fly operationally again.

'A' Flight of 73 Squadron, recently arrived in the Debden Sector, had only mustered three serviceable Hurricanes to join 'B' Flight's full complement of six to patrol Chelmsford at 15,000ft. In the subsequent combat over the Thames Estuary, Squadron Leader Maurice Robinson, a supernumerary officer on 73 Squadron, claimed an Me 110 destroyed, as did Flight Lieutenant Michael Beytagh, who saw his victim 'hit the dock near Billericay [ORB]', this being the *Gruppenadjutant* of I/ZG 2, *Oberleutnant* Gerhard Granz, who baled out, as did his *Bordfunker*, *Feldwebel* Willi Schutel, both men being captured. Pilot Officer Neville Langham-Hobart also claimed an Me 110 destroyed, and Sergeant Geoffrey Garton a probable He 111. Sergeant Alfred Marshal damaged an Me 110 but was hit by return fire, as a result of which his engine cut-out, the pilot being slightly wounded and gliding down to make a wheels-down forced-landing at Burnham Marshes.

For all of these pilots, fresh to the air battle over 11 Group, these were their first recorded combat claims – although this was tempered by a sad loss: Flight Lieutenant Reginald Lovett, commander of 'A' Flight, was missing:

> a grand fellow – a good pilot – intrepid and as keen on his job as it is possible to be. He was last seen in the Billericay district, since when

> nothing has been heard. If only we could hear something of him, tension would be relieved. The uncertainty of his fate troubles all. [ORB]

News would be received – but sadly Lovett was dead, shot down and killed, his Hurricane crashing at Stock, near Billericay.

As the enemy's relentless assault on target '*Loge*' continued, the first RAF squadrons to have engaged were soon back on the ground, urgently refuelling and rearming before hurriedly returning to the fray. Having already been in action, by 17.30 hrs the Spitfires of 72 Squadron were back at Croydon and being feverishly 'turned around' by their dedicated groundcrews.

At 17.45 hrs, Pilot Officer 'Dutch' Holland and Sergeant John Gilders took off again, with orders to patrol base, followed ten minutes later by Sergeant Basil Douthwaite, on what was also his second scramble, and two fresh pilots, Sergeants Norman Norfolk and Norman 'Sticky' Glew; the latter reported:

> With three more aircraft we climbed to 15,000ft and met a large force of bombers and fighters at 16,000ft. We delivered an attack from underneath and towards starboard beam. I picked out a force of three bombers and sprayed them. Incendiary bullets were going into the E/A. I held the fire on for five seconds, then broke away on being attacked by five Me 110s. Later, I attacked an Me 110 but broke away upon seeing a Spitfire being attacked by Me 110s. The Spitfire was flown by Sergeant Norfolk who had just shot down a Do 17. I saw it going down with both engines smoking.

Glew was accredited with a damaged Do 17, and Norfolk one destroyed. By 17.55 hrs, all of 72 Squadron's Spitfires were safely back at Croydon.

Similarly, fifteen minutes after returning to North Weald, at 17.50 hrs six serviceable Hurricanes of 249 Squadron scrambled again, ordered to London. As the Hurricanes took-off, a wave of German aircraft passed over the aerodrome at 15,000ft, but no bombs fell until the enemy reached north-east London.

At 18.00 hrs, 249's small force caught up with the raiders, Sergeant Fred Killingback subsequently claiming an Me 109 probable – but Sergeant John Beard's Hurricane was hit by AA fire, forcing him to take to his parachute, fortunately unhurt. The remaining five Hurricanes all returned safely to base by 18.30 hrs. Certain officers, however, had a less pleasant experience:

> It is worthy of note that during this, the enemy's largest full-scale attack on the London Docks, Pilot Officers Meaker and Loweth had motored to Maidstone to collect the CO from hospital there. On their return they arrived at Surrey Docks about five minutes before these attacks took place and spent a very undignified forty-five minutes lying on the pavement at the entrance to the Blackwall Tunnel. [ORB]

Thankfully, Squadron Leader John Grandy and the two pilot officers survived the traumatic experience unscathed.

The events of 7 September 1940 – which has gone down in history for the British as 'Black Saturday' – would represent a depressing day indeed for 43 Squadron, three sections of which had left Tangmere with orders to patrol Beachy Head at 15,000ft. At 17.25 hrs, up to twenty-five Do 17s, escorted by some fifty Me 109s, which milled about above the bombers, were sighted flying north-west over Folkestone. Further north, two similar formations could be seen, flying west towards London, over the south bank of the Thames.

It was noted by the squadron's combat report that the German bombers 'kept a very tight formation and proceeded on their course without the slightest deviation, even when subjected to intense AA fire, some of which appeared to be bursting amongst them.' The CO, the South African Squadron Leader Caesar Hull DFC, ordered Yellow Section to climb and engage the enemy fighters while he led the other two sections to attack the bombers. Yellow leader, Flight Lieutenant John 'Iggy' Kilmartin, climbed his section as ordered 2,000ft higher – then the attack went in.

Immediately, three Me 109s pounced on Yellow Section, but one was hit by Kilmartin and 'went down completely out of control', emitting white smoke. Kilmartin, however, was then attacked by a *Schwarm* of 109s, only escaping their attention through violent evasive action. Meanwhile, the bombers proceeded towards London, their formation impeccable, and Kilmartin next positioned himself to attack their leaders' port side.

One of these bombers suddenly left the formation, turned about and headed for the sea – pursued, needless to say, by Yellow leader who managed to hit the Do 17 before the escorting 109s lost no time in chasing him away. Other 43 Squadron pilots managed quick attacks before the 109s also intervened; indeed, the squadron after action report observed that 'owing to the large number of enemy there was no opportunity to observe the effect of their fire, and the enemy fighters seem to have been extremely active in keeping our fighters away from the bombers.'

Sergeant Alan Deller, however, was shot down by Me 109s over Ashford, baling out unhurt, and soon checked in confirming his status and that he was returning to Tangmere. Flight Lieutenant Richard 'Dick' Reynell, a former member of the Oxford University Air Squadron, and a highly experienced test pilot currently serving on 43 to gain operational experience, was dead, having fallen victim to the lethal 109s over South London and was killed when his parachute failed to open. The CO, Squadron Leader Caesar Hull DFC, a friend of Reynell's, had gone to his assistance – but was shot down and killed by a 109 in the process, his Hurricane crashing in the grounds of Purley High School. Hull was also an experienced fighter pilot, awarded the DFC for his successes during the ill-fated Norwegian campaign, during which he had survived being shot down and wounded. When Squadron Leader John 'Tubby' Badger was badly wounded leading 43 Squadron on 30 August 1940, Hull had been promoted and sent to command the unit; exactly one week later, this gallant South African was dead. Men like Hull and Reynell were exactly the kind of experienced pilots Fighter Command could simply not afford to lose.

Six Hurricanes of 79 Squadron's 'A' Flight had taken-off from Biggin Hill at 16.40 hrs to:

> attack enemy over aerodrome. Believed Ju 88 and 86 [*sic*]. Some Do 17 or 215 [*sic*] and fighter escort. At 17.30 hrs Pilot Officer Tracey landed with oil on his windscreen, he took off again in another aircraft. At 17.55 hrs Squadron Leader Heyworth landed. He, together with Pilot Officer Stones DFC, got one Ju 88 probable. All aircraft landed by 18.21 hrs. Pilot Officer Peters got a bomber probable, believed Do 17. Pilot Officer Stones DFC: missing, later reported to be shot in leg and landed safely at West Malling. He got a Do 17 probable or damaged. [ORB]

The thirteen Spitfires of Squadron Leader John Hill's 222 Squadron, up from Hornchurch, also intercepted a wave of bombers and fighters approaching London, going into action over Maidstone at 18.00 hrs.

In the arising melee, Pilot Officer John Broadhurst, Sergeants Iain Hutchinson, Rainford Marland and John Burgess all claimed Me 109s destroyed; Johnson and the South African Flying Officer Brian van Mentz claimed probables. Pilot Officer Tim Vigors claimed a Do 17 destroyed, but, bizarrely, Hill claimed a damaged 'Glenn Martin (in French markings) [ORB]'. Van Mentz was also credited with a 'Do 215' probable, as was Pilot Officer Laurie Whitbread, a Ludlovian, who reported:

> We engaged an enemy formation of Me 109s. I became separated from the rest of the Squadron so I climbed back to my original altitude and flew round looking for a target. I found one in a formation of 25–30 Do 215s [*sic*], which appeared to have no fighter escort. Keeping in the sun, I dived down on the last aircraft which was straggling behind some 100 yards at the rear of the formation and flying at 20,000ft. I carried out a quarter attack from the port side (formation was flying westwards along south bank of the Thames at Dartford). I opened fire at 300 yards, range closing rapidly. The starboard engine set on fire and I broke away, the return fire from the rear three gunners and my closing range making it advisable.

No.22 Squadron suffered no losses in the engagement.

At 18.00 hrs, the Spitfires of 10 Group's 609 Squadron, being led in the air by Flight Lieutenant James MacArthur, 'Sorbo Leader', were patrolling Brooklands at 10,000ft as ordered when, according to Flight Lieutenant Frank Howell, Red 1, the pilots saw 'many enemy aircraft and AA bursts over London':

> I lost sight temporarily of Sorbo Leader, so climbed to 20,000ft. Large formation of Me 110s coming in from North. I told each Red aircraft to pick own target as E/A were flying in wide formation. I dived and attacked one Me 110, giving three-second burst from about 350–150 yards. Broke away, narrowly missing it as it turned in same direction. I looked above me and saw one Me 110 spinning down with one wing

> completely broken away, and another explode in mid-air, engine cowling and pieces of aircraft flung in every direction. I presume one of these was the one I attacked.
>
> I climbed into the sun and was attacked by another Spitfire, tracer bullets going past my starboard wing. Climbed into sun and attacked one Ju 88 of large formation. Smoke came from one engine, three-second burst. Climbed again and attacked another Ju 88 of same squadron. This was coloured completely black all over. One-second burst at close range, but had to break away as I was myself attacked by yellow-nosed Me 109s. Ju 88 claimed probably destroyed because this type believed almost unmanageable with one engine u/s.

The Polish Flying Officer Tadeusz Nowierski, Blue 2:

> I followed leader and attacked a big formation of Do 17 (or Me 110, type of E/A is not definitely known). Beam attack developing from astern. Two bursts of two-seconds, no results observed. I dived away and then climbed up to 15,000ft and saw an Me 109. A dogfight developed but I lost sight of the E/A. I then saw a Do 17 and attacked from astern at 150 yards range, three bursts of two-seconds. The last burst caused the E/A to catch fire between the starboard engine and fuselage. A Me 109 then attacked me and I broke away downwards and evaded him.

Nowierski claimed 'either a Do 17 or Me 110' probable. In total, the reinforcing 10 Group squadron claimed three Me 110s, an Me 109 and two Do 17s destroyed, two Me 110s, an Me 109 and a Ju 88 probably destroyed, and one Me 110 and a Ju 88 damaged. No.609 Squadron, which had been roughly handled at the beginning of the Battle of Britain, suffered no losses in the engagement.

Although the Canadians of 1(RCAF) Squadron had been ordered to remain patrolling over Northolt, the CO, Squadron Leader Eric McNab, somehow found himself separated from his unit and flying east over Maidstone in company with a Spitfire at 18.10 hrs:

> when approximately five Me 109s, with yellow colouring reaching from the front of the cockpit windscreen to the airscrew boss, crossed in front

> of me flying in line astern at about 18,000ft towards the Channel. I attacked the rear one with a deflection shot and followed into line-astern, using my excess speed, due to height, to follow. The Me 109 climbed and I fired 150 rounds from each gun dead-astern from about 150 yards. The E/A suddenly climbed vertically and fell straight down. I got a glimpse of white vapour from below his fuselage before breaking off.

McNab claimed the 109 as a probable.

Having refuelled and rearmed after their initial combat, five Hurricanes of Northolt's 1 Squadron, led by Flight Lieutenant John Finnis, returned to the battle, Finnis claiming a 'Do 215 [*sic*]' damaged over Sevenoaks at 18.15 hrs, and Pilot Officer Michael Homer another over Tilbury.

At 18.15 hrs, 234 Squadron, the other reinforcing unit from 10 Group, finally engaged the retiring raiders in a running battle between London and Brighton. On the subject of reinforcing 11 Group, Pilot Officer Keith Lawrence, a New Zealander, recalled:

> I would say that whenever we were vectored to the Brooklands area, we climbed to 20,000ft, so as to reach the patrol line at a reasonable altitude before action. My recollections of Middle Wallop scrambles in August and September 1940 is that they were generally ordered in good time for us to climb to an appropriate height for interception while en route.

Pilot Officer Bob Doe, also of 234 Squadron:

> After 234 Squadron was scrambled from Middle Wallop, I climbed like mad in an attempt to avoid the trauma of the previous two raids where I had been at a disadvantage from the very start, and managed to reach London at a reasonable altitude where I could have a go at the bombers on my terms.

On this occasion, twelve Spitfires of 234 Squadron were ordered to patrol Kenley and Biggin Hill at 10,000ft – but actually climbed to 20,000ft. Arriving over their patrol line, the pilots saw many enemy aircraft, between 16,000–22,000ft, retreating to the south and south-east. According to the squadron's subsequent report to Fighter Command HQ: 'Red Section must have been attacked by a formation of Me 109s which were escorting about 150 bombers. Red 1 was shot down in a manner not ascertained.'

This was a blow to the Squadron: 'Red 1' was the CO, Squadron Leader Joseph 'Spike' O'Brien DFC, who had received his decoration at an investiture held by King George VI at Buckingham Palace only four days previously. The 28-year-old was mortally wounded when attacked and found dead when his aircraft crashed near Biggin Hill.

> Red 2 [Pilot Officer Doe], when the attack was made, dived on the rear Heinkel of a bomber formation and gave port engine a one-second burst. This burst into flames at the same moment as three Me 109s attacked Red 2. Red 2 dived, pulled up underneath the enemy bomber and gave the starboard engine a one-second burst. This also caught fire and one person baled out of the rear cockpit. The three 109s were still firing at Red 2 and he avoided them in the region of Dover and joined up with Red 3 [Sergeant Harker]. When the Heinkel was last seen, both engines were well on fire.
>
> Red 3 had meanwhile attacked an Me 109 over South London, gave him a three-second burst which set fire to the port wing of the E/A which went down in a vertical dive. Red 3 then observed a Hurricane attacking Red 2. The Hurricane had red, white and blue roundels.
>
> Red 2 avoided this attack and, Red 3 joining up with Red 2, both attacked a formation of Me 109s in line abreast. Red 3 gave the outside starboard Me 109 a three-second burst and E/A dived into the sea. The remaining six Me 109s turned to attack and Red 3 saw an Me 109 about to attack Red 2. Red 3 attacked from the beam and the Me 109 turned and made a head-on attack on Red 3. Red 3 dived and again saw him on Red 2's tail. Red 3 again attacked from the beam and saw his bullets hitting the cockpit of the E/A. When he broke away the Me 109 was not in sight.
>
> Green Section had sighted five Me 109s about 5,000ft above them north-west of Dover, proceeding south-east. Green 1 [Pilot Officer Dewhurst] climbed and attacked the Me 109s with two very short bursts from slightly above and from the port beam. The E/A went steeply downwards with smoke coming from the fuselage. Green 1 was

> then attacked by two Me 109s and did not, therefore, see the result of his first engagement.
>
> Yellow 2 [Sergeant Klein], south-east of London, attacked a Do 17 from astern and put all his ammunition into his fuselage and engine. The port engine started smoking and the rear-gunner stopped firing, then starboard engine began to smoke and the E/A started to lose height over the Channel. Yellow 2, at 1,000ft, had to break away owing to lack of fuel. The E/A was still losing height and smoking from both engines.
>
> Blue Section had meanwhile engaged a formation of Do 17s. Blue 1 [Flight Lieutenant Hughes] made a quarter attack on a straggling Do 17 below the rest of the formation and Blue 2 [Pilot Officer Lawrence] saw large pieces fly off the E/A, then a wing crumple and finally the E/A went into a spin. Immediately afterwards, Blue 1 went spinning down with about one third of a wing broken, and crash.

This was another grievous blow to 234 Squadron: the Australian commander of 'B' Flight, Flight Lieutenant Paterson Clarence Hughes (who would receive a posthumous DFC), was a highly popular member of 234 Squadron – and a fighter ace recalled by Doe as a 'go-getter'. Exactly what happened to Hughes, the last RAF pilot to die on 7 September 1940, remains unclear but, known for closing very closely with the enemy, it is probable that his aircraft was damaged by pieces breaking off the bomber, or collided with the enemy aircraft when it suddenly lost control.

The Australian baled out but his parachute failed to open and he was killed, falling to earth, his descent unchecked, into the garden of 16 Main Road, Sundridge; the Spitfire, X4009, crashed at nearby Dark's Farm (and, at the time of writing, is in the process of being re-built to flying condition as a memorial to this gallant fighter pilot from 'Down Under').

Sad indeed was the fact that Hughes had only married Kay, his English sweetheart, just five weeks before, the young widow now having the tragic duty of burying her 22-year-old husband at St James's churchyard, Sutton-in-Holderness, near Hull – a long way from his birthplace at Cooma, New South Wales.

The Do 17 involved belonged to *Stab* KG 76 and was on a mission to photograph the damage to London's dockland. One of the crew baled out and was captured, slightly wounded, but the other two crewmen were killed when the bomber crashed into the river Darent at Sundridge.

Returning to the air battle, Pilot Officer Keith Lawrence, Blue 2:

> carried out an attack on another Do 17 on the right flank, at the rear, but with no visible result. He broke away and saw about twelve Me 109s being engaged by fighters above this formation of Do 17s. Blue 2 singled out an Me 109, which, after a turn, dived for the coast. Blue 2 caught it at 10,000ft and after three bursts it caught fire.

Short of fuel, Lawrence landed at Croydon, and remained there overnight before returning to base. The other nine survivors all returned safely to Middle Wallop by 20.00 hrs.

After the enemy's retirement, it was clear that the main attack on '*Loge*' had occurred between 17.45 and 18.10 hrs – and after the enemy had been harried across Kent to the coast and withdrew across the Channel to France, apart from several fighter forces sweeping the Channel, seeking to protect straggling bombers, RDF screens were otherwise blank for several hours.

During this attack, Londoners had witnessed combat on a hitherto unseen scale. Through sheer weight of numbers the Germans had reached their target, starting huge fires in the docklands and East End. Vast areas were devastated and nearly 1,800 Londoners either lost their lives or suffered injury. The majority of damage was caused to the Commercial and Millwall docks, West Ham and Barking, and bombs also fell on Purfleet, Grays and, yet again, the oil tanks at Thameshaven.

Undoubtedly, this was the most devasting conflagration London had seen since the Great Fire of 1666. Indeed, although penned 700 years previously, Dante's dark poem *Inferno* could well have been written for this moment, and as Londoners looked up at the 'fleets of wonderous birds', they doubtless wondered whether Britain ever would 'reign the sovereign of the conquered air', as Thomas Gray had so far-sightedly prophesised in 1737.

Fire Chief Aylmer Firebrace:

> The Surrey Commercial Docks had been attacked simultaneously with those north of the River. Here are situated many basins, and vast stores of soft woods, mostly imported from the Baltic … The vast area of

some two hundred and fifty acres, containing thousands of standards of timber, including a lot of pitch pine and other resinous woods stored in sheds and on open ground, burst into flame.

Incendiary bombs ignited the built-up deck cargoes of the many ships in the docks. They lodged, burning, in inaccessible places in the huge piles of timber stacked twenty feet high; they fired the carpet of tindery wood chips, which had accumulated on the timber storage foundations, so spreading the fire with the rapidity of flashing gunpowder. In a very short time, the heat was so intense that even the wood paving blocks in the roads were burning. A tempestuous roaring sea of fire increasing in violence every minute, stormed its way into the heavens.

The Fire Officer, faced with this inferno and waiting impatiently for bulk reinforcements, may be excused a lapse from standard phraseology when he sent an exasperated message: 'Send all the bloody pumps you've got; the whole bloody world's on fire!' As far as could be seen, it was.

Firemen drenched the timber stacks with water, but the moment they moved their jets to a new area, the soused wood steamed, dried, and once more burst into flame. Four auxiliary fire stations were engulfed and obliterated. Pumps became surrounded by fire and had to be abandoned, their crews only just making their escape in time.

On the river bank, people were in imminent danger of being driven into the water by the flames, and had to be evacuated by boat. Those cut off by fire at South Wharf, which lies to the east of the dock area, sought refuge in a barge; with difficulty it was towed to safety by a fire boat, nosing its nightmare way between groups of moored small craft, most of them alight, and some burning furiously.

Forty-two huge fires were now raging; one was being fought with three hundred pumps and another required one hundred and thirty. Reinforcements poured in, some eventually coming from as far afield as Birmingham and Bristol. Throughout the frightful night Pageants Wharf Fire Station remained in action and became the focus for the direction of operations. Firewomen on duty here, well led by their woman officer, stuck to their job and put out fires threatening to destroy their building. They established a well-organised dressing station for the many firemen, some smoke blind, others in great pain from sparks from the burning wood having lodged in their eyes, who came in from the fire ground. For several weeks the firewomen were to be the only representatives of their sex in this neighbourhood; all others had been evacuated.

Of the million and a half tons of soft wood timber concentrated in the Surrey Commercial Docks, four-fifths was destroyed. Daylight, so longed for by firemen on a big job, was to reveal a smoking wilderness; huge warehouses stood gutted; ships, which only a few hours previously had been discharging their cargoes, now lay, some on fire, some torn by blast, some sunk with only parts of their funnels and superstructure showing above the water.

The enemy had certainly done their work with thoroughness.

Another big conflagration area created by the attack of 7–8 September, 1940, was in the territory in which Woolwich Arsenal stands. Here land firemen and the crews of fire boats had to face the additional dangers of exploding ammunition. Projectiles from burning dumps of 'fixed' ammunition hurtled through the air turning base over nose in their flight, threatening fire boats and land fire engines impartially. Fire mains soon went out of action, and fires had to be fought with water obtained from the many dykes and ditches that abound in the Arsenal.

A message was received by the L.F.B. control stating that half a square mile of danger buildings containing H.E. shells was well alight, and the fire liable to spread to a large magazine. All fires must eventually go out; but strenuous efforts were required before this one conformed to the general rule.

As firemen toiled to extinguish the flames, debris crashing all around them, ambulances raced hither and thither, bells clanging away, and rescue parties did their best to extract survivors from their shattered homes and work places, the sky over London's docklands pulsed with the fierce blaze, glowing like a massive homing beacon into the darkening sky. There would be no respite, though: shortly after 20.00 hrs, RDF indicated three enemy formations fifteen miles north of Cap D'Antifer, flying north – '*Loge*'s' fires guiding these night-bombers of *Generalfeldmarschall* Sperrle's Luftflotte 3 back to London.

It was now that the Chiefs of Staff, shaken by the enormity of the attack on the capital, issued a simple code word: CROMWELL – invasion imminent.

The word filtered down through the army command and, unofficially, to the Home Guard. Such was the state of confusion, however, that some commanders misunderstood the order, wrongly believing that an invasion was in progress: the Home Guard vigorously rang church bells throughout the land, and in some places the army blew bridges in the hope of impeding the enemy's advance. Whatever was actually happening, all through that night and the next twelve days, regular and part-time troops remained on full alert.

It certainly appeared as though the invasion was indeed 'imminent', given the scale of this visceral attack on London – and reconnaissance aircraft of Coastal Command ominously reported the assembly of 100 invasion barges at Dunkirk, and many more at Ostend, while four *Kriegsmarine* destroyers were sighted at Cherbourg.

The renewed attack began at 20.10 hrs, lasting until 04.30 hrs the following morning, Sperrle's bombers flying shuttles, back and forth across the Channel. The RAF's nocturnal defences, however, were in their infancy: Airborne Interception radar had yet to be perfected, and dedicated night-fighting aircraft had not yet appeared in numbers, meaning that although bombing accuracy was compromised, the raiders were able to operate after dark with comparative impunity. Even so, it is surprising that Fighter Command made no attempt to intercept the first incoming waves of bombers – and the first raiders dropped bombs on Battersea, Hammersmith and Paddington, and turned for home, without even being engaged by AA fire. Indeed, the guns of the Inner Artillery Zone only opened up twenty-five minutes after Battersea was first hit, and during the night, the Blenheim night-fighters of 25 Squadron patrolled without success. In short, the Germans had it all their own way.

Of the night raid, Firebrace recalled that:

> The Thames as it flowed through the fire-ravaged docklands was experiencing the wildest night in its history. Along the south bank there was an unbroken wall of flame a thousand yards long. The fire blew half-way across the river, and such passing shipping as there was had to keep well over towards the north side, three hundred yards away. Even then some vessels could not face the heat and turned back; those that went on had their paint badly blistered.

More than sixty craft were sunk or destroyed on the river during this night of 7–8 September. Numerous blazing barges, a number of them laden with inflammable copra (the inside of coconuts), their moorings having been burnt through, drifted down the river with the tide, threatening riverside wharves; they were to be borne back, still blazing, when the flood tide made.

Half a dozen London fire boats which had been at the Thames Haven oil tank fires were ordered back to London to join in the battle. Here is how the officer in charge afterwards described the journey:

> We kept close formation until we reached Woolwich, and then we saw an extraordinary spectacle. There was nothing but fire ahead, apparently stretching right across the river and burning on both its banks. We seemed to be entering a tunnel of fire – no break in it anywhere. All the usual landmarks were obliterated by walls of flame. Burning barges drifted past. For many hours no contact with the shore was possible. We did what we could where we could as we slowly worked our way up river.
>
> At one time we were just getting into position to fight a fire in a large warehouse when the whole of the riverside front collapsed into the water with a mighty splash. The contents of the building, bags of beans, pouring into the river made a sound like a tropical rain storm. Soon after, we were surprised to see two firemen and three firewomen picking their way along the shore in the direction of Southwark Bridge; they told us they had been cut off in a control room for several hours. They had undoubtedly had a rough time of it, but did not seem unduly perturbed.

This raid gave the Regional Fire Control its first big task; soon reinforcements from all over the Region were pouring East towards a sky whose gorgeous colour told of the damage being done. Requests by West Ham for pumps gradually rose to the 500 mark. Barking and East Ham were also in difficulties and asking for help. The situation at the docks inside the L.C.C. area was so grave that 1,000 pumps were at work on these targets alone.

At last there was something very big and very fierce for firemen to get their teeth into; the lurid scenes of destruction that they were witnessing heartened them, and enabled them to exceed their normal powers of endurance.

North of the river the London and St Katharine's Docks were heavily hit and set blazing. At the West India Docks, Rum Quay, whose big peacetime fire in 1933 has been described, was burnt out. About a million and a quarter-gallons of rum were destroyed; torrents of blazing spirit flowed into the dock, while burning rum puncheons exploded, flinging jets of liquid fire in all directions.

The Royal Docks were very heavily bombarded, and not unnaturally in such circumstances, the information and reports trickling through from the Assistant Regional Fire Officer's Control in West Ham gave but a hazy picture of what was happening. It was almost impossible for those on the fire ground to size up the situation, let alone transmit a condensed report to the Regional Control. Here the only fact known was that West Ham was asking for phenomenal reinforcements; it was clear that a very serious situation had arisen.

Accordingly, at midnight I dispatched two staff officers, Mr F. Murrell, L.F.B., and Mr B. Forrester, A.F.S., to the area of the Royal Docks in order to reconnoitre the position. Their journey was rendered hazardous by the enormous craters in the roads, by getting tangled up in damaged trolley-bus wires, and by twice running over unexploded bombs. But their journey was helped for part of the way by their route being lit, as brightly as if it were day, by the colossal fires which were raging in the area of the Surrey Commercial Docks on the other side of the river.

The fires in the vicinity of the Royal Albert and King George V Docks were an awe-inspiring sight; the situation was completely out of hand. Superstructures of ships were blazing; acres of warehouses were on fire from end to end; molten tar was flowing alight over many of the roads, often filling bomb craters with liquid fire. It was a scene of weird and brilliant devilry. Many people had to be evacuated by water from their homes in the Silvertown area, driven out by the dense fumes of burning tar products.

It was one thing for staff officers to get into the fire-stricken area; it was quite another to get out again. Arriving at a bridge just as the fire was crossing it, the car accelerated and got by, the fire joining up immediately they had passed. It was their last chance of getting out; fires now blocked all exits. Bombs were still falling as they made for home, when they had an experience by no means unique in Fire Service war history.

Turning down a side street, they had to pull up sharply as an H.E. bomb cratered the road ahead of them; backing out they found that a bomb of the same stick had fallen on their route. However, their car was just small enough to squeeze past the crater. The information they brought back was of considerable value; one eye-witness account on such an occasion was worth many necessarily incomplete signals.

In the East End, Violet Regan and family had by now been evacuated to Glengall Road School. The school was crowded, 'with scarce room to move. The bedlam outside never ceased.' When the night raid began, it was 'terribly frightening … the little ones … began to scream'. Panic began rising – and so Violet's father,

> [the] possessor of a fine rich tenor voice, began to sing something they all knew, *Just a Song at Twilight*. It was touch and go at first … There was a sudden hush as they listened to him sing, then here and there a few voices around us joined in, then more, and soon it became and swell as they sang the lovely old refrain with him. What a tonic that was! To hear these tired folk lift up their voices in song, then more songs – and the wits amongst us with their spontaneous cockney humour had us all laughing in no time … When at last daylight came and the All-Clear finally sounded a gasp of sheer relief must have burst from one and all.

Such was spirit of Eastenders – who would defy and confound the air power strategists. Indeed, as Churchill later wrote:

> These were the times when the English, and particularly the Londoners, who had the place of honour, were seen at their best. Grim and gay, dogged and serviceable, with the confidence of an unconquered people in their bones, they adapted themselves to this strange way of life, with all its terrors, with all its jolts and jars.

The Battle of London had now begun, in terrifying style. As Angus Calder wrote:

> It was the battle of an unarmed civilian population against incendiaries and high-explosive; the battle of firemen, wardens, policemen, nurses and rescue workers against an enemy they could not hurt. The frontline troops were doctors, parsons, telephonists, and people in peacetime life had been clerks, builders' labourers and housewives.

The most unlikely people became heroes, or so it seemed, and without doubt *the* heroes of the hour were London's firemen, and those sent to support them.

Across the Channel, following Bomber Command's attacks on Berlin, the Nazi propaganda machine lost no time in trumpeting news of London's pain. Of this first *Vergeltungsangriff* – revenge attack – the OKW's communiqué read:

> This afternoon, the Luftwaffe attacked the port and City of London for the first time with strong forces. The attacks were carried out as a reprisal for the intensifying night attacks during the last weeks by the English Air Force against non-military targets in the Reich. One single huge smoke cloud is spreading out from the centre of London towards the Thames Estuary. Reports so far show that thirty-one enemy aircraft were shot down in aerial combat. Six of our aircraft are missing.

The Luftwaffe's actual losses were somewhat more pessimistic, however: forty aircraft had in fact been lost, and fourteen more damaged, in addition to one destroyed and four damaged in flying accidents.

As a later OKW signal read: 'The *Reichsmarschall* is personally directing the attacks from the North of France.' Indeed, Göring, contrary to his claim at Nuremburg in 1945, was doing so enthusiastically, and cock-a-hoop when he broadcast to the German Volk on the evening of 7 September 1940:

> I now want to take this opportunity of speaking to you, to say this moment is an historic one. As a result of provocative British attacks on Berlin on recent nights, the *Führer* has decided to order a mighty blow to be struck in revenge against the capital of the British Empire. I

> personally have assumed the leadership of this attack, and today I have heard above me the roaring of the victorious German squadrons which now, for the first time, are driving towards the heart of the enemy in full daylight, accompanied by countless fighter squadrons.
>
> Enemy defences were, as we expected, beaten down and the target reached, and I am certain that our successes have been as massive as the boldness of our plan of attack and the fighting spirit of our crews deserve. In any event this is an historic hour, in which for the first time the German Luftwaffe has struck at the heart of the enemy.

By any standards, the attack had been an enormous success. London had been substantially bombarded and Fighter Command had lost twenty-eight fighters destroyed and sixteen more damaged; thirteen pilots had been killed – the highest number since the great battles of 15 August 1940 (also thirteen) and including experienced men like squadron leaders O'Brien and Hull, and Flight Lieutenants Hughes and Reynell. Dowding's 'Going Downhill' conference, therefore, was perfectly timed – the new policy implemented immediately.

Among Fighter Command's movements that day was 10 Group's 213 Squadron, which flew from the quieter sector of Exeter to the frontline 11 Group sector station at Tangmere. As Pilot Officer Alexander Osmand, who had already been wounded in action, wrote to his wife that day: 'The idea petrifies me, because it is about the hottest spot in England. I suppose we have to go along and lend support in an uneven battle.' According to the Prime Minister's speech of 20 August 1940, the airman of the RAF were 'unwearied in their constant challenge': but, realistically, how much more could they take?

During the day, unsuitable weather over enemy occupied Europe had seen 2 Group's Blenheim's abandon plans to attack enemy airfields, and that night, the mist over the French coast compromised Coastal Command's raid on Boulogne Harbour.

After dark, Bomber Command's Blenheims, Wellingtons, Whitleys and Hampdens attacked the invasion ports, Emden docks, and dropped incendiaries on the Black Forest, where military supplies were hidden. Ruhr marshalling yards, Gelsenkirchen's oil refinery and Essen's Krupp steel works were also bombed. The only loss was a single Whitley of 51

Squadron, which suffered engine failure while reconnoitring the enemy coast, and forced-landed in Suffolk. None of these operations represented any kind of 'knockout blow', of course, or anything like the scale of attack on London – but, nonetheless, even after such a traumatic day, these offensive raids proved that the lion still had both wings – and teeth.

Sunday, 8 September 1940

After the previous day and night's exertions, the Luftwaffe largely spent the day regrouping – instead of continuing the daylight hammer blow on London. That morning, Air Vice-Marshal Park – the only RAF High Commander able to fly modern fighters – took-off in his personal Hurricane, 'OK1', and, according to his flying log book, flew from Northolt to Stapleford Tawney airfield, thence to the North Weald Sector station before returning to Northolt via South London.

From the vantage point of his fighter's cockpit, Park could clearly see the damage and destruction wrought by Göring's unprecedented assault of the previous day. By flying doggedly and directly to their target in close formation, thereby protected by their mutual, withering, cross-fire and hundreds of escorting fighters, the Germans had bludgeoned their way through to and grievously hurt London – which Fighter Command had failed to prevent. The still burning docklands and East End below was something Park would never forget:

> It was burning all down the river. It was a horrid sight. But I looked down and said 'Thank God for that', because I knew that the Nazis had switched their attack from our fighter stations, thinking they were knocked out. They weren't, but they were pretty groggy.

Churchill's predication that by bombing Berlin, Hitler would retaliate and bomb London – thereby saving the airfields from further damage and, having a longer flight to their target, provide Fighter Command with more opportunities to intercept, had been grimly proved correct. As previously explored, the fighter stations were not, as Park said, 'knocked' out, but as he also commented, 'they were pretty groggy'.

For all the pain Park felt viewing London's agony below, he also knew that the enemy's change of strategy represented a major turning point in the battle – and a reprieve for both his airfields, and, most importantly, his pilots – although the loss of thirteen the previous day was unsustainable going forward, if the enemy continued this scale of attack. Only time would tell what the Germans would do – but now, the Battle of the Airfields over, Park knew that he faced the greatest challenge yet: the Battle of London.

As Park's lone Hurricane flew over the capital, down below Fire Chief Alymer Firebrace visited the Royal Albert and King George V docks:

> and toured the scene of the night's disaster in company with the Chief Officer of West Ham, Mr H. Johnson. A gallant imperturbable commander of a small brigade, he was carrying a very heavy burden. His communications shattered, reliance had to be placed on dispatch riders, some of whom had come from a distance and therefore did not know the ground.
>
> Merely to keep track of the reinforcements sent to him and to provide for their feeding and relief was an administrative task of considerable magnitude. But the spirit of those still fighting fires – some of them had been continuously at work for nearly twenty-four hours – had to be seen to be believed. I had a word with a fire-blackened auxiliary who was at work on a branch, and expressed regret that it had not been possible in the circumstances prevailing, to relieve crews, or even to feed them adequately. He said:
>
> 'Don't you worry about us, Guv'nor; we've 'ad nine months without a decent fire and this is 'eaven!'
>
> It seemed more like hell to me, but there was room for both opinions.

Churchill sped to the East End, with his entourage, to see the damage for himself. According to an eyewitness, Colin Perry:

> He looked invincible, which he is. Tough, bulldogged, piercing. He made his way through the smoke, the City workers all crying 'Good old Winston' … and the culminating cry of 'Are we downhearted?' to the heaven-rising response of 'N-o-o-o-o', which echoed around the city and, indeed, the world. It was magnificent, stirring, dramatic.

Harold Scott was with Churchill at Silvertown: 'Pessimists had predicted panic and bitterness in the East End, but I saw nothing of the kind. Smiles, cheers and grim determination showed already that "London can take it".'

Others were less enthusiastic, an anonymous East End lady apparently telling Church 'exactly would 'e could take!' Nonetheless, in the days and many nights ahead, London would have to 'take it' – and 'take it' Londoners did, confounding the pre-war predictions of bombing's effect on civilian populations. And, beyond doubt, Churchill, for all his now oft-mooted other flaws, was just the war leader Britain needed – and this day saw this human dynamo in his element, doing what he did best: leading by example and from the front.

Surely, even his most ardent critics could not help but admire this giant of a man, striding through the smoke and debris, inspiring the people, twirling his bowler hat in the air on his walking cane, giving his famous 'V for Victory' sign wherever he went. This, of course, was Churchill at his very best and in his own 'Finest Hour'.

Having moved from Exeter to Tangmere the previous day, Pilot Officer Alexander Osmand wrote to his fiancée, Miss Marjorie Hodgetts, in Bristol:

> We are just getting settled in our new home, bit by bit, our quarters here are quite sumptuous, as we live in the old married quarters, but we may not stay there long. There is a movement afoot to billet us out, or at least find some place away from the aerodrome. Then if the Huns choose to flatten the place off, we won't be in such danger. There's no sense in risking pilots, as long as their near enough to be got at in an acute emergency.
>
> The Mess here is pretty good, and well up to the usual RAF station standard, it's a typical Mess, of course, unlike our place at Exeter, which was the old Exeter Flying Club place. Really, at Exeter we were sitting pretty; the place was really comfortable, and quite nicely decorated. It was a change from the general run of messes, which are always depressing in their drab sameness. But a pukka Mess has certain advantages, meals can be got conveniently at all hours, and the service is exemplary. All our cares are meticulously attended to … which is just as it should be!
>
> I had a good long night's rest last night, and today I feel a whole heap better and more cheerful … I'm afraid I let things get me down

a bit, but I guess it was the suddenness of the blow of our move. We only had six hours' notice to get away, and that's enough to tax anyone's imagination, especially if the person concerned is inclined to be sensitive!

Anyway, here I am and, as I say, we are getting rapidly settled in our new home. I suppose we have come in at the critical period of the war, and will have more than enough to keep us busy, but that will give us the chance to do our share unstintingly. I shall take every possible care of myself … and for the rest, I entrust myself, and all my love, into God's care.

Darling, I have just heard about the bombing of London, yesterday and last night. It was terrible, and utterly ruthless, and if that doesn't make us mad, heaven knows what will! This is war, and we must fight these Germans with everything in our power. We must meet ruthlessness with ruthlessness, for they must be brought to account for their inhumanity. I can only pray that in the midst of everything you have been safe, and your courage strong. It would be more than I could stand if anything happened to you.

I worry a lot at this hour when things have been even worse than they have been in past weeks, and I wish with all my heart that you were away from it all, you and all your family. Can't you, and your mother and Joan, get away to Sudbury at once? At the earliest opportunity, I am going to phone home, and ask them to see if they can put you up. However bad things are round home, it must be paradise compared to poor old London, I should know, I've seen what's been happening from the air!

Well, whatever plans and schemes I may have – I can't do anything about them at the moment. Our meals are severely curtailed owing to the hectic state of affairs, and we have had to resort to having our meals sent over to our flight dispersal points. We can then take bites between flights! Or, take a plate with us!! Actually, with alarms and excursions, the time is nearly 2.30 pm now, and we haven't yet had lunch. We live in hope that it will turn up within the next few hours … Hurrah! Here it is and I am hungry! Excuse me darling, while I eat, won't you!!

Ah! That was most welcome and I feel a much better man for it. I'm just wondering if it will ever be worthwhile going to the Mess for our food, if our feed can come to us. Must be influence or something, but

> it's a darned good idea, We'll just have to lie in luxury, and make them wait on us hand and foot, just exerting ourselves when flying must be seen to. If it wasn't for the flying, we could live the ideal life of eating and sleeping, and all without having to move more than a few feet!!
>
> But enough of this frivolity! My dearest love, I'm not going to say much more for the moment. Things are pretty hectic, and if I get this finished and into the Mess post, while I have the chance, you won't be left waiting for it ... This and my last two notes have been rather brief, and hardly up to my usual standard ... But I think you understand. It's been a bit upsetting, having to move hastily and so very unexpectedly, but I'm gradually gaining my usual composure.

The lull after the enemy exertions enabled Air Chief Marshal Dowding rotate more of his squadrons: 43 Squadron, leaderless and decimated, was pulled out of the line and replaced at Tangmere by 607 Squadron.

Pilot Officer Harry Welford:

> I shall always remember 8 September 1940, because it was the day after the evening that Betty Elise and I became engaged, but our move to Tangmere was confirmed that day. We were to relieve 43 Squadron, which had barely half the intended complement of pilots left capable of operational duties.
>
> Of course it was a tragedy so far as my fiancée was concerned and, though I felt the same, there was a war to be fought and we were trained fighters. This was the beginning of the end, and, as we all climbed into our Hurricanes, having bid our adieus that fine Sunday morning, I wondered how many of us would see Usworth or Newcastle again. Strange as it may seem, dirty, smoky old Newcastle was suddenly a seventh heaven compared to the green fields of southern England.
>
> We arrived at a completely blitzed aerodrome and were greeted by the remains of 43 Squadron, some on crutches, others with arms in slings, and yet another with his head swathed in bandages having had his face torn by an exploding enemy cannon shell. Though they had so many casualties it was amazing to see them walking about. Needless to say, they were very pleased to see us, having just been up on the third sortie of the day and waiting for news of their latest casualties. We only

had time to refuel before being called upon to fly an operational patrol that evening. There was no interception and no casualties.

Another change in 11 Group was that 79 Squadron was rested, the twelve remaining operational pilots flying from Biggin Hill to Pembrey in South Wales, swapping places with the rested 92 Squadron.

The day began very quietly, with only occasional German fighter patrols sweeping the Channel, photographic reconnaissance flights, and an unsuccessful attack on a convoy in the St George's Channel. By late morning the enemy fighter forays over the Dover Straits had increased, suggesting that a threat was building up.

In anticipation, 11 Group scrambled ten squadrons with orders to cover the ring of sector stations around London, but the first enemy incursions were a fighter sweep only as far inland as Ashford, and the rather pointless dropping of a few bombs on the coast at St Margaret's Bay. At 11.35 hrs, however, RDF indicated a formation of fifty plus which crossed the coast over Ramsgate at midday, flying west, parallel with the Thames Estuary – the whole of II/KG 2, heading for London's docklands, escorted by the Me 109s of JGs 2, 3, 26, 27, 51 and 53.

The escort mission, however, began badly for I/JG53, as *Oberleutnant* Wittmeyer, the Adjutant of I/JG 53 recalled:

> Off Dungeness we were met by a flight of three fighters at low altitude. I reported them to *Hauptmann* Mayer by radio: he replied 'Let's have a closer look at them!' The entire *Gruppe* descended to investigate these aircraft. We soon recognised the approaching fighters as Me 109s – but we were now so close that we were racing towards each other. The leader of the other flight and his *Rottenflieger* were able to break away in time but I collided head-on with No 3. The other machine went down immediately but its propeller had badly damaged my cockpit – one blade had struck the cockpit immediately in front of me, while another severed my seat harness directly behind me and I was thrown out of the cockpit.
>
> I was able to open my parachute over the water and a strong wind carried me far to the East, toward Cap Gris-Nez. I landed in the water just off the coast and soon rescued by a boat belonging to the Todt

> Organisation. I had serious injuries to both eyes and my face from tiny aluminium fragments from the other aircraft's propeller; even after convalescence I never fully regained my sight and lost stereoscopic vision.

The pilot of the other 109, *Oberleutnant* Kunert, *Staffelkapitän* of 8/JG 53 was less fortunate: he fell from his parachute harness and drowned.

At 11.20 hrs, eleven Spitfires of 41 Squadron had left Hornchurch to patrol Dover, where, at 12.15 hrs, the Spitfires were ambushed by Me 109s, one of which shot down Flying Officer William 'Scotty' Scott who was seen going down in flames. Scott went into the Channel, from which his body was only recovered on 1 November 1940. There was no other contact and the Spitfire pilots made no combat claims.

Interestingly, according to the ORB, 46 Squadron, based at Stapleford, was ordered to form a wing with Hendon's 504 Squadron – further evidencing the fact that Air Vice-Marshal Park was not averse to using such formations when appropriate. At 11.30 hrs, twelve Hurricanes of 46 Squadron scrambled to patrol base at 10,000ft and rendezvous with 504 Squadron over North Weald.

At 12.15 hrs, the incoming raid was sighted flying north-west, towards North Weald, at 18,000ft, ahead and to port, the thirty Dorniers in three waves, the fighter escorts flying astern and stepped up from 25,000–30,000ft. No.46 Squadron managed to get at the bombers before the Me 109s came down, after which a dogfight developed south of the Thames Estuary, over the Isle of Sheppey. Leading 46 Squadron was Flight Lieutenant Alexander Rabagliati, flying the experimental Hurricane armed with four 20mm cannons. According to the squadron's subsequent Intelligence Patrol Report, Rabagliati 'opened fire at 250 yards and after firing eighty rounds his guns packed up. He continued right through the formation of bombers, throwing his machine about in an endeavour to get the guns working again, but without success.'

Sergeant Stanley Andrew had more luck flying a conventional machine-gun-armed Hurricane, who attacked a Do 17 of 5/KG 2 which went into a spin before exploding in mid-air over Maidstone, killing the four-man crew. Andrew also damaged another bomber, as did Pilot Officers Peter Lefevre, Peter McGregor and Charles Ambrose. Sergeant William Peacock hit a 109 of 3/JG 53 which crashed at Seal, near Sevenoaks, killing the pilot,

Unteroffizier B. Adelwart; Ambrose claimed a 109 probable and a damaged 110, and McGregor a damaged 109.

In turn, the Me 109s of 4 and 6/JG 2, roughly handled 46 Squadron: Sergeant Andrew's Hurricane was shot-up, although the pilot was unhurt and returned safely to base; Pilot Officer McGregor was shot down and crash-landed at Happy Valley, Meopham, and Flying Officer Roy McGowan forced-landed his damaged aircraft at Biggin Hill.

Two pilots, however, were missing. Flight Lieutenant Norman Burnett, the commander of 'B' Flight, had baled out over Sheppey, news being received of his admission to Queen Mary's Hospital, Sidcup, suffering from burns – but of Sub-Lieutenant Jack Carpenter there was no such welcome news. A Canadian serving in the FAA and who was among those gallant nautical airmen who volunteered to fight with Fighter Command, it was ascertained that Carpenter had also baled out – but had fallen dead near Maidstone.

No.504 Squadron did not contact the enemy and all pilots returned safely to Hendon.

Twelve Hurricanes of 605 Squadron had left Croydon at 11.50 hrs to patrol base with Kenley's 253 Squadron. Yellow Section of 605's 'A' Flight flew at 17,000ft, above the remaining Hurricanes, providing top and rear cover. Having been vectored hither and thither, 605 Squadron was heading north between Maidstone and Tunbridge Wells, also sighting the enemy formations flying west. Before the Hurricanes attacked, a Do 17 was seen to be hit by AA fire, which went down in flames. There were, in fact, two Do 17s destroyed by the Thames and Medway gunners, one of which crashed near Farningham Road railway station, the other exploding over it.

According to 605 Squadron's Intelligence Patrol report, 'B' Flight, which was ahead and led by Flight Lieutenant Archie McKellar, immediately prepared to attack the bombers from abeam but as the Hurricanes approached the Germans changed course, towards the Hurricanes. 'B' Flight therefore attacked head-on, McKellar raking the leader with a five-second burst. The remainder of 'B' Flight and Red Section of 'A' Flight then attacked the Do 17s on the port side, breaking up the formation. Inevitably, Me 109s intervened, diving on 'A' Flight. Pilot Officer Christopher 'Bunny' Currant, Red 1, fired a two-second burst at a 109, which broke away, badly damaged, and Yellow 2, Pilot Officer Tom Cooper-Slipper claimed a 109 destroyed. Yellow 1, Pilot Officer Alec Ingle, hit a Dornier which dived, emitting black smoke, and other bombers were damaged by Currant and Cooper-Slipper, while Green 1, Pilot Officer James Humphreys, a New Zealander, damaged a 109. Yellow 3, Flying Officer John Fleming, also a New Zealander, was shot down in flames, however, baling out horrendously burned over Tunbridge Wells.

No.605 Squadron's spirited head-on charge had broken up the enemy KG 2 formation, which wheeled about, retreating eastwards without reaching its target or dropping any bombs. Given that cloud was 10/10ths, however (501 Squadron ORB refers), the Germans very likely simply aborted the mission, being unable to bomb blind.

At 12.20 hrs, twelve Hurricanes of 501 Squadron scrambled from Gravesend, led by Squadron Leader Harry Hogan, Red 1, to patrol base. When climbing at 5,000ft the Hurricane pilots saw forty withdrawing enemy aircraft high above them but were unable to climb fast enough to intercept. Instead, 501 Squadron was sent to patrol Hawkinge where a single Me 109 attacked Green Section, the unit's rearguard. Green 1, Pilot Officer Byron Duckenfield, dived away, his assailant suddenly appearing in front of him: two short bursts sent the 109 into the sea – marking the end of the day's fighting.

The only other combat during the day had been off the Scottish coast, at 13.12 hrs; while on patrol, Pilot Officer Jas Storrar and Blue Section of Dyce's 145 Squadron sighted a lone Dornier twenty-five miles east of Montrose and gave chase. Already low on fuel, however, the Hurricanes only managed three short bursts, two of which were seen to hit the reconnaissance bomber, which made good its escape into cloud.

During the day, there was plenty of action for Coastal Command and the Blenheims of 2 Group, Bomber Command. At 10.35 hrs, fifteen German ships were reported off Cap Gris-Nez – prompting an immediate attack by Blenheims of 53 and 59 squadrons. The results of this bombing was not observed, however, because the bombers were suddenly attacked by Me 109s returning from their escort mission to London docks: two Blenheims of Detling's 53 Squadron were destroyed, the crews of which were reported missing.

Coastal Command also lost a Hudson of 224 Squadron, based at Leuchars, which failed to return from a patrol over the North Sea, having also fallen victim to Me 109s. There were daylight losses too for Bomber Command: the Watton-based 82 'United Provinces' Squadron lost two Blenheims to Me

109s, their crews, both on reconnaissance flights of the Dutch and Belgian coasts, also disappearing without trace. So too did a crew of 40 Squadron, raiding Ostend, and two 101 Squadron Blenheims attacking Boulogne. *Gefreiter* Erhardt Scheidt of 1/JG 26, *Oberleutnant* Ludwig Franzisket of 7/JG 27, *Oberleutnant* Rudolf Busch of 3/JG 51 and *Leutnant* Heinz Altendorf of 7/JG 53 all claimed Blenheims destroyed.

No.107 Squadron, based at Wattisham, also lost two Blenheims and crews raiding Ostend, and a 218 Squadron Blenheim disappeared without trace on a North Sea reconnaissance sortie. By night, 130 Bomber Command Blenheims, Wellingtons, Whitleys and Hampdens targeted the invasion ports of Ostend and Boulogne, enemy shipping at Bremen and Hamburg docks, and marshalling yards in Germany. Ostend and Boulogne were successfully attacked, but as the night wore on, deteriorating weather frustrated most other raids.

That night German bombers returned to London. By morning, twelve more fires had been started, and another 412 Londoners were dead; the survivors were not to know that they would have to endure a further fifty-five consecutive nights of such torment and anguish before the *Nachtangriff* abated.

No.605 Squadron's ORB:

> German bombers came over London district again at night, dropping bombs apparently indiscriminately: raids did not cease till dawn. Flight Lieutenant McKellar, Pilot Officer Humphreys and Pilot Officer Forrester stole or borrowed the Station Bedford truck, which Flight Lieutenant McKellar drove to enable them to enjoy the fleshpots of London – owing to the air raids they never slept a wink and returned in truculent mood having found no consolation for lack of sleep, whereas we at Croydon slept soundly!

Monday, 9 September 1940

The new day dawned with a 9/10ths covering of cloud over southern England, the overcast only diminishing to 7/10ths by late afternoon. The lull in the fighting provided another opportunity for Air Chief Marshal Dowding to rotate certain squadrons: at 13.45 hrs, nine Hurricanes of 229 Squadron's 'A' Flight and ten of 'B' left Wittering in 12 Group to change places with

Northolt's 1 Squadron. No.229 Squadron's CO was Squadron Leader Arthur Banham, previously among the first ever Spitfire pilots when 19 Squadron received the new type at Duxford in August 1938, who had later served as a flight commander on 264 Squadron, flying the ill-fated Defiant turret-fighter, surviving being shot down on 26 August 1940; it was Banham's third day in command of 229 Squadron.

Having been relieved at Kenley by 66 Squadron six days earlier and repaired to Coltishall, on this day the remnants of 616 Squadron, now categorised a 'C' unit under the auspices of the 'Going Downhill' policy, were replaced at Coltishall by 74 Squadron and withdrew further north to Kirton. Between June and August 1940, 74 Squadron had flown from the Hornchurch sector in 11 Group, then, after a brief stay at Wittering, had rested and also received and trained replacements at Kirton. Now a 'B' unit, the South African Squadron Leader Adolph Gysbert 'Sailor' Malan rotated his 74 Squadron with newly promoted Squadron Leader Billy Burton's 616. It was a clever system – which worked. No.74, of course, was a famous squadron; their South African leader already a legend in Fighter Command and a leading ace.

Apart from fighter patrols over the Dover Strait, there was little enemy activity until 16.05 hrs when, like the day before, these sorties began increasing. Air Vice-Marshal Park reacted in strength: at 16.30 hrs, the Spitfires of 92 Squadron were scrambled from Biggin Hill with orders to patrol Canterbury; and at 16.44 hrs those of 41 Squadron went up from Hornchurch to patrol Maidstone.

The previous day, Park had ordered that wherever possible, 46 Squadron at Stapleford would form a wing with North Weald's 249 Squadron and Hendon's 504; at 16.45 hrs, therefore, the Hurricanes of 46 and 249 squadrons took off, rendezvoused and headed for Rochford. At the same time, the Spitfires of 66 Squadron scrambled from Kenley to reinforce 41 Squadron over Maidstone.

By 16.50 hrs, RDF screens were indicating six separate enemy formations, each with an average estimated strength of thirty plus, either off Calais or the Dover Strait. Four of these raids were on course for northern Kent and the Thames Estuary, suggesting that London or the sector stations in that area were the intended target.

Four large enemy formations were also approaching the Sussex coast, so 12 Group was requested to cover the airfields north of the Thames: at 16.50 hrs, 'B' Flight of Squadron Leader James McComb's 611 Squadron was scrambled from Fowlmere to patrol North Weald, first below cloud-base, then at 27,000ft (although a distant enemy formation was sighted, wisely McComb remained on his allotted patrol line and these 12 Group Spitfires were not engaged). No.10 Group was also requested to assist; at the same time 12 Group's first fighters left Duxford, the Spitfires of 234 Squadron left Middle Wallop in Hampshire, followed by those of 609 at 17.00 hrs, to patrol Brooklands. Simultaneously, Squadron Leader Douglas Bader led the Hurricanes of 242 and 310 squadrons off from Duxford – contrary to widely held but mistaken belief, however, there was never any time wasted orbiting the airfield and awaiting the arrival of Squadron Leader Brian Lane's 19 Squadron Spitfires from nearby Fowlmere: Bader simply set course and everyone else fell in behind, the Spitfires easily catching up the slower Hurricanes and providing top cover.

On this occasion the Duxford Wing's orders were to patrol North Weald at 20,000ft. According to Bader biographer Paul Brickhill, the instruction Bader received from Duxford's Station Commander and Sector Controller, Wing Commander Alfred 'Woody' Woodhall, was '*Will* you patrol between North Weald and Hornchurch, angels twenty?' This 'order', if true, was open to personal interpretation by the Duxford formation leader. Indeed, Bader ignored the given height by climbing to 22,000ft, and led the Duxford Wing not towards North Weald, as instructed and required by 11 Group, but south-west and over London. Air Vice-Marshal Park, of course, had every right to expect that supporting groups would obey his orders – but here we have the first example of 12 Group's growing confidence that 11 Group's orders could be bypassed.

No.11 Group also scrambled more fighters: 257 Squadron's Hurricanes at 16.53 hrs, sent from Martlesham, to patrol West Mersea, and 603 Squadron's Spitfires hurriedly left Hornchurch at 16.55 hrs to patrol the East Sussex coast, and at 17.00 hrs, the Hurricanes of 605 Squadron hastened from Croydon to Maidstone, those of 607 Squadron were sent from Tangmere to Mayfield and at 17.04 hrs, the Spitfires of 602 Squadron left Westhampnett with identical orders. A minute later, 17 Squadron's Hurricanes left Tangmere to cover base, and at 17.12 hrs 253's Hurricanes scrambled from Kenley to patrol base and Biggin Hill. The Northolt Wing, comprising 1(RCAF) and 303 Squadrons, then took-off at 17.20 hrs to rendezvous over and patrol their airfield.

At 17.35 hrs, by which time German formations had already crossed the coast, 72 Squadron were sent from Croydon to patrol Biggin Hill, and five minutes later the freshly arrived 229 Squadron left Northolt to patrol base.

Some 300 plus German aircraft were now over south-east England; Air Vice-Marshal Park had reacted in strength, thanks to the new 'Going Downhill' policy – and his tactic of squadrons fighting in pairs was paying off – much to the enemy bomber crews' dismay, who continued demanding closer fighter protection. This was a mistake: as we have seen, consistent with lessons of the First World War, fighters were actually more effective when free to hunt and engage the enemy, not when shackled to a close escort role – reassuring though the sight of so many friendly fighters clustered closely around the bombers must have been for those units.

With so many aircraft of both sides airborne, the fog of war hangs densely over the exact sequence of subsequent interceptions. Although detail for both squadrons is scant regarding this particular action, it would seem from the information available that the Spitfires of 41 Squadron were first to sight and engage the enemy in the South London – Maidstone area, at or around 17.00 hrs. According to the ORB, 41 Squadron 'sighted large formation of E/A and engaged them. Enemy casualties one He 111 destroyed and one damaged; seven Me 109s destroyed and one damaged. Our casualties nil.' None of these claims can be definitely verified, however.

No.92 Squadron Intelligence Patrol Report:

> The Squadron got split up and the first to attack seems to be Flight Lieutenant Kingcome who first saw a large formation of enemy bombers being attacked by a squadron of Spitfires [41 Squadron]. He climbed up and saw twelve yellow-nosed Me 109s circling in line astern. He joined in on the end of the formation and gave the last E/A a short burst. E/A dived away from the formation with smoke emerging. He was attacked by the rest so he dived away and later climbed back and attacked another Me 109 with no apparent effect. Was again attacked by the remainder so he dived away and returned to base.

> The Bomber formation was now out of sight of the fighter formation. Squadron Leader Sanders saw Green Section behind him being attacked by Me 109. He got in a short burst at one of them but could not see the effect as his turn was too tight and he spun out of it.
>
> On instruction returned to base and encountered a formation of He 111s about ten miles SSE of Biggin Hill, heading North. Attacked the left one head-on, closing to 100 yards, broke away upwards and saw E/A slide out of the formation, going down in a left-hand turn. Immediately afterwards he saw an Me 109, got on its tail and got in a deflection shot by turning inside it. E/A half-rolled and dived. Black smoke coming out behind it. He followed it and fired several short bursts from 200 yards, diving very fast. He eventually left E/A at 2,000ft in cloud.

Sanders, the CO, and Kingcome, commander of 'A' Flight, made 92 Squadron's only claims, the former for a He 111 destroyed and an Me 109 probable, the latter also for a 109 probable. The squadron lost two Spitfires: Pilot Officer Cecil Saunders was shot down over Rye and baled out with shrapnel wounds to his legs; Pilot Officer William Watling was also hit over Rye, baling out off Winchelsea and being rescued from the sea, badly burnt. Pilot Officer Alan Wright's Spitfire was severely damaged, although he returned safely to base and was unhurt. All three had been hit by that master of the ambush from on high and out of the sun: *Oberleutnant* Gerhard Schöpfel, *Kommandeur* of III/JG 26.

No.501 patrolled Canterbury at 25,000ft, but only Flight Lieutenant John Gibson, Red 1, who had become separated from the rest of his squadron, sighted a formation of enemy bombers, one of which he attacked, but without any apparent result. All eleven Hurricanes landed safely back at Gravesend at 18.08 hrs.

According to 310 Squadron, a large enemy formation was sighted, 'South of the Thames Estuary, heading north-west … The attack was delivered South of London' – this being a raid heading for RAE Farnborough. This was, however, exactly the scenario Dowding and Park had sought to avoid: the sector stations north of the Thames were now unprotected – and yet the possibility of a threat against them could not be discounted.

While evidence exists confirming that 12 Group was on occasion called for too late, this equally demonstrates that 12 Group's contribution was often self-serving: instead of patrolling the airfields north of the river, as instructed, Squadron Leader Bader had led the Duxford Wing on what amounted to a fighter sweep over London – which was hardly likely to improve relations between the two groups.

The usual confused fight developed. Although 310 Squadron reported attacking 'Do 215s [*sic*]', it actually became embroiled with Me 110s and He 111s, the latter of KG 1 and RAE Farnborough bound. During the initial charge, Flight Lieutenant Gordon Sinclair collided with Flying Officer Johnnie Boulton; the former safely took to his parachute but the 20-year-old Boulton was killed. His Hurricane, in fact, collided in turn with an Me 110 of 9/ZG 76 which crashed at Woodmanstone – some thirty miles south-west of North Weald. The Me 110 attacked by Flying Officer Bergman and Pilot Officer Fejfar exploded over Worcester Park; Pilot Officer Zimprich fired at a 3/KG 1 He 111 already engaged by 607 Squadron's Sergeant Burnell-Phillips, the bomber forced-landing near Sundridge.

Given their Spitfires' superior performance at high altitude, 19 Squadron had been detailed to protect 242 and 310 Squadrons from high-flying German fighters. Having climbed to 23,000ft, the Spitfires were soon in action, subsequently making various claims. Pilot Officer Wallace 'Jock' Cunningham left an Me 109 'enveloped in flames' and which crashed at Ditcham. Sergeant David 'Little Boy' Cox left another diving in flames. Sub-Lieutenant Giles 'Admiral' Blake, however, pursued the raiders across the Channel, leaving an He 111 with both engines stopped and descending seawards.

When the Duxford Wing attacked, Bader himself fired a long burst at the leading He 111, which he left 'turning on its back', later writing in his log book that he had, 'Got the leader in flames.' Pilot Officer Willie McKnight claimed a Dornier in flames and the destruction of an escorting fighter. Flight Lieutenant Ball also claimed an Me 109 flamer.

No.242 Squadron, however, lost a pilot killed in this action, the Canadian Pilot Officer Kirkpatrick Sclanders being shot down and killed, his Hurricane crashing near Caterham. Another Hurricane was also destroyed when Sergeant Robert Lonsdale, also a Canadian, was badly shot-up by a bomber's return fire, forcing him to bale out over Kenley; the pilot was unhurt. No.310 Squadron had lost Flying Officer Boulton in the collision with Flight Lieutenant Sinclair, and the Czech Pilot Officer Frantisek Rypl's Hurricane was damaged when he forced-landed at Oxted, out of fuel. Two of

19 Squadron's Spitfires were also damaged: Sub-Lieutenant Blake returned to Fowlmere with a damaged gravity tank and windscreen, and Pilot Officer Cunningham's aircraft had taken a bullet through the all-important mainspar.

Upon conclusion of this engagement, the wing's squadrons claimed as follows:

19 Squadron: 5 (and 2 shared destroyed), 3 probables, 0 damaged.
310 Squadron: 3/3/1.
242 Squadron: 10 destroyed.

Wing total: 20 (and 2 shared destroyed), 6/2.

The wing's score of twenty destroyed and two shared, along with six probables and two damaged, made impressive reading. Soon, 242 Squadron received further congratulatory signals from Leigh-Mallory and the CAS. Those in high places were becoming increasingly convinced that 12 Group had got it right.

The reality, however, was that only four enemy aircraft were definitely destroyed that day in combat with the Duxford Wing (and another through the collision with Boulton). The available evidence, therefore, suggests that on this occasion the wing over-claimed by some 5:1, it being noteworthy that 242 Squadron's claims were already consistently and substantially higher than the wing's other squadrons.

By now, the fighting was very confused, with combats swirling, ebbing and flowing between Guildford and the Sussex and Kentish coasts.

No.605 Squadron's ORB states that,

> the Squadron took off and intercepted seventeen He 111s with large numbers of Me 110, Me 109 and He 113 [*sic*] protection near Farnborough, Kent. By constant attack the enemy formation was broken up and prevented from attacking London. Other attacks took place as far away as Farnborough, Hants. Flight Lieutenant McKellar destroyed three He 111s and one Me 109; Pilot Officer Currant and Sergeant Wright destroyed an Me 110 and Pilot Officer Currant had a share in destroying an Me 109 with another Hurricane squadron. Pilot Officer Humphreys baled out near Borden with a small wound in his hand.

Pilot Officer George Forrester, however, was missing, it later being established that having been hit by return fire from a *Stab* III/KG 53 He 111, his Hurricane collided with the bomber and crashed at Shalden, killing the pilot; the bomber crashed near Alton, one of the crew baling out to become a POW, the other three crewmen dying in the crash.

No.72 Squadron, up at Angels 15, sighted the enemy bombers and fighter escorts over Biggin Hill, but owing to R/T malfunction, when Flight Lieutenant Ted Graham ordered an attack in sections line astern, this went unreceived. Consequently the Spitfires failed to contact the enemy, although Sergeant Basil Douthwaite, who was weaving behind the squadron, was fortunate to encounter and engage an Me 110, which he 'shot down in flames near Lewes [ORB]'. This 110, of 9/ZG 76, was retiring from London and ditched in the Channel off Newhaven; the pilot, *Feldwebel* Hermann Koops being captured, but his *Bordfunker*, *Unteroffizier* Christian Weiher (unusually a member of another *Staffel*, namely 7/ZG 76) was killed.

The Spitfire pilots of 222 Squadron found the enemy while patrolling at 27,000ft over Ashford; Pilot Officer Laurie Whitbread:

> Whilst on patrol over East Kent we sighted a formation of enemy bombers flying West at 20,000ft, above cloud. It had an escort of Me 109s, flying above and behind at 26,000ft, and also another formation of fighters flying to one side, at the same height as the bombers. The fighters were engaged. I had a combat with an Me 109. A burst of roughly four seconds from my guns appeared to shoot off the starboard aileron when the 109 went into a spin. It continued to spin downwards into the cloud layer when it disappeared from view. My flight leader stated that he observed the 109 spin down and the pilot bale out.

In his diary, the young Ludlovian wrote: 'One Me 109 claim, confirmed by van Mentz.' The enemy fighter belonged to 6/JG 27 and crashed at Mounts Farm, Benenden, at 18.15 hrs, the enemy pilot, *Unteroffizier* Georg Rauwolf, being captured.

Pilot Officer Tim Vigors also claimed a 109 destroyed but was shot-up himself, his Spitfire's engine hit by three cannon rounds, forcing him to crash-land at Southfleet. Pilot Officer John Broadhurst claimed a 109 damaged before 'having a large part of the tail of his aircraft shot away, successfully landed at Rochford [ORB]'; Sergeant Ernest Scott also damaged a 109.

At 17.40 hrs, 253 Squadron's Flying Officer Roy Watts returned to Kenley when a cockpit side panel inexplicably broke open, leaving the eight remaining Hurricanes patrolling base and Biggin Hill at 6,000ft, below cloud. The enemy was then sighted approaching from the east at 15,000ft: seventeen bombers and heavy fighter escort, which 253 Squadron sighted above them and through a gap in the clouds. The squadron reported the enemy's presence, then turned west, climbing to 14,000ft before being vectored to intercept a bigger raid. According to the squadron's Intelligence Patrol Report:

> a formation of thirty-four Ju 88s at 15,000ft escorted by a large number of fighters were sighted five miles off the starboard bow. Squadron turned West and climbing to 16,000ft turned towards bombers delivered a diving beam attack on the bombers starboard bow in sections line astern, opening fire at about 450 yards closing to fifty yards. The attack was apparently most successful as the bombers broke formation and turned South, jettisoning their bombs.
>
> It was observed that as the squadron was about to attack, the bombers signalled to their fighters by firing a red star cartridge and the second attack was prevented by enemy fighters engaging the squadron until the bombers were out of range. No individual claims are made but several pilots agree that five Ju 88s broke off and dived away as though destroyed.

One 253 Squadron Hurricane 'forced-landed at Cobham Farm' after the engagement, 'pilot safe [ORB]'.

There was also action over West Kent and East Sussex. The first defending squadron to engage the incoming enemy was the newly arrived 607 Squadron. Previously, based at Usworth in Northumberland, the squadron had been involved in the 'Junkers Party' off the north-east coast on 15 August 1940, when 12 and 13 Groups squadrons routed Luftflotte 5. Those enemy bombers, however, were escorted by Me 110s, so 607 Squadron had no experience of fighting the Me 109 during the Battle of Britain – and like various other units would find the change in the battle's tempo traumatic.

No.607 Squadron's CO, Squadron Leader James Vick, led the full operational complement of twelve Hurricanes on patrol over Mayfield at 17,000ft – when at 17.30 hrs enemy aircraft were sighted flying north. According to the ORB, these numbered '60/70 E/A, possibly Ju 88 and Do 17', and '40/50 Me 109s were seen both sides of and astern of the bombers at about 19,000ft'. According to Sergeant Peter Burnell-Phillips, however, the enemy numbered '150, including fighters escort and bombers', the latter being 'Do 17s and 215s [*sic*]'. There was no ambiguity over the identity of the German fighters: 'Me 109s', although Burnell-Phillips timed the action at 17.20 hrs and occurring in the 'Tunbridge Wells locality'.

While Vick's Hurricanes were 2,000ft higher than the enemy bombers, the Me 109s had a height advantage over 607 Squadron of 2,000ft – and substantially outnumbered the 'County of Durham' fighters. Blue Section attacked the bombers from below without any apparent result, while Vick ordered Green Section to provide a rearguard. After this initial attack, the bombers were out of reach, so Red and Yellow Sections were ordered to engage the Me 109s.

Sergeant Burnell-Phillips, Yellow 2, also managed to attack the bombers, however,

> accompanying Yellow 1, Flying Officer Foster, I made a quarter attack from below. First attack unsuccessful. Made a second attack from approximately 5,000ft above, diving under fighter escort from out of the sun. This attack was successful. The E/A, a Dornier, broke away with both motors on fire. I continued to attack, firing approximately 1,500 rounds.

This was not a 'Dornier' but a 3/KG 1 He 111 en route to bomb London and which forced-landed near Sundridge, having subsequently been attacked by 310 Squadron's Pilot Officer Zimprich.

Inevitably, though, the 109s rained down; Burnell-Phillips continues: 'At that point I was myself attacked by three Me 109s. A bullet in my oil tank forced me to land near Knockholt with a seized engine. The E/A landed about four miles away. This was confirmed by the local police.'

Burnell-Phillips made the squadron's only combat claim in this action – which proved catastrophic for 607 Squadron due to the Me 109s' attack. Pilot Officer Stuart Parnall was shot down and killed at Goudhurst; Pilot Officer John Lenahan at Cranbrook; Sergeant Richard Spyer was shot-up and baled out slightly wounded, his Hurricane crashing at East Peckham. Pilot Officer George Drake, however, was missing.

Pilot Officer Harry Welford, 607 Squadron:

> That fateful day, much to my disappointment, I was not called upon to fly and inevitably the squadron later went off. As it happened I was the most fortunate, as in this, the squadron's first engagement since arriving in 11 Group, our Hurricanes were well and truly bounced by Me 109s: we lost six out of twelve aircraft; two NCOs were wounded and three officers killed. Among the latter were my best friends, Stuart Parnall and 'Scotty' Lenahan, and as no more was ever heard of young George Drake, his death was presumed. We were shocked, we just couldn't take it all in. No one talked of it but we all hoped for news of the missing from some pub or hospital.
>
> No news came and so we bit back our tears and sorrow. It was 'You heard about Stuart and Scotty? Rotten luck, wasn't it?', and someone would add, 'And young George Drake, bloody good blokes, all of them.' After that epitaph the matter would be dismissed with the ordering of another round of drinks to avoid any further evidence of sentiment. The truth of it, though, still hurts me to think of it even now.
>
> After the Battle of France, we had received a number of replacement pilots, straight from OTU; among them was Pilot Officer George Drake, a 19-year-old South African. He had such a boyish face that I always thought he was too young to be pitched into battle, but then so too were many others. He was very inquisitive, always interested in how we 'Brits' thought and lived. No bad thing that, as I daresay he expected to be among us for some time. Sadly he wasn't.

Pilot Officer Drake was destined to be the first of The Few reported missing during the Battle of Britain to be discovered by aircraft recovery enthusiasts long after the war. In 1972, George Drake's remains were found with his aircraft, Hurricane P2728, at Goudhurst in Kent. The pilot's brother, Arthur, provides a little detail regarding his long-lost brother's short life:

> Our family lived at Kroonstad, in the province of Pretoria, where our father was Stationmaster. George matriculated at Paarl Boys' High

School in 1938, and was a member of the Paarl branch of the St John Ambulance Association. He always wanted to fly but was rejected by our own air force for being colour blind. Appreciating that in the event of war Great Britain would desperately need pilots, he then successfully applied for the RAF.

To his younger brothers, Eric and myself, George was very much the hero; our father was secretly very proud but mother was naturally much concerned for her eldest son. George worked his passage to England and achieved his ambition to become a fighter pilot. Joining the RAF to fight for Britain was George's only ambition. He went out to the fighting knowing that the odds were against him and his friends. He was very proud of what he was doing and we have always been proud of him down the years.

Pilot Officer George Drake was buried with full military honours at Brookwood Military Cemetery on 22 November 1972.

For 607 Squadron, 9 September 1940 would be remembered as a dark day indeed – and was an exceptionally violent introduction to the fighting over 11 Group.

Returning to the action that day, at 17.35 hrs, according to the 66 Squadron Intelligence Patrol Report, Squadron Leader Rupert 'Lucky' Leigh was leading 'Clickety-Click' and orbiting Maidstone at 22,000ft and above cloud. Enemy bombers were seen travelling north-west, 4,000ft below. Suddenly there was a warning shout of enemy fighters above and the Spitfires dived in pairs, as had previously been arranged, for thick cloud at 6,000ft.

During this evasive action, Sergeant Matthew Cameron lost the squadron but suddenly saw three Me 109s just 30 yards ahead of him. Opening fire immediately at the closest 109, it belched 'considerable black smoke'. In less time than it takes to tell, Cameron broke vertically down – nearly colliding with another 109, at which he fired two bursts which hit their mark, knocking pieces off the enemy fighter. A loud explosion from behind, however, sent Cameron wisely diving steeply into cloud, and, having expended all his ammunition, he returned to Kenley.

Having passed through the thick cloud, Squadron Leader Leigh shouted up on the R/T for his Spitfires to re-form on him, but not all heard or could find him, including Flight Lieutenant Ken Gillies, who:

> saw a British pilot bale out, and he circled round him till he was down to 1,000ft and saw him land West of Tunbridge Wells. He then climbed to 15,000ft in an endeavour to find a friendly fighter formation, when an Me 109 passed him in a dive; he turned onto its tail and chased it, but its speed was too great for him to catch up.

Gillies then returned to base, as did Pilot Officer Johnny Mather, who had also failed to find the squadron and was too low to rejoin the fighting high above. Similarly, Pilot Officer Crelin 'Bogle' Bodie saw no one when his CO called up, but was informed by 'Runik' (Kenley Sector Control) of 'bandits' at 15,000ft. Bodie climbed to 23,000ft and spotted Me 109s 3,000ft below – which he attacked.

On breaking away at 15,000ft, he saw a 109 'crash in a field. He had no idea of the exact position and on looking round he saw another fight going on: uncertain whether or not he was responsible, he makes no claim.' (Certainly *Unteroffizier* Massmann of 7/JG 3 was shot down and forced-landed near Hawkhurst, where he was captured, but given the number of claims for 109s destroyed it is impossible to say by whom.)

Pilot Officer George Corbett claimed an Me 109 destroyed but was shot-up himself and baled out, landing near Cowden. Two 109s were claimed damaged by Pilot Officer Arthur Watkinson, and Pilot Officer Bob 'Oxo' Oxspring damaged a 'Do 215 [*sic*]' over Seaford, setting both engines alight before breaking off when attacked himself by a 109.

Four 66 Squadron pilots, namely Pilot Officers Hubert 'Dizzy' Allen and Ian Cruickshanks, and Sergeants Dudley Forrest and Douggie Hunt did manage to contact Squadron Leader Leigh, and together the five Spitfires climbed towards the battle ongoing above. At 8,000ft 'they saw a large formation of E/A flying South with one He 111 well away on the port side, just above the clouds at approximately 6,000ft. The CO delivered three attacks on this solitary plane before breaking off as it entered cloud.' Allen and Cruickshanks then attacked: 'The plane crashed in a ploughed field near the East Sussex coast; three men climbed out and were arrested by soldiers who ran up.' (Yet again, this enemy aircraft had been misidentified, though: it was actually a Ju 88 of *Stab* II/KG 30, which forced-landed at Barcombe, near Lewes – one of the crew was killed in the Spitfires' attack, the remaining three captured unhurt.) Sergeant Forrest attacked a 'He 111 [*sic*]' alone, watching his tracer enter the port wing without any other apparent effect before losing his target in cloud. Forrest then landed at Westhampnett where he refuelled before returning to Kenley.

At 17.40 hrs, the Spitfires of 602 Squadron, also orbiting Mayfield, sighted the same formation of bombers attacked by 66 Squadron, recorded in the Intelligence Patrol Report, compiled by Flying Officer Herbert Ashley, as '30/40 Do 17s. Some He 111s believed also present [*sic*].' The Germans were flying north-west, Me 109s seen so far away and above that the Spitfire pilots were unsure whether they were on a sweep or escorts. Before Squadron Leader Sandy Johnstone could lead his men to attack, 607 Squadron got in first, dispersing the 'Do 17s', some of which the Spitfires then engaged.

Squadron Leader Johnstone and Pilot Officer Archibald Lyall attacked a 'Do 17', which had turned about and was heading south; this was another Ju 88, however, this time of *Stab* III/KG 30, the aircraft of *Major* Hackbarth, the Gruppenkommandeur, which crashed into the sea off Pagham. Johnstone was then attacked by an Me 109, which Lyall shot down into the sea, this most likely being *Feldwebel* A.W. Müller of 3/JG 3 who ditched six miles off Newhaven and was captured. Flight Lieutenant Paul Webb was then hit by a 109, consequently crash-landing near Boxgrove, slightly wounded and suffering a broken wrist.

Green Section of 602 Squadron was late arriving on the scene owing to its Spitfires being taxied by non-operational pilots still in training. Combat-ready pilots rapidly took possession and hastened to Mayfield, arriving at 15,000ft to find:

> 15/20 Do 215s [*sic*] at 10,000ft on southerly course, escorted by 30 Me 109s in tiers up to 15,000ft. Top tier, fifteen in number, went into defensive circle. Green 1, Sergeant Andrew McDowall, turned outside circle in opposite direction and was attacked by two leading Me 109s; he dived and one Me 109 passed behind, from right to left. Green 1 turned left and fired at 150 yards, two seconds. Pilot of Me 109 baled out.

This was *Feldwebel* Höhnisch of 1/JG 53, which was providing a rearguard for the KG 1 He 111s briefed to attack London. Having reached the target, the Germans turned around and in so doing Höhnisch drifted away from his fellow pilots. Upon sighting the Spitfires, he accelerated and tried to reach them – but was too late:

> I thought I had made it. But in the same instant there were explosions in my machine. Flames shot into my face with the force of a blowtorch. I managed to bale out with extreme difficulty. I then spent two months in a hospital at Woolwich with first and second degree burns on my face and hands, and bullet wounds in my legs.

During this escort sortie, 4/JG 53 lost its *Staffelkapitän*, *Oberleutnant* Schulze-Blanck in combat off Hastings, and 8/JG 53's Gefrieter Becker also went into the Channel: the enemy losses were stacking up.

No.602 Squadron's Sergeant Basil Whall claimed a 'Do 17' destroyed in this action, although no such enemy casualty cross-references; the pilot 'ricked his neck and was not able to furnish details on landing'.

Squadron Leader 'Uncle' George Denholm was leading the twelve Spitfires of 603 Squadron over Sussex around this time, although the exact time appears unrecorded and detail generally scant. According to the squadron's Intelligence Patrol Report, 'when ten miles North of Ford saw about twenty-five Me 109s in vics of three at 25,000ft and below them fifteen He 111s in vics of three, line astern, heading North … The squadron attacked the bombers out of the sun and turned them around.'

Flying Officer James Morton claimed a He 111 destroyed (circumstances unknown and no apparent casualty correlates), and Pilot Officer James MacPhail claimed one damaged; 603 Squadron suffered no loss (there was another reason for celebration in the Hornchurch Mess that night: Flying Officer George 'Sheep' Gilroy and the New Zealander Pilot Officer Brian Carbury were both awarded the DFC on this day, and Pilot Officer James Caister the DFM – although the latter, now a POW, would be unaware of the decoration for some time).

The now retiring enemy was also intercepted by Squadron Leader Eric McNab's 1(RCAF) Squadron at 17.40 hrs, south-east of Guildford:

> While climbing to manoeuvre for a position of advantage a protective screen of Me 109s were encountered above and proceeding south. These aircraft attacked the squadron and Pilot Officer Miller was shot down.

> He baled out but was found to be wounded in the leg and to have sustained burns. Pilot Officer Peterson accounted for one E/A, Pilot Officer Lochnan damaged two E/A and Squadron Leader McNab damaged one.

By 18.00 hrs, according to 303 Squadron, the German formation, comprising 'about forty bombers, Ju 88 and He 111, Me 109 and Me 110 in large numbers' was over Beachy Head and 'escaping southwards at great speed, losing height [ORB]'. The enemy, however, were 1,000ft above the Poles, and only the leading Hurricanes were able to climb in time to engage at 13,500ft:

> Flight Lieutenant Kent damaged a Ju 88 which escaped in cloud and it fell in sea, mid-Channel, rubber boat seen [possibly a machine of *Stab* II/KG30, which failed to return to France and the crew of which remain missing]. Flying Officer Zumbach was attacked by Me 109s. He destroyed one which disappeared in cloud and caught another banking in front of him, and fired into the cockpit and engine from above at 30 yards, seeing tracers hit. E/A turned on its back and fell into cloud. [ORB]

Flying Officer Jan Zumbach was credited with one Me 109 destroyed and a probable (although why, given that both aircraft disappeared into cloud and were not seen to crash by Zumbach or anyone else, is difficult to understand – but, like the Duxford Wing, it is a demonstrable fact that such accreditations are commonplace with 303 Squadron).

Attacked by other 109s, however, Zumbach managed to extricate himself and landed at White Waltham, spending ten minutes collecting his thoughts and recuperating slightly before heading back to Northolt. Sergeant Kazimierz Wunsche was less fortunate: shot up by a 109, he baled out over Newtimber, north-west of Brighton, slightly wounded. The Czechoslovak Sergeant Josef František had tried to intervene, attacking Wunsche's assailant, which he set on fire; no mistaking this combat claim: 7/JG 27's *Unteroffizier* Karl Born attempted to abandon his stricken fighter but was killed in the process, when another burst from František tore into his cockpit area; the 109 crashed in flames at Roman's Gate Cottage, Rudgwick.

The Czech then pursued a retiring He 111 but was intercepted by two escorting 109s and forced to seek refuge in cloud, nearly colliding with another He 111. Upon leaving his safe refuge, František was immediately attacked again by 109s, his Hurricane battered by four cannon shells: one in the port wing, one through his left fuel tank – which fortunately failed to ignite – another through his radiator and the fourth was stopped by the steel armour plate behind the pilot's head – which saved his life.

František spiralled away from the action to crash-land in a cabbage field next to Woodingdean's Downs Hotel, described in the 303 Squadron ORB as an 'excellent landing' which avoided injury or further damage to the aircraft. In addition to the 109, which was definitely destroyed, František was also credited with a He 111 destroyed – which was not, in fact. No He 111s were lost during this action, which found 303 Squadron in a poor tactical position and in which the Me 109s once more ably protected their charges, although a III/KG 53 He 111 returned to base badly damaged, with a dead crewman aboard and two more wounded. Being unable to catch the fleeting Germans, there were no other claims by 303 Squadron.

As the Germans landed back in France, both sides counted the cost. Small numbers of bombs had been dropped on the southern London suburbs of Kingston, Barnes, Richmond, Epsom, Walden, Purley, Surbiton and Norbiton, and closer to the centre, Wandsworth, Lambeth, Fulham and Chelsea were also hit. This, however, was nothing like the sustained and devastating attacks in previous days on London's docklands, and, although the raiding formations were collectively only a third of the size of those which successfully bombed *Loge* on 7 September 1940, it was still capable of inflicting heavy damage – but it did not. Fiercely determined fighter opposition had turned the enemy about – which was doubtless bent on another major raid on London.

Overall good controlling and aerial reporting had seen twenty-two defending squadrons scrambled; six covered aircraft factories and airfields, and of the remaining sixteen, only one failed to intercept. In this action thirteen British fighters had been destroyed and thirteen more damaged; six pilots were killed and ten wounded. The Germans, however, had lost twenty-seven aircraft destroyed and twelve more damaged.

While the Kanaljäger enjoyed certain technical advantages given that the Me 109 already had a constant speed propeller, fuel-injection and 20mm cannon, and were able to climb very high on their cross-Channel journey to southern England, the main disadvantage of using a short-range defensive interceptor as a long-range escort fighter was now very apparent: lack of range.

The range of the Me 109 E-3 and E-4 was some 410 miles; the distance from St Omer in the Pas-de-Calais, around which were clustered various airfields, temporary and otherwise, was directly 140 miles; the German fighters, however, had to climb and rendezvous with the bombers, then fly a throttled-back, zig-zag, course to keep station with their slower charges – all of which burned up precious fuel. On a good day without complications, such as a pure fighter sweep, the 109 pilot could spend just twenty minutes over London – and even that limited time meant for a nerve-wracking flight home across the Channel.

On 9 September 1940, *Oberleutnant* Hans Ohly, 1/JG 53's new *Staffelkapitän*, recorded that day's escort flight at 97 minutes, and 4/JG 53's *Oberfeldwebel* Stefan 'Steff' Litjens at 115 minutes – a very long flight for a single-engine fighter faced with two sea crossings. Indeed, on this, and many other days, JG 53's pilots reached France on their last reserves of fuel, forcing them to land at St Inglevert, near Calais, instead of their home bases around Le Touquet, further South. Many a 109 pilot would head for those airfields closer to England – or the French beaches.

Oberleutnant Ulrich Steinhilper of 3/JG 52 had already seen his friend, *Oberleutnant* Hinnerk Waller, become his unit's first case of Kanalkrankheit – 'Channel Sickness' – caused by the ongoing and acute stress and exhaustion of continual combat flying. Diagnosed with a stomach complaint, Waller had been prescribed a special diet and advised to abstain from excess alcohol. Unlike Fighter Command, the Luftwaffe did not rest pilots after tours of duty in the frontline, nor were units rotated to quieter sectors, and leave was a rarity. Arguments between Kamaraden became more common, as taut nerves led to quick tempers, and the consumption of alcohol significantly increased. For those who survived, upon return to base adrenalin dissipated, leaving pilots physically exhausted and having to come to terms emotionally with the loss of friends: there was no respite for the young aircrew either side of the Channel – and it was not only certain German pilots becoming disconsolate.

At 19.30 hrs on 9 September 1940, Pilot Officer Alex Osmand of 213 Squadron wrote to his beloved Marjorie from the Officers' Mess at RAF Tangmere:

> Well, things do seem to be happening, don't they! This time we hadn't a thought of what was coming to us, but things happen fast in this game, and we have to be able to act on a moment's notice. So, here we are now, right in the line of fire – so to speak. We shall be taking on the job of going after the raiders who go for London. I'm afraid it's going to be a stiff job, as they are at it absolutely continuously, we shall be occupied all the while – and we shall be battling against considerable numbers.
>
> To be absolutely blunt, this sudden change in our station doesn't appeal to me one bit … However, one cannot pick and choose, and if the job is hard, it will at least be well worth facing. The outlook is far from rosy – but the consolation is we're only here temporarily. At a guess, I'd say we'll have two to three weeks in this lovely spot, and then return to Exeter. It isn't as I first assumed, a permanent move … but that's only slight consolation.
>
> Darling, I'm tired, worried and rather despondent. Everything seems to have gone wrong for me, all of a sudden. It's very trying, but I must be brave and face it, I know what great faith you have yourself, and I must try to live up to all that we two believe, and know to be best. For you, my darling, I carry on! I shall pray for you, with all my heart and soul, and I pray that I shall fulfil my duty, and yet be spared to bring you the fullest happiness. Oh, I know that will mean my own whole life will be glorified … But it's just you I'm caring for and thinking about, If it weren't for you, I would not care so much for life. but you make it so worthwhile!

There was no sign of defeatism, however; Flight Sergeant George Unwin DFM, 19 Squadron: 'We never considered being beaten. It was just not possible in our eyes'.

Earlier in the day, Coastal Command reconnaissance aircraft returned from the enemy coast with disconcerting news: some 200 invasion barges were off Ostend and 70 German ships were at anchor off Flushing. The vessels off Ostend were immediately attacked, with a hit reported on an auxiliary ship, and by night Blenheims of 53 and 59 Squadrons successfully attacked invasion shipping at Boulogne, as did Beauforts of 22 Squadron, which also bombed Calais, losing one aircraft and crew in the process.

Rain squalls and thunder storms, however, prevented Bomber Command Blenheims completing their reconnaissance sorties of the Dutch and Belgian coasts. For 105 Squadron's Sergeant Dennis Hodson and his crew, namely Sergeants Edward Palmer (observer) and Rendle Green, this was their first operational sortie – from which they failed to return. Last seen by Flight Lieutenant Swain 'pursued by two enemy fighters eight miles south of Den Helder [ORB]', the Blenheim had been shot down into the North Sea by *Leutnant* Waldemar Wübke of 9/JG 54 – a first for the German too, this being his first aerial victory; Palmer and his crew were never found.

As darkness fell, responsibility for attacking the invasion ports passed to the Fairey Battle squadrons. Three Battles of Bircham Newton's 103 Squadron were despatched to bomb:

> enemy shipping concentrations in Calais Harbour. Two aircraft successfully bombed the target area. Sub-Lieutenant R.A. de Sandoval-Sievier, Pilot Officer W.A. Cooper and Sergeant F. Drinkwater in Battle L5010 did not return to base and were reported missing. Information since received from Red Cross, Geneva, indicates that this crew were killed, their aircraft being shot down by enemy AA fire. [ORB]

The missing 103 Squadron crew also disappeared, never to be seen again.

Three Battles of 150 Squadron were also tasked with bombing the concentration of barges at Calais, each aircraft carrying sixteen 40lb and two 250lb General Purpose bombs:

> Taking off from base at 18.48 hrs and setting course via Orfordness, Squadron Leader Carter and crew arrived over the target at 20.45 hrs where they launched three attacks against the harbours and barges at Calais. The detonations of the bombs released on the first attack were not observed but on the second attack all five were seen in the outer concentration of barges.
>
> The bombs released on the third attack detonated close to the fire caused by the first attack and the crew report that they clearly saw the outer of three barges joined together on fire. This fire spread rapidly and was followed by a number of explosions, thought to be ammunition barges.

> Pilot Officer Elliot and crew took off at 18.57 hrs for the same target at Calais where they arrived at 20.41 hrs. On release the bombs were seen to detonate on the jetty North of Calais, in barge concentrations but the results were not observed. The weather conditions over the target were found to be good, the moon being of considerable assistance to the pilot in locating his target. No enemy vessels were observed and our aircraft landed back at base at 23.15 hrs.
>
> The last aircraft to leave for the target was captained by Flight Lieutenant Beall and manned by his usual crew. Arriving over the target at 20.32 hrs the pilot employed a steep dive from 2,500ft to 1,700ft, releasing half his bomb load, then repeating these tactics on a second run. Although no actual results were observed the pilot is convinced that his bombs fell on the target.
>
> All of our aircraft returned safely to base. [ORB]

The 'Battle of the Barges' was now well and truly on.

For eighteen Bomber Command Wellingtons the target was marshalling yards in Belgium and Germany, naval installations at Wilhelmshaven, and the airfields at Schiphol and Bucken – all targets being hit. The Whitley force headed for industrial targets in Germany, including a gas works in Berlin, and Hampdens attacked Hamburg and Kiel in addition to sowing mines off the Gironde and scattering propaganda leaflets over France. Just one aircraft failed to return from these operations, a Whitley of 51 Squadron which ditched in the North Sea while returning from Berlin to Dishforth – one of the crew drowned but two were rescued by the Royal Navy.

The enemy was also active that night, from 20.00 hrs onwards various raids heading for London via the Isle of Wight and Dungeness, this unwelcome activity increasing from 02.30 hrs on 10 September 1940. The Daily Home Intelligence Report, however, tells us that, contrary to what Göring hoped to achieve by this sustained bombing:

> In the areas which have been heavily raided there has been little sign of panic and none of defeatism, but rather of bitterness and increased determination to 'see it through'. There is widespread and deeply felt apprehension, which is apparent mostly in the London Dock area, of

> a continuation of raids, and much anxiety about the chaos in domestic affairs which has resulted from the activities of the last few nights.
>
> As far as the East End is concerned, this is beginning to show itself in an aimless evacuation to what are believed to be safer places, e.g. the St James's Park shelters and Paddington Station … Men working in factories in the East End are encouraging their wives and families in this haphazard escape, but express their own willingness to stay and face further raids if they can be sure that their relations are in comparative safety.
>
> … The gallantry of both the RAF and AA crews continues to receive great praise. There is continued criticism of the BBC's method of announcing casualties and raid details. Special exception was taken to Charles Gardner's broadcast on Saturday, and it is suggested that what is wanted by the public in its present frame of mind is the kind of encouragement which can only be given by a real working-class man who has himself been through the worst of recent raids.

In Bristol, 'Rumours of invasion' were 'rife … following the ringing of church bells and the calling out of the Home Guard'.

Certainly, the situation was becoming increasingly critical – but more so, it seems, for the enemy.

Tuesday, 10 September 1940

By now, some 2,000 barges had been concentrated in the invasion ports, ready for the execution of Operation *Seelöwe*. Churchill was under no misapprehension as to the enemy's intention:

> a heavy full-scale invasion of this island is being prepared with all the German thoroughness. It does not seem it can be long delayed … we must regard this week as a very important period of our history. It ranks with the days when the Spanish Armada was approaching … or when Nelson stood between us and Napoleon's Grand Army at Boulogne.

The *Kriegsmarine*, however, pointed out an increasingly obvious fact on 10 September 1940: there was still 'No sign of defeat of the enemy air force', even though the Luftwaffe possessed 'considerable German fighter superiority', *Reichsmarschall* Göring had 'not yet attained … operational conditions … essential to the enterprise – undisputed air supremacy in the Channel area and elimination of enemy air activity in assembly area of German naval forces'. The OKM opined that *Seelöwe* would be better served 'if the Luftwaffe now concentrated less on London, more on Portsmouth, Dover and other naval ports'.

Hitler, however, supported the view that the bombing of London could still force the required decision, thereby rendering the perilous *Seelöwe* unnecessary. Again, as he had earlier in the summer, Hitler hesitated. Reports from the *Reichsmarschall* spoke of great execution to the RAF by the Luftwaffe – but the inescapable fact was that Luftwaffe losses were heavy and there was no sign of the RAF being substantially depleted, much less defeated.

Indeed, of the fighting on 9 September 1940, *Major* Hannes Trautloft, *Kommodore* of JG 54, wrote that 'The sky was full of roundels … For the first time we had the feeling that we were outnumbered.' Fighter Command was proving an obstinate foe and, moreover, the wider RAF, through bombing and mine-laying, was disrupting the invasion ports – and by night Germany – including Berlin – was still being attacked. The writing, it seemed, for *Seelöwe*, was now on the wall.

The *Kriegsmarine* chief, Admiral Raeder, required ten days' notice before launching *Seelöwe* – and Hitler had set 11 September 1940 as the day of decision, meaning 21 September was the earliest date for *Seelöwe*; moon and tide, however, made 24 September a more favourable day, giving Hitler several extra days of deliberation. Consequently, with no sign of the RAF being defeated, he postponed his decision until 14 September. From the German perspective, therefore, everything depended on the Luftwaffe – and time was running out. Soon, the day of decision, one way or another, would be at hand – and the *Führer* would have to either unleash *Seelöwe* or miss what had been a unique and unprecedented opportunity. The next few days, as Churchill knew full-well, were critical.

The morning of 10 September 1940, however, dawned with low cloud covering most of northern Europe, completely unsuitable conditions for major air operations, consequently providing an unexpected opportunity for both sides to draw breath.

Writing from his office at 11 Group HQ, Uxbridge, Air Vice-Marshal Park reported to Air Chief Marshal Dowding on the enemy's tactics during this phase:

> The normal attack was formations of long-range bombers, escorted by strong formations of fighters as experienced in the previous phase of operations up to 10 September 1940. Bombing attacks were mostly high-level, with only a few at medium altitudes.
>
> **Method of Attack**
>
> The enemy has attempted in this phase to draw our fighter patrols off from his bombers by high altitude diversions, as he had attempted to do, unsuccessfully, prior to 10 September. Increasingly high fighter screens were sent inland to draw off and contain our fighters, while the bomber formations, closely escorted by further fighters, endeavoured to sweep in some 6,000–10,000 feet below.
>
> The majority of attacks approached in two or three waves at varying intervals of time, on a much wider front and at heights varying between 16,000 and 20,000 feet for bomber formations. Small formations sometimes broke off from the main raid immediately fighter opposition was encountered and, descending to lower altitude, made clever use of cloud cover to attack objectives in the London area. Owing to extreme difficulty in reporting the tracks of these split raids, they frequently reached their objectives without effective interruption, and sometimes made their escape to the coast without being engaged.
>
> As our success against these bombers increased, there was a noticeable increase in the ratio of enemy fighters to bombers, the ratio in the later part of the phase being about four fighters to one bomber.
>
> **Employment of Enemy Fighters**
>
> The favourite practice was to send a very high fighter screen over Kent from 15–45 minutes ahead of bomber attacks, presumably to draw up our fighter squadrons and exhaust their petrol before the main attack crossed the coast. At other times the high fighter screen arrived only a few minutes in advance of the bomber formations with close escort.

> Fighter escorts normally consisted of two parts: (a) a big formation above and to the flank or in rear of the bombers, and (b) smaller formations of fighters formating with the bombers on the same level or slightly below. The latter formations endeavoured to prevent head-on attacks by our fighters against the incoming bombers.

Regarding the deployment of 11 Group's squadrons, Park added:

> The general plan adopted was to engage the enemy high fighter screen with pairs of Spitfire squadrons from Hornchurch and Biggin Hill, half-way between London and the coast, and so enable Hurricane squadrons from London sectors to attack bomber formations and their close escort before they reached the line of fighter aerodromes East and South of London. The remaining time to intercept the first wave of the attack by climbing in pairs formed a third and inner screen by patrolling along the line of aerodromes East and South of London.
>
> The fighter squadrons from Debden, Tangmere, and sometimes Northolt, were employed in wings or three squadrons in pairs to form a screen south-east of London to intercept the third wave of the attack coming inland, also to mop up retreating formations of the earlier waves.
>
> The Spitfire squadrons were redisposed so as to concentrate three squadrons at each of Hornchurch and Biggin Hill. The primary role of these squadrons was to engage and drive back the enemy high fighter screen, and so protect the Hurricane squadrons, whose task was to attack close escorts and then the bomber formations, all of which flew at much lower attitude.

This response reflects a flexible approach – not a fixed mindset, especially regarding formation-size and the fact that the Spitfire's high-altitude facility meant that the type performed a crucial function.

Regarding 11 Group's use of wings, Park added:

> When early warning had given adequate time, and cloud conditions were suitable, squadrons were employed in wings of three against enemy bomber formations and their close escort. Being located outside the area normally patrolled by enemy fighter screens, the squadrons from Debden,

> Northolt and Tangmere were not infrequently employed in wings of three squadrons. These wings were successful in engaging retreating bomber formations, which normally lost their escort before reaching London, because of the vigorous action of Spitfire and Hurricane squadrons working in pairs against incoming raids.
>
> Experience showed that even small wings of three squadrons were not effective against high fighter patrols, and the Spitfire squadrons were therefore used in pairs.

Again, though, the limitations of aerial radio telephony meant that these 11 Group wings were really only arriving over the battle area together, before fighting independently. Also, three squadrons were only operating against bombers at medium altitude, while pairs of Spitfire units patrolled at high altitude. The important thing to appreciate, and which becomes relevant shortly, is that 11 Group's sector controllers and the Observer Corps were aware of the existence, position and intention of these friendly formations.

Sinister moves, however, were afoot in 12 Group. The unexpected lull in the fighting enabled Air Vice-Marshal Leigh-Mallory to summon Squadron Leader Douglas Bader to his 12 Group HQ at Hucknall. The AOC listened while Bader explained his belief that it was the formation leader in the air – not the sector controller on the ground – who should decide when and where to attack, on the grounds that height information received from RDF was frequently inaccurate and because, in any case, the controller could not see the enemy personally. This, however, was absolutely and completely contrary to Fighter Command's System.

According to Bader's early biographer Paul Brickhill, Leigh-Mallory agreed with Bader and said, 'I'll put this to the right people and in the mean-time you might as well carry on with your theory. It seems to work.' So convinced, in fact, was Leigh-Mallory that 12 Group knew better than both Air Chief Marshal Dowding and Air Vice-Marshal Park that he added two more squadrons to the Duxford Wing. This was now not just a wing, but a *big* wing of five squadrons – a 12 Group Corps d'élite indeed. Nothing could have been more contrary to how Dowding had expressly ordered the battle to be fought. Even Bader himself was 'startled'. So now, 12 Group awaited an opportunity to pitch this massive formation of fighters into battle.

Down at Tangmere, two Polish fighter pilots reported for duty with 607 Squadron, namely Pilot Officers Franek Surma and Jan Orzechowski. These pilots had flown Hurricanes with 151 Squadron at North Weald since 25 August 1940, seeing action on 30 August, 1940 Pilot Officer Surma claimed a He 111 probably destroyed, and the following day Pilot Officer Orzechwski was shot-up by an Me 109, crash-landing at Foulness. On 1 September 1940, however, 151 Squadron was withdrawn to Digby, but the two Poles were considered sufficiently fresh to return to 11 Group.

Pilot Officer Harry Welford, 607 Squadron:

> I recollect a short, stocky, rather serious man who would have been Jan Orzechowski. He smoked cigarettes incessantly and used a cigarette holder. The Polish officers tried to strike a pose, I imagine, to keep their end up with us rather casual Brits. They were extremely good pilots, but quite mad and totally fearless. Franek Surma, who was with me in 'B' Flight, was a bit more relaxed and met us half way, probably because he spoke more English than the others.

AC1 Bob Morris, Fitter IIE, 66 Squadron:

> On this day, we of 'Clickety-Click' moved from Kenley to Gravesend, which was no more than a civilian flying club airfield. We were the only squadron there, at what was Biggin Hill's satellite. At Gravesend we looked down the River Thames, opposite Tilbury, and I remember bombs hitting large floating oil tanks in the river there. I always admired the sailors of the little boats, tugs and the like that used to pull out these tanks, which were on fire, to stop the flames spreading.
>
> Unlike at Kenley, however, we were not bombed at Gravesend. There was only one hangar there, our dining room, a small hut for flying control and a pilots' crew room. Without much to hit on a grass airfield we would have been difficult to put out of action anyway.
>
> We had half a day off every ten days, which we used to spend fast asleep. We were exhausted, working dawn to dusk. As we had lost so many pilots at Kenley we began receiving replacements at Gravesend.
>
> At Gravesend we used to watch the German aircraft coming in, heading for London or elsewhere, the trails in the sky, and how relieved

we were when they passed overhead and went straight on! Being close to the river there would often be a ground mist, which could last all day, meaning that no aircraft could take off, but at least the Germans couldn't see us.

On such days we always used to get our work done by early afternoon when, inevitably, a football would appear and a game would start on the edge of the aerodrome. We never used to pick a side, you just joined in with whichever side seemed to be winning, and that was the way you kicked! On one occasion we were busy playing when we heard these German aircraft circling around overhead, looking for something to bomb. Suddenly, right through the fog, came a parachute flare which landed on our football pitch – someone kicked some dirt onto it and we just carried on playing. No one ran for shelter, that was how used we had become to it all.

You never heard anyone talk about defeat. Of course we were not conversant with all the facts, though occasionally we would get some air force 'big wig' come and give us a pep talk. Our entertainment was to walk to Rochester or Strood, to the pictures, then walk back again. We also went to dances at the Co-op Hall in Gravesend. Life went on.

So far as air operations over England were concerned by day on 10 September 1940, with cloud preventing major raids, various Do 17s, Ju 88s and He 111s of KGs 2, 54 and 76 made nuisance raids on Yarmouth and Newhaven, and bombs were randomly dropped in Kent and Sussex, killing eleven civilians.

At 16.15 hrs, Flight Lieutenant Norman Ryder was leading Red and Blue sections of 41 Squadron up from Hornchurch, when at 20,000ft, ten miles south-east of base, a small formation of Ju 88s was sighted. Immediately, Ryder led the Spitfires in a diving attack, intending to cut the formation in two, firing as he passed through the Germans at a Ju 88, glimpsing smoke issuing from an engine. Ryder:

then attacked another 88 by joining a circle and experienced very great return fire and good evasion of E/As' part, had to break off engagement. I fired at a third and was fired on from astern, part of my hood at this moment flew off. Ordered by control to patrol home base and engage 50+ E/A, I returned but did not engage before pancake order.

The Ju 88 was credited as damaged.

At 17.40 hrs, five Spitfires of 72 Squadron scrambled from Croydon to patrol Redhill, and received information from 'Rastus' (Biggin Hill) that bandits were approaching that aerodrome at Angels 10. Red Section orbited and saw a 'Do 215 [*sic*]' at the predicted height, flying south-west. Flying Officer John 'Pancho' Villa, leading Red Section, ordered a Fighter Command No.1 Attack, resulting in the Dornier being shot down, army officers confirming that it crashed in a field near East Grinstead. This was actually a Do 17 of 9/KG 76 engaged on a reconnaissance of London, two of the crew being killed, two others wounded and captured.

Meanwhile, 72 Squadron's Yellow Section, led by Flying Officer Norman Robson, saw AA fire bursting over Weybridge, and upon investigating discovered a Dornier flying south. Robson attacked the raider from astern as the enemy pilot dodged in and out of cloud, until it disappeared into cloud at 4,000ft. This was confirmed as destroyed, on the basis of a Dornier reportedly crashing in the vicinity of the combat, but that would have been Red Section's kill.

In this exchange, 72 Squadron's Pilot Officer Ernest Males' Spitfire was damaged by return fire, his aircraft being further damaged when he consequently forced-landed at Etchingham, collapsing the undercarriage; the pilot, however, was unhurt.

Pilot Officer Trevor Wade and Sergeant Ronald Fokes of Biggin Hill's 92 Squadron had taken off at 17.50 and 17.55 hrs respectively to patrol base. At 17.55 hrs, Wade, Yellow 2, was ordered to intercept a bandit approaching from the south-east, which the Spitfire pilot sighted at 7,000ft, flying north, six miles east of Biggin Hill. The Dornier's rear-gunner opened up on the approaching fighter, but was killed by Wade's first burst. The bomber turned for cloud, pursued by Wade – just ten to fifteen yards behind.

After expending all his ammunition, Wade 'saw E/A lose height and speed, and that his starboard engine was on fire. He therefore called up Red 2, Sergeant Fokes, and vectored him onto the bandit.' Fokes found the Dornier ten miles south-west of base, which he also attacked; the 'E/A crashed near Gatwick and broke up completely'. This, however, was the same Do 17 attacked and also claimed by 72 Squadron – once more illustrating how a single casualty could be multiplied many times on the balance sheet, thereby giving a false indication of fighter pilots' performance and execution to the enemy.

These were the only daylight combats of the day.

At 19.30 hrs that evening, Pilot Officer Alex Osmand once more sat down in the Officers' Mess at Tangmere and wrote to his beloved Marjorie:

> My darling Marjorie,
> Things are all very quiet, and we begin to wonder what the catch is. Truly, the whole state of affairs is very surprising, and rather ominous, and this is most probably the lull before the storm. These are crucial days in the Battle for Britain, for winter will soon be with us. If the Germans intend to invade us this year, they will have to get a move on ... and if they don't invade us this year they are forfeiting their chances of success.
>
> It's an unbelievable conclusion to reach – because it all points to the fact that we can expect the worst they can give us, any time now. Our enemies are no fools, and they know their own weaknesses as well as our own. They are bound to take what chances they have of succeeding – and it will be a hard task to fight them off.
>
> At this particular moment, it looks as if Hitler is trying to undermine our morale, by continual indiscriminate bombing. London in particular seems to have been picked as the chief objective I suppose he feels that London with its millions of inhabitants can easily be brought to its knees, and that the people will only stand so much. We, of the Air Force, do what we can to stop the raiders, and to prevent their return to Germany, but when they come in large numbers, it isn't humanly possible to stop the lot. Then, when they come at night, our task is magnified a thousand-fold ... looking for a plane in the darkness is comparable to the proverbial needle in the haystack. With the help of searchlights, we can get some success – and there lies our hope.

It was a perceptive letter.

At night, the German bombers returned, resulting in thirty-seven red air-raid warnings being issued. Again, the primary target was London, major fires being started at St Katharine's Dock and London Dock, and both Cardiff and Sheffield were also attacked. Biggin Hill's 92 Squadron's diarist noted that 'Enemy activity at night continues. AA barrage is terrific, like bursts of machine-gun fire sometimes, it is so intensive. Squadron personnel acclimatizing to this barrage at night and managing to get some rest.'

'Intensive' though the barrage was, not a single German bomber was hit. Still lacking dedicated night-fighters and effective airborne interception radar, Spitfires and Hurricanes were pressed into patrolling the night skies – a role for which neither fighter was designed or intended. Indeed, the Spitfire was a poor night-flying aircraft, owing to its narrow track undercarriage, its long nose providing limited forward visibility during taxiing, take-off and landing, and the banks of exhaust on either side of the nose glowed in the dark, compromising the pilot's night vision.

That night, 602 Squadron at Westhampnett practiced night-flying: one Spitfire was written-off and another damaged in forced-landings, and a third was damaged when landing at nearby Tangmere; fortunately none of the pilots were hurt, but this certainly indicates the hazards involved with flying Spitfires by night.

For Coastal and Bomber Commands, the focus was now primarily on the Battle of the Barges. PRU aircraft returned with evidence of thirty ships at anchor in Boulogne Harbour, and more enemy shipping off Flushing and Ostend; 140 invasion barges were counted at Calais, and more enemy shipping was seen approaching Calais via Cap Gris-Nez. Two Blenheims of 53 Squadron reconnoitred the Dutch coast, and three more joined five of 59 Squadron 'to bomb merchant vessels between Calais and Dunkirk [53 ORB]'. A further reconnaissance of the Dutch coast by Bomber Command was frustrated by bad weather, however, although a reconnaissance of the North Sea was flown without incident.

By night, Coastal Command Beauforts sowed mines off Cuxhaven, but Blenheims and antiquated Swordfish were thwarted by the weather when sent to attack the barges at Calais and naval shipping off Le Havre. The barges were also Bomber Command's primary nocturnal target, and for the first time all bomber groups, 1, 2, 3, 4 and 5, were engaged in this offensive activity.

Three Battles of 103 Squadron attacked barges at Calais, over which the Germans now flew a balloon barrage as a defensive precaution. Blenheims of 2 Group attacked the barges concentrated at Flushing, and the long-range gun batteries near Calais. Barges at Flushing and Ostend were also attacked by twenty-six 3 Group Wellingtons – a sizeable force – and 'Whimpeys' also hit enemy airfields.

The Whitley force of 4 Group bombed both Bremen docks and Berlin's Potsdamer railway station – but two aircraft were lost: a 58 Squadron Whitley forced-landed in enemy-occupied Europe, the crew becoming prisoners, and a 77 Squadron crew was also incarcerated after crashing near Zwolle. Another sizeable force comprising twenty-one 5 Group Hampdens also attacked barges at Calais and Ostend, one aircraft failing to return from the latter target, the crew all missing.

Daily Home Intelligence Report:

> Morale remains unchanged today. Voluntary and unplanned evacuation of East End families continues … There is, however, little evidence that these efforts to escape are due to defeatist feelings, but are simply because the people are thoroughly frightened.
>
> Now that they are beginning to feel, and are being referred to, as 'soldiers in the front line', everything should be done to encourage this opinion of themselves. It would undoubtedly help if the public were made to feel that their friends and relations had died for the country, in the same sense as if they were soldiers, sailors or airmen.
>
> It might be a small but extremely telling point if, for instance, the dead were buried with Union Jacks on the coffins, or if the Services were represented at their funerals. Attentions of this kind would undoubtedly mean much at this time.

South-Eastern (Tunbridge Wells):

> Morale is extremely high in the Region, and everyone if full of praise for the RAF. People are still going out into the streets to witness thrilling dog-fights overhead.

There would be no shortage of 'thrilling dog-fights' for the good folk of Tunbridge to marvel at in the week ahead.

Wednesday, 11 September 1940

On this day, Air Vice-Marshal Park issued 'Instruction to Controllers No.16', making clear how the AOC 11 Group wanted the battle in the air to be fought:

Readiness Squadrons
Despatch in pairs to engage first wave of enemy. Spitfires against fighter screen, and Hurricanes against bombers and close escort.

Available 15 Squadrons
a) Bring to Readiness in pairs;
b) Despatch in pairs to engage second wave.

Available 30 Squadrons
a) Bring to Readiness;
b) Despatch singly to protect aircraft factories or sector aerodromes, or to reinforce squadrons already in the air.

If there is a third wave and it is necessary to despatch these squadrons, they should be sent in pairs as follows:

Debden and North Weald squadrons together.
Hornchurch and Biggin Hill squadrons together.
Kenley and Northolt squadrons together.

Tangmere Squadrons
When not required to protect the Portsmouth-Southampton area in conjunction with 10 Group squadrons, the Tangmere squadrons should be employed within Kenley or back Tangmere Sector to engage enemy formations that approach London from the South, or endeavour to pass round the South of London to attack aircraft factories at Kingston, Brooklands and Langley. Whenever time permits, the Readiness squadrons and the Available 15 squadron should be despatched to work as a pair after having rendezvoused at base.

Rendezvous of Squadrons
The Group Controller must name the base over which pairs of squadrons are to rendezvous, as they normally occupy separate aerodromes within a Sector. Sector Controllers should inform Group Controller immediately a pair of squadrons have rendezvoused over any given point. Group Controller should then detail these squadrons to a raid and leave the rest to Sector.

> <u>Selection of Squadron to Lead a Pair of Squadrons</u>
> The detailing of the directing squadron should be done by the Sector Controller, who should know which squadron is best suited to lead. Sector controllers must also repeat to the squadron being led all orders issued to the directing squadron in case these units become separated by clouds. Sector commanders must impress upon squadron commanders the importance of leading squadrons in a pair joining up and maintaining contact with the squadron being led.

Air Vice-Marshal Park also reported favourably to Air Chief Marshal Dowding regarding the level of cooperation received from 10 Group:

> During this phase of heavy attacks on the London area, there were occasionally heavy diversionary attacks on the Portsmouth area, when 10 Group rendered invaluable assistance by despatching squadrons singly or in pairs to reinforce Tangmere Sector. During mass attacks over London, valuable reinforcements were provided by 10 Group for the close protection of aircraft factories and airfields West and south-west of London. These squadrons several times intercepted bomber formations that had broken away from the main raids and endeavoured, without escort, to attack aircraft factories and aerodromes, making use of cloud cover.

Among Air Vice-Marshal Sir Quentin Brand's 10 Group squadrons was 238, freshly returned to Middle Wallop from a two-month sojourn at Cornwall's St Eval airfield, with which served Sergeant Gordon Batt:

> When we returned to Middle Wallop in September, the size of the German formations had increased: the bomber formation was usually fifty-sixty strong, in an oblong block and close formation, and above them were Me 110s, and Me 109s higher still.
>
> To counter this we often flew accompanied by one of Wallop's Spitfire squadrons. Our CO was the senior squadron commander and so we usually led, our Hurricanes attacking the bombers while the Spitfires held off the escort. It certainly did my morale a lot of good; God and Hitler know what it did to theirs! The only snag was that as 238 was

> first to attack, I never had the opportunity to look back – there must have been chaos!
>
> Towards the end of August and throughout September, we were frequently called to the West of the London area. The Controller would give us a commentary regarding what was going on generally, and while holding off at 20,000ft, we could hear him directing 11 Group's squadrons into action. From our position West of London, we could see ack-ack bursting over the capital, and condensation trails of the Spitfires, Hurricanes and Me 109s. The boys of 11 Group were obviously holding their own and we were sensibly being held in reserve.
>
> When we were vectored, the Controller would say something like: '25 Bandits, Angels 20, heading straight for you, they're all yours!' It really was slick control. All of the sorties, though, were quite frightening and fraught with danger!

Up in 12 Group, 242 Squadron again remained at Coltishall, in fact whenever CO Squadron Leader Douglas Bader was absent, as he still was, at 12 Group HQ, the unit did not proceed to Duxford. Squadron Leader 'Sailor' Malan, however, led 74 Squadron to join 19 and 611 Squadrons at Fowlmere. One flight of Wittering's 266 Squadron, now a 'B' unit, which had operated from 242 Squadron's dispersal at Coltishall for the last three days, also flew to Fowlmere.

At Duxford, the Polish Hurricanes of 302 'Poznań' Squadron were also on readiness for the first time, putting three Spitfire and two Hurricane squadrons, some fifty fighters in all, at the Duxford Sector Controller's disposal. All involved eagerly awaited the call to reinforce 11 Group.

The lull of the previous day, though, continued until 14.50 hrs on 11 September 1940 – when RDF detected formations off Cap Gris-Nez estimated at twenty plus and twelve plus. These raids flew over the Dover Strait between 15.00 and 15.10 hrs, crossing the south-east Kent coast at Folkestone before flying inland to Maidstone, where they both turned and flew out over North Foreland. Rightly, 11 Group guessed that this was a feint, as no bombs were dropped, and so it proved to be: at 15.00 hrs, large German formations began forming up over the Pas-de-Calais. In addition to Luftflotte 2's Maidstone feint, Luftflotte 3 was assembling formations to strike against Portsmouth, which, after the drubbing received on 9 September

1940, may also have been intended to divert the defenders' attention from the main raid: target London.

Between 15.00 and 15.20 hrs, RDF plots made clear, however, that the major raid was coming across the Dover Strait. In anticipation of the capital being the intended target and complying with Air Vice-Marshal Park's latest instructions, three pairs of 11 Group squadrons were scrambled to provide a defensive screen between the south-east Kent coast and London: at 15.10 hrs, 46 went up from Stapleford to join up with Hendon's 504 Squadron over North Weald, thence to patrol Gravesend; five minutes later, Kenley's 253 and 501 Squadrons took-off and headed for Maidstone, and from Hornchurch the Spitfires of 41 and 603 squadrons made for Maidstone. The final initial disposition was 92 Squadron scrambling from Biggin Hill at 15.20 hrs, also heading for the Maidstone line.

Again responding in strength, Air Vice-Marshal Park requested assistance from 10 Group, which sent 238 Squadron, at 15.25 hrs, from Middle Wallop to patrol Brooklands and Weybridge, and at the same time 11 Group scrambled more squadrons: 72 Squadron left Croydon, initially to patrol base, then to patrol Gravesend, and at the same time 249 left North Weald to patrol the eastward approach to London's docklands. Also at 15.25 hrs, 229 Squadron left Northolt, five minutes later forming up with 303 Squadron to form the 'Northolt Wing' and patrol Biggin Hill.

At 15.28 hrs, 222 Squadron took-off from Hornchurch to patrol base, and, assistance having been requested from 12 Group, at 15.30 hrs, Squadron Leader Brian Lane DFC led eight Spitfires of his own 19 Squadron, together with six of 266, off from Fowlmere as the lead unit in an all-Spitfire wing, the other squadrons being Squadron Leader 'Sailor' Malan's 74 and Squadron Leader Jimmy McComb's 611. Lane's instructions were to patrol in a southerly direction towards the Thames Estuary.

By 15.35 hrs, 2 enemy formations of 100 plus and 50 plus were approaching the South Foreland, so at that time 66 Squadron was sent from Gravesend and vectored towards the incoming enemy. At 15.45 hrs a third German formation, of fifty plus, was between Folkestone and Dover. The northern enemy force comprised the He 111s of I and II/KG 1, the southernmost those of I and II/KG 26.

These raids were escorted by Me 110s of ZG 26, V(Z)/LG 1 and both II and III/ZG 76, and the Me 109s of at least JGs 2, 51, 53, 54 and LG

2. Although after the subsequent action various RAF squadrons claimed to have engaged and destroyed Ju 88s, there is no evidence whatsoever of that type being involved, so, again, this is a case of misidentification, the actual targets being Me 110, He 111 or Do 17 aircraft, the most likely type confirmed by the relevant combat's location.

At 15.40 hrs, Northolt's 1(RCAF) Squadron was scrambled to intercept the incoming raids, and three more 11 Group squadrons were then scrambled at 15.45 hrs: the 'Debden Wing' of 17 and 73 Squadrons to patrol Rochford, 605 from Croydon to patrol base, and 257 from Martlesham to patrol North Weald – a surprising commitment, considering that the Duxford Wing had been requested to cover North Weald and Hornchurch, begging the question, therefore, as to whether this deployment was an insurance policy in case 12 Group either failed to arrive in time or, indeed, not comply with the order and patrol elsewhere over the 11 Group area.

With so many units and aircraft involved, as is so often the case, owing to incomplete records and contradictory times having been recorded, it is impossible to construct a true chronological narrative of the ensuing air battle but it is clear that at least sixteen RAF squadrons intercepted the northerly He 111 raiders – which suffered particularly heavy losses. This was down to a faulty route planning, leading to the Me 109s burning up too much fuel early on and having to retire early – leaving the ponderous Heinkels alone over England with inevitable consequences.

Five defending squadrons attacked the southerly force of Do 17s, and three more, it seems, fell on retiring raiders from both enemy forces. What follows (as always, quoting pilots' personal combat reports, squadron ORBs and Intelligence Patrol Reports), is the most accurate interpretation possible given the evidence available. Indeed, so heavy was the fighting on certain other days until at least the end of September 1940 that such methodology, going forward, is a common theme.

As the He 111 force crossed the coast, the raiders were sighted at intercepted at 16.00 hrs by 92 Squadron, as the commander of 'A' Flight, Flight Lieutenant Brian Kingcome, reported:

> I was patrolling with Yellow 2 when I sighted a very large formation of enemy bombers with a large fighter escort of Me 109 and Me 110 above and behind. They were crossing the coast over Dungeness when

> I first sighted them. With Yellow 2 I made a head-on attack on the lower layer of the bomber formation. One aircraft, a He 111, started to smoke, but I had no time to notice whether it crashed or not. I broke away downwards, climbed up behind and started a stern attack on the lower layer of the bomber formation when my engine cut, so I broke off the attack.

Eighteen-year-old Pilot Officer Geoffrey 'Boy' Wellum:

> Having lost the squadron I was flying near the coast at 9,000ft when I saw and engaged a He 111. The port engine was out of action. I did one quarter attack and was met with fire from top and bottom guns of the E/A. I did a second quarter attack and this time met with fire from the top gun only. Black smoke began to come from the starboard engine. I did one more quarter attack and then went in astern. White smoke came from the starboard engine and the enemy aircraft lost height slowly. Having finished my ammunition, I broke off the engagement.

This was the first time Wellum had fired his guns in anger, and the He 111 was subsequently claimed as destroyed. Out of ammunition, having emptied 2,740 rounds into the raider, Wellum, 'Gannic Red Two', was heading home when:

> A flash, bright like magnesium and a sharp, very loud explosion. Something red streaks past the cockpit from somewhere astern … My own fault. Elementary rule number one: never relax vigilance … So this is how a fighter pilot dies. Looking back over my shoulder, an Me 109 sitting on my tail thirty yards away … turning with me. I see the flash from his cannons and puffs of greyish smoke as he tries a quick burst … more hits …
>
> I keep turning, keep going, the 109 tucks in behind me. Round and round and still he sticks there, glued to my tail. This chap can fly … an old hand. I hold on to the turn … and even tighten it. Must be pulling six G. The Spit judders, a high-speed stall … hold on … fly her like hell. As I watch the 109, I now know the meaning of the word 'fear', real stark staring fear, the sort of fear that few people possibly ever experience.

> Round and round we go. The Hun fires again ... Missed me. Maybe I've gained a little on him. I'm starting to calm down and think logically. The German pilot is trying to tighten his turn ... I see the 109 flick. You won't do it, mate ... I can see his head quite clearly, even the shape of his oxygen mask.

Turning, turning, always turning, tighter and tighter; the 109 came out of the turn, pulling up to gain height before turning again. By now, the Spitfire had gained too much, and was behind the 109 – but out of ammunition. Carefully awaiting his moment, the 109 low on fuel, the second the German broke away Geoffrey was rolling out and away in a vertical dive. It was a lucky escape – and a baptism of fire, if ever there was one: 'When that 109 caught me after that Heinkel, I remember thinking "If you can get away with this, you can get away with anything" – because he should have killed me.'

It was a lucky escape indeed.

In total, 92 Squadron claimed seven He 111s, one Me 109 and one Me 110 destroyed, and a 109 probable. Those He 111s attributable to 92 Squadron are a 6/KG 26 bomber attacked by Pilot Officer Allan Wright (and pilots of 66 Squadron) and which forced-landed at Camber, where the crew set fire to their machine before being captured, and a I/KG 26 aircraft shot down at Burmarsh by Pilot Officers Trevor Wade and Dennis Williams. Pilot Officer Fred Hargreaves, though, was missing; the Canadian Pilot Officer Harry Edwards was shot down and killed, crashing into a wood at Smeeth (where he would remain undiscovered for nearly a month), and Flight James Paterson, a New Zealander, was shot down by an Me 109, baling out near Ashford badly burned.

After a shaky start, losing two COs on the same day, 253 Squadron had settled down at Kenley under the leadership of Squadron Leader Gerry Edge, an experienced pre-war pilot and formerly a flight commander on 605 at Croydon. Edge had led his new Squadron off from Kenley to orbit base before being vectored to Angels 20 and ordered to intercept Raid 44.

At 15.45 hrs, 253 Squadron sighted, according to the Intelligence Patrol Report, 'some thirty He 111s and Do 215s [*sic*] escorted by approximately fifty Me 109s and Me 110s, were sighted at 16,000ft some thirty miles east over Dover, heading NW'. This was the northern force, and, given the reported presence of 'Do 215s', possibly part of the slightly more southerly force. Edge climbed his Hurricanes NNE, delivering a beam attack by sections from 1,000ft above – out of the sun. The Germans were effectively ambushed, three bombers bursting into flames while several more were left 'smoking badly'. During the attack, the bombers fired red flares – the signal summoning urgent assistance from their escorts.

Squadron Leader Edge, Red 1, dived away after the initial charge, then climbed to 18,000ft, diving onto a He 111 and attacking head-on, 'seeing bullets entering cockpit, smashing the Perspex and probably killing the pilot. E/A spiralled away'. (Edge was a leading exponent of the head-on attack, in fact, as he explained to me in 1992: 'Surrounded by all that Perspex, the German bomber crews didn't like the head-on attack at all, you know – so we of 253 Squadron used that fact very much to our advantage'). Having engaged the bombers, Edge then despatched a 109 with a single one-second burst, setting the enemy fighter alight, which subsequently crashed in flames near Wadhurst – this being *Feldwebel* Hermann Siemer of 8/JG 51, that Geschwader's fifty-ninth fatality since the war began.

Yellow 2, Sergeant William Higgins, also set a 109 alight, which was seen to crash 'near Newhaven'; this was the *Staffelkapitän* of 2/JG 51, *Hauptmann* Ernst Wiggers, who was killed in the crash at Houndean Bottom, Lewes. In total, 253 Squadron would claim the two Me 109s destroyed along with 'three Do 215s [*sic*]', a He 111 probable, and two He 111s, a 'Do 215' and an Me 110 damaged, these claims offset by a slightly damaged Hurricane.

Squadron Leader Harry Hogan's 501 Squadron had arrived over Maidstone only to be vectored to Chatham, where the Hurricanes turned south-west, towards a point between Biggin Hill and Maidstone. About ten miles south of Biggin Hill, Hogan's formation was attacked by a *Schwarm* of four Me 109s, breaking up the squadron. Again, the Intelligence Patrol Reports describes events:

> Seven of the Squadron re-formed and three of them, together with three Spitfires [probably those of 603 Squadron] attacked and destroyed a Do 215 [*sic*] [no Dorniers actually lost on this day]. This was a straggler from a force of twenty Dorniers which came in towards Kenley and turned towards the Thames Estuary. The remaining five Hurricanes attempted to join but could not find them.

> Yellow 3 sighted a formation of about 30+ He 111s with fighter escort, coming in from the East, and attacked the second vic of the bomber formation, damaging two of them. He then climbed to a height of 18,000ft and sighted a force of He 111s coming in from the East, approximately over Maidstone and travelling South at 16,000ft. He did a beam attack on the leading vic of the formation, out of the sun, and damaged one of the bombers. His machine was hit in the oil tank.
>
> Blue 2 engaged a single Heinkel at 10,000ft near Biggin Hill and damaged it.

One Hurricane, however, failed to return – although the pilot was safe; Yellow 3, Sergeant Tony Pickering:

> Squadron Leader Hogan ordered a head-on attack against a formation of enemy bombers over London. We dived down on the Huns and I just pressed the gun button and shut my eyes! One of the nose gunners gave me a squirt and hit the sump, I started smoking but managed to spiral down away from the fight. It was a lovely day and I could see Kenley below quite clearly. As there was no one about I thought that I would just come down and make a normal landing. At about 3,000ft, however, the petrol caught fire and I was over the side pretty sharpish! My Hurricane went down and crashed, and I landed by parachute in a Guards Depot, where I was given a couple of whiskies. I was wearing ordinary uniform trousers, shoes, an open neck shirt with no tie as it was hot, and that was it. I hadn't even had a shave that morning and I remember being a bit singed around the face and hair but was otherwise uninjured.

The Spitfires of 41 and 603 squadrons were also patrolling South London, the latter engaging at 16.00 hrs, as Pilot Officer Brian MacNamara later reported:

> On sighting a large Balbo approaching London, the Squadron formed line astern, peeling off and attacking the bombers. I found a lone Heinkel and attacked it from above and behind, slightly on the port quarter. After a prolonged burst, I saw black smoke from the starboard engine. I broke away and again attacked from below and abeam, giving it a burst

> of three or four seconds. I was then forced to break away, as a number of other Heinkels and some Me 109s were firing at me.

Pilot Officer James MacPhail:

> I dived on a He 111 from its port beam. The enemy immediately took evasive action, turning sharply to its port and I was forced to break away to its rear. I saw my burst enter the fuselage.
>
> I climbed up and saw the enemy going southwards, losing height. A Hurricane and a Spitfire then dived and did stern attacks, one each, and the enemy turned to the right and I dived and did a head-on attack of two – three seconds, from a range of 150–50 yards, and saw tracer enter the centre of the fuselage.
>
> Two of the crew baled out, the wheels came down and the aircraft exploded on landing in the vicinity of Edenbridge. The crew landed in fields slightly to the SW of the aircraft. I received an Armour Piercing bullet in the gun channel heater of my inner starboard gun.

This He 111 belonged to 3/KG 26, and was attacked by pilots from at least five squadrons before exploding at Dormansland.

In addition to the foregoing, Pilot Officers Bill Read, 'Raz' Berry and the South African Basil 'Stapme' Stapleton all claimed Me 109s damaged, and the latter also a probable, while Flight Lieutenant John Boulter damaged a He 111. Apart from the bullet which hit MacPhail's Spitfire, 603 Squadron suffered no other damage or casualties.

Pilot Officer Gerald Langley, 41 Squadron, 16.15 hrs, at 20,000ft and fifteen miles south-east of London:

> I was Red 2 in the leading section … when we sighted the enemy 5,000ft below us. We dived out of the sun and I fired a five-second burst on a Ju 88 [*sic*] hitting it on the port side – may have damaged port engine.
>
> As I turned away I saw tracer bullets coming over my port wing, my machine went out of control and although I juggled with the controls for some time nothing happened. I baled out at approximately 6,000ft to the North of Sevenoaks.
>
> I finally landed in the middle of a large garden in Sevenoaks, none the worse for wear.

Pilot Officer George Bennions was also shot up, after damaging an Me 110, returning safely to base, as did Sergeant Isaac Howitt, who was surprised by a 109 over Dungeness and also got his damaged Spitfire back to Hornchurch.

The Hurricanes of 605 Squadron also entered the fray at 16.00 hrs, fighting a running battle between Rochester and Beachy Head for the next thirty minutes; Flight Lieutenant Archie MacKellar:

> I was leading the squadron from Blue Section and was told to rendezvous with another squadron 15,000ft above base, I to lead both squadrons. This other squadron never, so far as I could see, joined me. At 14,000ft I saw large bomber formation, plus escort flying WNW. I informed the squadron and Runic of this and carried on climbing.
>
> When I gained 1,000ft above the bombers I instructed the squadron to prepare for a beam attack out of the sun, which was just behind us and of great value, as I consider that the bomber formation never saw our approach due to the sun in their eyes. The bomber formation was composed of vics of five aircraft in squadron formation.
>
> A little South of Gravesend I therefore attacked the leader of the port outside vic from quarter ahead to beam and saw it break out of formation and spiral down, confirmed by Green 1. As I was fairly close I had to break through the formation. On climbing up again I noticed near Chiselhurst one E/A at 15,000ft, much behind, and carried out a beam attack from the West and stopped his starboard engine. I did one more attack from a slight dive as the E/A was heading South, and behind, in an attempt to put out the port motor, thereby expending all my ammunition, and then saw the top rear gunner bale out and another crew member as well.
>
> What appeared to be maps etc were also being thrown overboard some miles South of Tunbridge Wells. I also noticed another Hurricane flying near me during these attacks (Blue 3). As by now I had no ammunition left I called up this other aircraft, who I knew to be one of my Flight, to finish the E/A off, but was informed that he also had no ammunition. We both then kept diving very low over him in an endeavour to force him lower and down on land. He was losing height very rapidly even on one engine. This machine, however, crashed on the water South of Beachy Head, having crossed Beachy Head at 1,000ft.

Historically, it has been accepted that MacKellar and Pilot Officer Robert Jones had shot-up a He 111 of 1/KG 26, the pilot of which, *Feldwebel* Jabusch, baled out having been wounded and was captured; the observer and aircraft captain, *Leutnant* Zimmermann, however, took control of the aircraft and made a controlled forced-landing near Dieppe. The He 111 attacked by MacKellar, though, was seen to crash into the Channel, so more likely this was one of three He 111s from I and II/KG 26, which went into the sea.

The German formation had turned about before reaching London, and just before it did so 605 Squadron's Pilot Officer Christopher 'Bunny' Currant attacked and damaged two He 111s, and Pilot Officer Tom Cooper-Slipper another. The Polish Pilot Officer Anton Glowacki claimed an Me 110 destroyed (possibly the machine of 9/ZG 26 which crashed at Harvel, having also been attacked by pilots of 19 Squadron). After the formation turned south, 'those on the ground at Croydon saw Pilot Officer Currant destroy a He 111 which crashed a few miles to the East, and he damaged two more He 111s [ORB]'.

The Polish Sergeant Jan Budzinski attacked a He 111 without apparent effect before taking an Me 109 head-on, which dived away, pursued by the Hurricane pilot. South of Bexley, Budzinski opened fire from astern, as a result of which the 109 'broke up and dived down to the ground SE of Gravesend' – the pilot, *Unteroffizier* Anton Hechmaier, of 3/LG 2, crashed in flames at Wrotham and was killed.

No.605 Squadron's only casualty was the CO, Squadron Leader Walter Churchill, who 'received a slight flesh wound in his arm [ORB]'.

Having taken-off at 15.40 hrs, Squadron Leader Brian Lane DFC climbed the all-Spitfire 12 Group Wing to 23,000ft over North Weald:

> I then sighted AA fire South of Gravesend and observed a large formation of E/A flying North at 20,000ft. I turned South and dived in a head-on attack on the leading formation of approximately twelve He 111s. I turned to port and observed E/A turning south-east over Sittingbourne. There were now only seven He 111s in formation with two more half a mile ahead and two Me 110s, one astern and one to port.
>
> I attacked rear Me 110 and saw large pieces flying off his starboard engine, which stopped. I broke away and attacked again from astern. The starboard engine caught fire and the E/A was last seen in a dive.

> The second Me 110 then opened up and left the He 111s. I carried out head-on and beam attacks on E/A without visible effect, and then an astern attack on rear He 111. The starboard engine was seen to catch fire. I had no more ammunition left and returned to base.

In his log book, the young CO wrote that he had 'Never had so much fun before!'.

Sergeant Bernard 'Jimmy' Jennings (Red 2):

> at 16.15 hrs we intercepted twelve He 111K, we did a head-on attack. I turned after firing and saw my He 111 with his starboard engine burning. I fired again and he went down, apparently out of control. So much tracer was whizzing past that I didn't stay to watch him. I lost the rest of the formation, so I attacked a rear-end Me 110, of a formation of about fifteen. This one fell back from the rest of the formation with smoke pouring out of his starboard engine.
>
> I did another attack from behind and he crashed in a wood, south-east of the Ashstead railway line, between Sittingbourne and Maidstone. I didn't see anybody jump by parachute. I chased eleven Me 110s out to sea, finished my rounds without any visible result and returned home.

The Me 110, of 9/ZG 26, crashed at Barnes Cote, Harvel. The pilot, *Oberleutnant* Junghans, was killed; his gunner, *Gefreiter* Paul Eckert remains missing.

Sergeant Adrian Roden was also flying in Red Section:

> Made an astern attack on the rearmost machine of about thirty Me 110s which were milling around in a large circle. I was about 100ft higher and dived with the sun behind me – came up from below into the astern position. I gave him a burst of about five seconds and as other aircraft were coming up behind I broke away down.
>
> Pieces of the target aircraft flew off from the port mainplane and he continued straight and level for about another fifty yards, and then smoke came from his port engine and he started a shallow dive.
>
> My position was not very healthy and I had to remove my attention from him. I tried to follow his flight a minute or two later but could see no sign of him.

Flight Lieutenant Jack Lawson was also successful, destroying a He 111, while Flying Officer Leonard 'Ace' Haines got an Me 110, Sergeant David 'Little Boy' Cox a probable 'Do 215', and the Czech Pilot Officer Frantisek 'Dolly' Dolezal an Me 109. Flight Sergeant George 'Grumpy' Unwin was shot down, but 'made a wizard forced-landing with undercarriage down!!! [ORB]'.

Flight Sergeant Unwin:

> I was at about 20,000ft, flying my usual Spitfire, P9546, QV-H, and I suddenly saw this lone Dornier. How he was on his own I'll never know, but he was off home. So I went after him. Now the drill against a Dornier was he had a dustbin rear gunner, a dustbin hanging down below the fuselage and so you had to fix him first before closing in for the aircraft. This I did, very cleverly of course. I could see him shooting at me and so closed in and gave him a burst and shot him up.
>
> At least I thought I had, I'll never know to this day whether I did or didn't, or whether someone took his place. Because as I closed right in on him and started shooting I saw his rear gunner shooting back at me, the little red sparks you could see. I didn't pay much attention to it, thinking that after a quick spray from the spread of my guns he would stop. I carried on firing for quite a while, when suddenly I was covered in smoke.
>
> To my horror a hole appeared in my windscreen – I was leaning forward of course, one did to peer through the gunsight which was fortunately in the middle of a piece of armour plated, bullet resistant glass about an inch and a half. A hole appeared in front of my face. I thought, 'Good God I must be dead, or something' – no blood, no nothing, but I'm covered in smoke, I thought I was on fire. So I whipped the hood back, undid my straps and started to get out.
>
> By this time I'd broken away, I was going downhill. I was halfway out of the cockpit when I suddenly saw that the smoke was coming from the top of the engine through the engine cowling which is where the glycol pipe is, the coolant pipe. The smoke was a really browny colour, it wasn't black smoke. I could smell it too, it was glycol. So I got back in and strapped myself in again, leaving the hood open, still going downhill in case somebody was following me. Then I started looking for a field, finding one to land in near Brentwood in Essex. In those

> days you were supposed to get it down without hurting the aircraft. So I waited until I'd found my field and got down to about a thousand feet, dropped the undercarriage and did a forced landing in this field which had a few cows in it. Quite a big field, it was. No trouble at all.
>
> I hadn't even got out of the cockpit before a jeep with a young subaltern and two soldiers with fixed bayonets came roaring through the gate. As soon as they saw it was one of ours they changed their attitude. I got a screwdriver from one of the soldiers and we took the top off, and there it was – a bullet had gone through the glycol pipe.
>
> As I had first served in the RAF as an engineering apprentice at Halton before the war, my technical knowledge was good, and so I knew what needed to be done to get me airborne again. The soldiers took me to North Weald, where I got help from a fitter plus spares and repaired the aircraft, which I flew back to Duxford two days later. The windscreen, however, could not be repaired on station and so P9546 was sent off to a Maintenance Unit (MU).

Landing an aircraft with narrow-track undercarriage in a rough field required great skill – and George's flying prowess had saved a valuable fighter. Unwin, 19 Squadron's 'High Priest', was an aggressive fighter pilot; as Squadron Leader Lane wrote, 'Grumpy with some 109s always reminded me of a terrier amongst rats!'

When Lane led the Spitfires of his 19 Squadron into the attack, 74, 611 and 266 Squadrons executed a left-hand turn, attacking on the beam of the enemy formation. In what was 611 Squadron's first experience of engaging amassed formation, Squadron Leader Jimmy McComb's pilots were soon in the battle's midst: Sergeant Stephen 'Sandy' Levenson attacked several enemy aircraft, including a 'Ju 88' which he actually flew alongside as the raider lost height. As he did so, his Spitfire was hit by AA fire and with black smoke pouring from beneath the instrument panel he broke off to forced-land near Kenley.

A nearby searchlight post then informed Levenson that the bomber concerned had crashed in flames a few miles south of Kenley – the He 111 of 3/KG 26 which came down at Lingfield (and which features in the combat reports of at least eight other RAF fighter pilots). The squadron's Sergeant Frederick Shepherd, however, was shot down in flames, the pilot abandoning his Spitfire over Croydon – but his parachute was on fire and he was killed. Unfortunately Shepherd's aircraft crashed onto 49 and 51 Hartland Way, Shirley, killing two civilians.

When the 12 Group attack went in, 266 Squadron attacked in two-line astern formations, from out of the sun, the Wittering Spitfire pilots claiming three enemy aircraft destroyed and five damaged. Pilot Officer Robert Roach claimed a He 111 probable but was himself shot down over Billericay, baling out safely and landing unhurt.

The South African Squadron Leader 'Sailor' Malan was leading 74 Squadron:

> I was Dysoe Leader operating from Duxford aerodrome as rear squadron of three-squadron wing led by 19 Squadron, with 611 Squadron [including the flight of 266 Squadron aircraft] in the middle. Detailed to intercept raids over London at 20,000ft. It was arranged that the two leading squadrons should keep fighter escort at bay while I attack bombers with 74 Squadron.
>
> We intercepted long rectangle of bombers at 20,000ft over London at approximately 16.30 hrs. We were flying in three fours, sections line astern. I gave order for head-on attack but before I could get far enough ahead I saw He 113s [*sic*] coming down onto us and turned towards bombers immediately, in order to deliver some form of attack before engaging fighters. I could not turn in the space and quite accidentally delivered a very effective beam attack at close range by turning across bows of formation and opening fire at 150 yards, closing to 50 yards.
>
> I saw my ammunition pouring into two E/A as I raked across formation, which was tightly packed and, because of close pursuit of enemy fighters, continued down in fast spiral to 13,000ft and climbed into sun at 20,000ft. Proceeded towards one turning onto southerly course but spotted a Ju 88 at 20,000ft which had either engine trouble or was observing results of bombing.
>
> I delivered a head-on attack and blew large pieces from port engine. I turned and delivered beam attack at 100 yards as enemy fighter dived down onto me. I continued down but saw port engine well on fire and aircraft going down in gentle dive. Also thought I saw one parachute open close to the E/A.

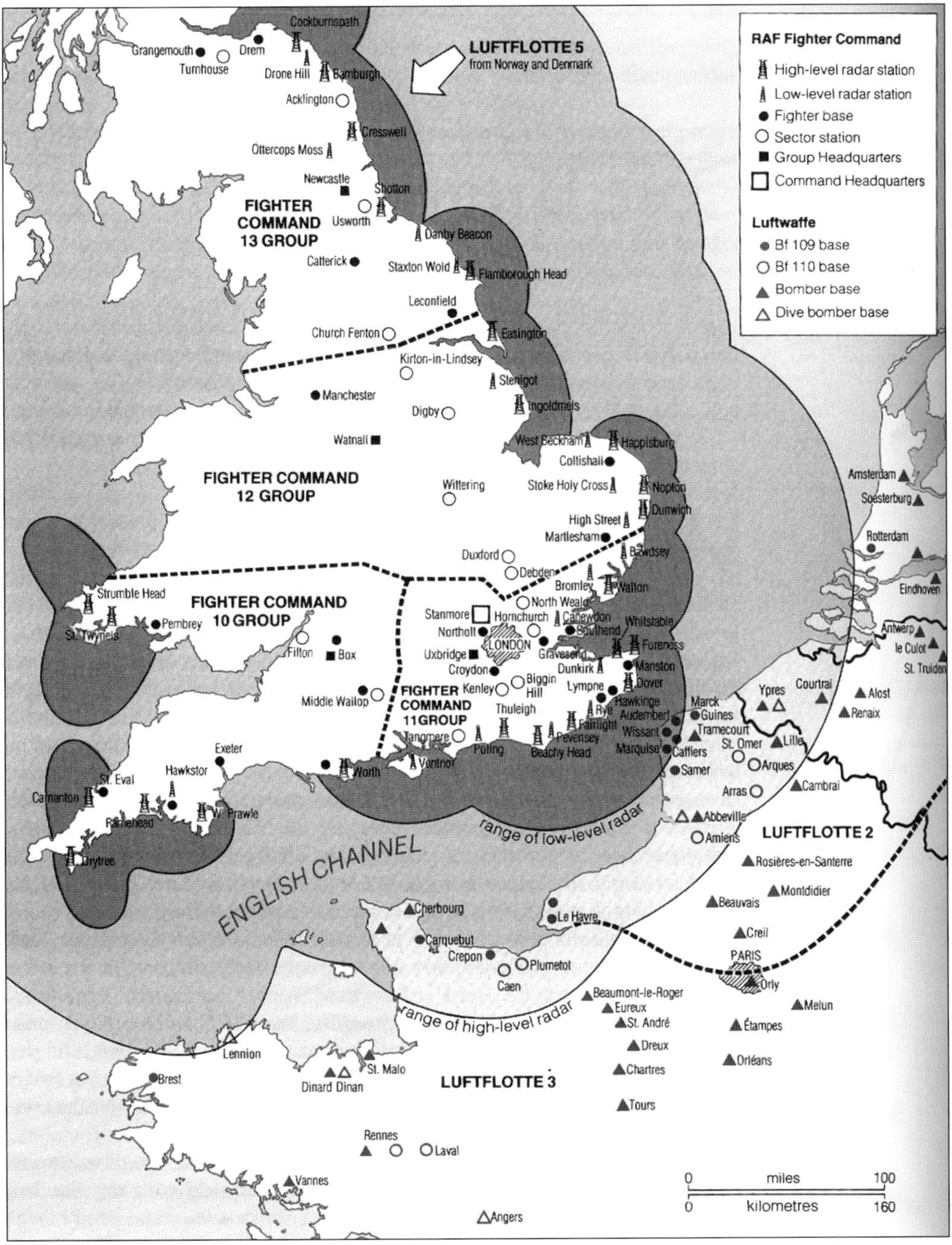

The opposing sides.

Hitler attending a conference with *Kriegsmarine* chief Grand Admiral Erich Raeder and *Feldmarschall* Walther von Brauchitsch, his army chief. Although cautious, both men supported the prospect of a seaborne invasion of southern England: Operation *Seelöwe*.

Hitler and Raeder on 21 May 1940, after the conference at which the possibility of invading Britain was first discussed.

German troops practice disembarking from an invasion barge at Calais.

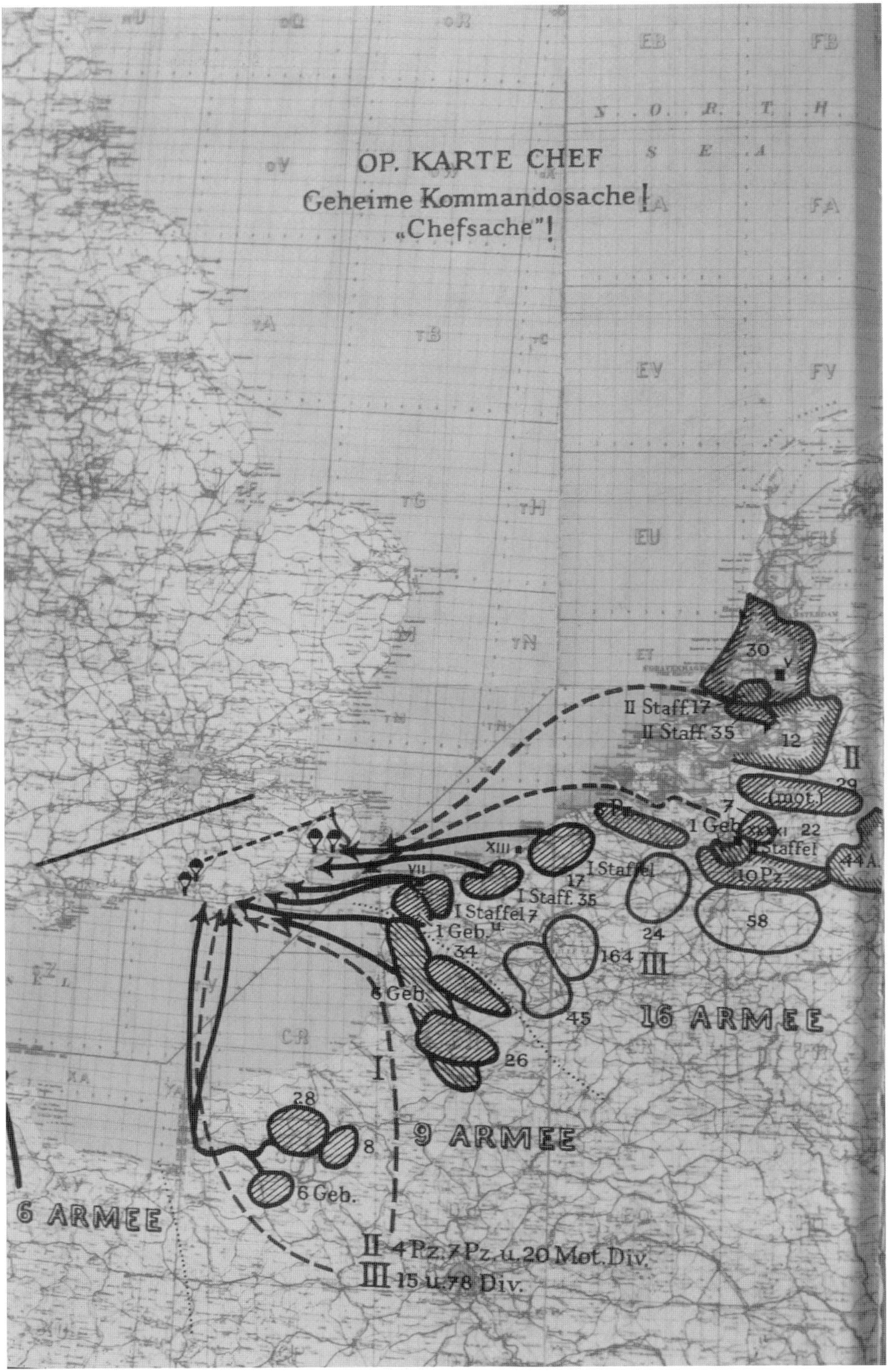

The German invasion plan.

An RAF bombardier's view of an invasion port and barges.

RAF photographic reconnaissance aircraft maintained a constant watch on the invasion ports, returning with essential intelligence.

A Coastal Command Lockheed Hudson – the aircrews of which flew countless ant-invasion, anti-submarine and shipping, convoy protection and reconnaissance sorties throughout the Battle of Britain.

A Coastal Command Avro Anson crew, complete with carrier pigeon, return from a reconnaissance sortie.

A Vickers Wellington – the RAF's best bomber in 1940 – which took the war to Germany by night.

A Bomber Command Handley Page Hampden being bombed up ready for an attack on the invasion ports – or perhaps an enemy airfield or even Germany.

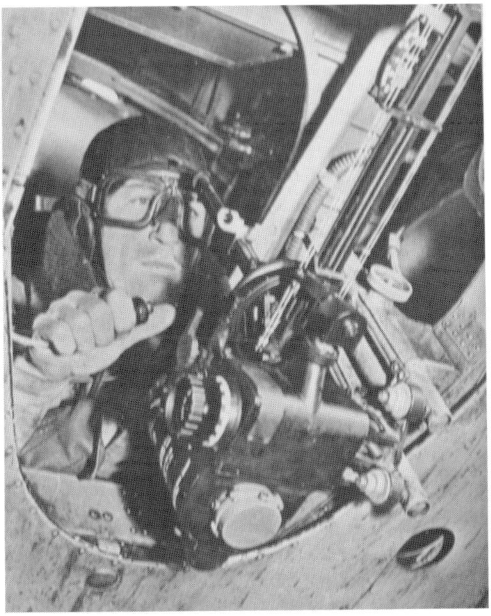

'Bombs gone!'

German bomber crews planning a raid on Southampton – an important deep-water port and home to the Vickers Supermarine Aviation Works, the main centre for Spitfire production.

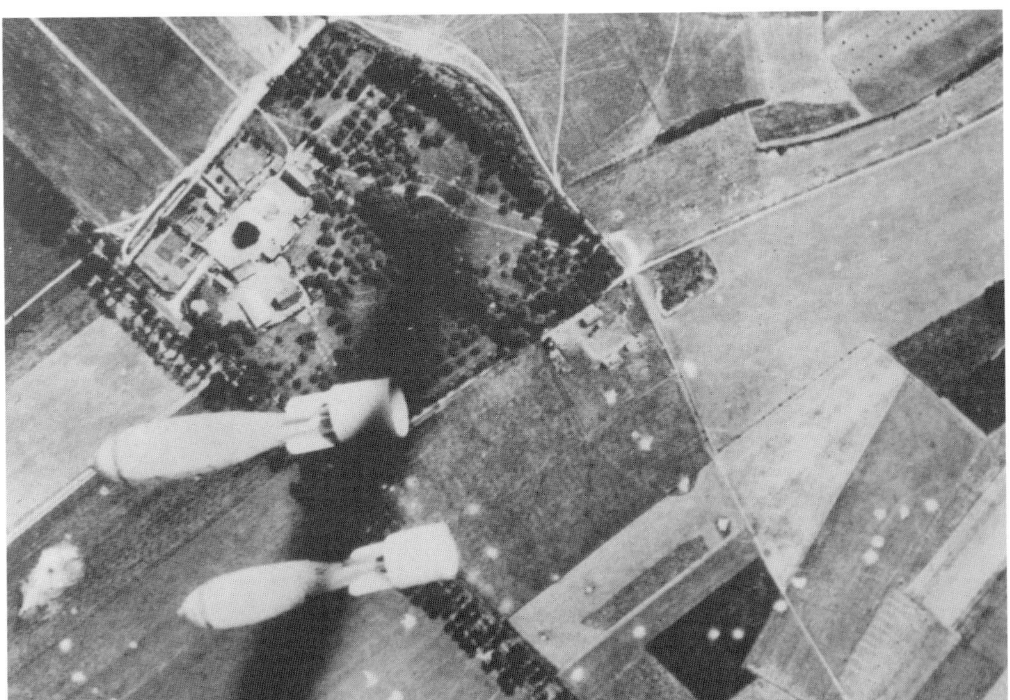

Bombs falling on Abbeville airfield from a 2 Group Bristol Blenheim – these unescorted bombers made innumerable attacks on enemy airfields in France and the Netherlands by day.

For the new phase of operations, the attack on London, Luftwaffe chief *Reichsmarschall* Hermann Göring (in white tunic) took personal command – and is seen here browsing a map of combat operations with other high-ranking Luftwaffe officers in France, September 1940 (Historic Military Press, HMP).

Göring (centre), observes the British South Coast through high power binoculars in September 1940 – possibly on 7 September 1940, the first day of the Blitz on London (HMP).

Göring, with *Generalfeldmarschall* Albert Kesselring, commander of Luftflotte 2 and to whom the destruction of London and 11 Group Fighter Command was entrusted, at Kesselring's field HQ on Cap Gris Nez, September 1940 (HMP).

Göring and Kesselring at Luftflotte 2's field HQ on Cap Gris Nez, September 1940 (HMP).

Göring and his staff watch the air operations from the outpost at Cap Blanc Nez, 13 September 1940. (Bundesarchiv; Bild-146-1976-043-24)

Men of the Observer Corps at a typical post – their visual tracking of the enemy was essential, given the radar only looked outwards and was of no use once the Germans had crossed the British coast.

A heavy anti-aircraft battery in the London area.

General Sir Frederick Pile, Commander-in-Chief of Anti-Aircraft Command visiting a London battery.

Local Defence Volunteers of the Home Guard practice repelling invaders during the autumn of 1940 – when the threat of invasion was very real indeed.

The hammer-blow fell on London's docklands on 7 September 1940 in an unprecedented attack – the East End seen still ablaze in this iconic photograph a day later.

Air Vice-Marshal Sir Keith Park, a New Zealander who commanded 11 Group, defending London and the south-east, with his personal Hurricane at RAF Northolt during the Battle of Britain. To Park goes the credit for the tactical victory.

King George VI visiting bomb-damaged Lambeth – Buckingham Palace was hit several times during the Battle of Britain and the Blitz, confirming that King, Queen and Londoners were all 'in it together'.

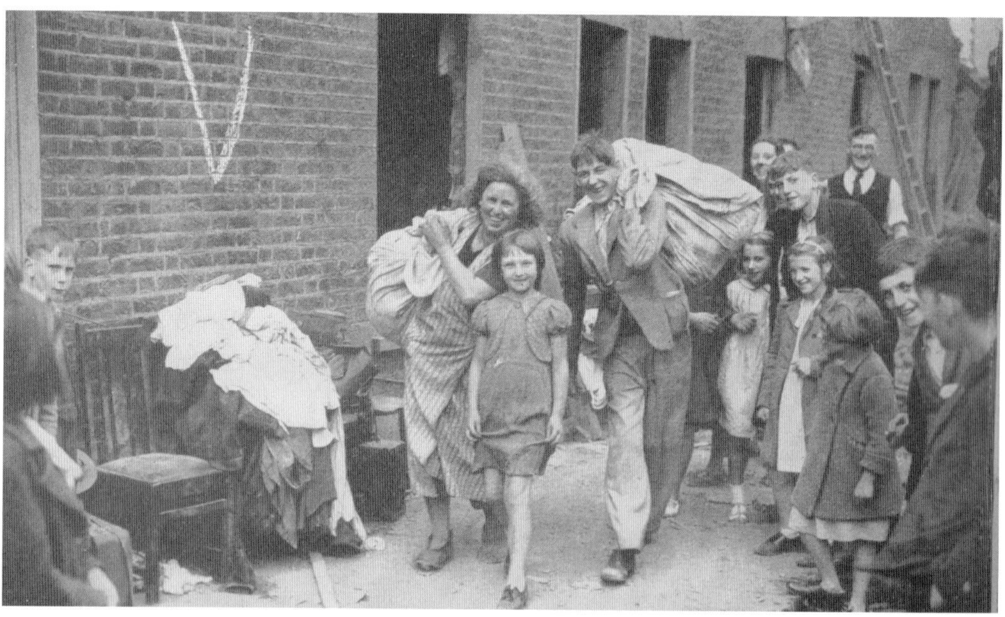

Bombed out Londoners, their catchphrase being 'London can take it' – thereby confounding the Italian air strategist General Douhet who believed that an air force alone could win a war by bombing and demoralising a civilian population.

London street scene, 8 September 1940.

RAF armourers at work on a Hawker Hurricane, Fighter Command's most numerous fighter throughout the Battle of Britain.

The legless Squadron Leader Douglas Bader DSO, commander of 242 Squadron and leader of 12 Group's controversial, Duxford-based, 'Big Wing' of first three then five squadrons.

The Duxford Wing first went into action over London on 7 September 1940. 242 Squadron's Pilot Officer Denis Crowley-Milling's Hurricane was shot-up, the armoured windscreen stopping a machine-gun round.

Crowley-Milling's Hurricane at Duxford.

Squadron Leader Brian Lane DFC (third from left), the 23-year-old commander of 19 Squadron, with some of his Spitfire pilots and those of 616 Squadron at Fowlmere, the Duxford satellite airfield, whilst contributing to 'Big Wing' operations in September 1940.

Wing Commander John Scatliff Dewar DSO DFC, Station Commander of RAF Exeter and the highest-ranking RAF officer killed during the Battle of Britain, when shot down over the Solent on 11 September 1940.

Flight Lieutenant Richard Carew Reynell, known to all as 'Dick', flew Hurricanes with 43 Squadron at Tangmere. A former Oxford scholar and test pilot, he was killed in action defending London on 7 September 1940.

Squadron Leader Caesar Hull DFC, a South African, the commander of 43 Squadron, also killed in action defending the capital on 7 September 1940.

Such was the shortage of pilots that Fighter Command was reinforced by volunteers from Coastal and Bomber Commands, and the Fleet Air Arm. Sub-Lieutenant Richard 'Dicky' Cork flew Hurricanes with 242 Squadron and is seen here after the Battle of Britain with his former 12 Group commander, Air Vice-Marshal Sir Trafford Leigh-Mallory – who support of Squadron Leader Bader's 'Big Wing' tactics would see a scandalous row develop between high commanders. (*Kate Ashby*)

A I/KG 26 He 111 burns at Burmarsh on Romney Marsh, 11 September 1940, its crew led away into captivity whilst the victorious Spitfire pilot circles overhead. The attack on London meant that the Germans had further to fly to their target, thereby providing more opportunities for Fighter Command to intercept them.

The iconic cathedral of St Paul's, wreathed in smoke and flame.

A He 111 over the famous 'S' bend in the Thames and London's docklands.

The attack on London also meant that the single-engined Me 109 fighter escorts were operating at the extremity of their range, with only a few minutes of fuel to spare for combat – many only just made it back to France.

A Me 109E down in Kent.

Air Vice-Marshal Sholto Douglas, Deputy Chief of the Air Staff, was a personal friend of Air Vice-Marshal Leigh-Mallory and also harboured enmity against Air Chief Marshal Dowding and Air Vice-Marshal Park – and his support of the 'Big Wing' would be a major contributory factor to the developing internal row over tactics.

Fighter pilot: Flight Lieutenant Eric 'Tommy' Thomas, a flight commander on 222 Squadron, flying Spitfires at Hornchurch. Thomas became an ace and later Wing Leader at Biggin Hill; he survived the war.

Bomber pilot: *Hauptmann* Hermann Kell, a He 111 pilot and *Staffelkapitän* of 3/KG 4, shot down over London on the night of 14/15 September 1940 by the New Zealand night-fighter ace, Pilot Officer Michael Herrick. Kell would spend the rest of the war as a prisoner in Canada, where he later settled.

The Canadians of 1(RCAF) Squadron were based at Northolt during the Battle of Britain, this snapshot of Flying Officer Arthur 'Art' Yuile having been taken previously at Prestwick. It should be remembered that the RAF was a multi-national force during the Battle of Britain.

Canadians: snapped at Northolt of 1(RCAF) Squadron pilots Flying Officer Blair 'Dal'; Russell (right) and 'Art' Yuile. Both were successful fighter pilots, Russell becoming a highly decorated wing leader, and survived the war.

Flight Lieutenant Paterson Clarence Hughes DFC, an Australian flight commander on 234 Squadron, killed in action defending London on 15 September 1940.

Pilot Officer Richard Jones, who flew Spitfires with both 64 Squadron at Kenley in 11 Group, and with 19 and the Duxford Wing; he survived the war.

Two Polish squadrons fought in the Battle of Britain, the first made operational being 302, based at Duxford, and then Northolt's 303 Squadron. English-speaking British or Commonwealth officers became commanding officers and flight commanders of these foreign-speaking squadrons, shadowed by their Polish and Czechoslovak counter-parts. Eventually, full command would be handed over, once the English language and RAF procedures were mastered. In this photograph, the British commander of 303 Squadron, Squadron Leader Ronald Kellett DSO (second left) listens whilst Flying Officer Jerzy Jankiewicz describes his latest combat. During the Battle of Britain, Sergeant Stanislaw Karubin (second right), often flew as Kellet's wingman. The pilot at extreme right is Pilot Officer Franciszek Korniki. 303 Squadron would gain a reputation for unparalleled ferocity when engaging the enemy.

The Canadian ace, Flight Lieutenant Johnny Kent DFC (second left), a flight commander on 303 Squadron at Northolt, with his Polish pilots after a sortie.

Some of 303 Squadron's Polish groundcrew at Northolt.

Other Polish pilots, with a good grasp of English, were embedded in RAF fighter squadrons, including Pilot Officer Franciszek Surma (left), seen playing 'pax' at Tangmere with his 607 Squadron Flight Commander, Flight Lieutenant Charles 'Chatty' Bowen; neither would survive the war.

Free Czechoslovaks also made an essential contribution, these pilots of 310 Squadron snapped at Duxford in September 1940.

Pilots of 501 'County of Gloucester' Squadron at Kenley, September 1940.

An informal snapshot of some 501 Squadron Hurricane pilots, from left: Pilot Officers James 'Ginger' Lacey DFM, Ken MacKenzie DFC, Tony Whitehouse, Bob Dafforn and Vic Ekins. All survived the war – but Dafforn was killed test-flying on 2 December 1945.

Although Supermarine escaped serious damage on 15 September 1940, the adjacent district of Woolston did not.

Hawker Hurricanes being produced at Brooklands. Thanks to the energetic Lord Beaverbrook, Fighter Command was never short of aircraft, insufficient pilots was the problem. Luftwaffe intelligence, however, was woefully inaccurate, failing to understand this. Having failed to achieve a decisive victory by bombing London, on 17 September 1940 Hitler postponed Operation *Seelöwe*. The next phase would see attacks concentrated on the British aircraft industry.

All photographs Dilip Sarkar Archive, unless otherwise indicated.

> The enemy fighter, which appeared to be He 113, followed me down to 10,000ft where I did a steep left-hand turn, blacking myself out, and shook him off.
>
> As my ammunition was expended, I returned to Duxford. Position of last engagement was about over Biggin Hill.

The first enemy aircraft was credited as 'damaged', the second destroyed.

Ordered to patrol Biggin Hill, 229 and 303 Squadrons, making up a Northolt wing, at 16.10 hrs the northerly German raid was sighted over Reigate, flying towards London. The first wave of enemy aircraft then turned seawards, so 229 Squadron attacked the third wave – head-on. No.303 Squadron, on the left of 229, wheeled around and attacked the middle and rear waves, to 229's starboard side. Squadron Leader Arthur Banham, commanding 229, led his Hurricanes into the attack in two lines astern.

Flight Lieutenant Frank Rimmer, commanding 'B' Flight of 229 Squadron:

> I was leading Blue Section behind Red and Yellow, and carried out a quarter attack on starboard bomber of leading section. Tracer fire came from E/A rear-gunner but not accurate. I closed in from 200–50 yards, firing until all ammunition was exhausted. After about four seconds there was no more fire from E/A. I saw pieces break from starboard wing and engine, which was smoking and in flames. E/A was going down when I saw an Me 109 in my mirror. He got in a burst which shattered my hood, causing superficial facial injuries. I half-rolled out of the fight, taking evasive action, and returned to base.

In this action 229 Squadron's pilots would claim three bombers destroyed, three probables and five damaged. With so many fighters engaging simultaneously, these enemy aircraft were undoubtedly attacked and claimed by pilots of other squadrons too. Pilot Officer Malcolm Ravenhill, however, was shot down over Biggin Hill, baling out suffering from shock, and Pilot Officer Kenneth Carver baled out badly burned.

Attacking in 229's wake, the Poles of 303 Squadron, led by the British Flight Lieutenant Athol Forbes, claimed four He 111s, three Do 17s, three Me 110s and seven Me 109s destroyed, pursuing the enemy back to the Channel. The majority of these claims, unfortunately, do not stand scrutiny.

Although all squadrons overclaimed due to the confused nature of air fighting, 303 Squadron's overclaiming ratio, like that of the Duxford Wing and 242 Squadron in particular, is substantially and consistently higher than other squadrons.

At best, four He 111s, three Me 110s and one Me 109 could perhaps be attributed to 303 Squadron – most of which were also attacked by other RAF pilots and featured in their combat reports too. Offset against whatever successes there were in fact, Forbes was shot-up and wounded, forced-landing at Heston, Sergeant Stefan Wojtowicz was shot down and killed, crashing at Westerham, and Flying Officer Arsen Cebrzynski was also shot down, crashing at Pembury – the pilot was mortally wounded and died eight days later.

Having turned about, the Germans had failed to reach London; according to 303 Squadron, 'many enemy aircraft jettisoned their bombs on wooded country well to the South of London [ORB]'.

Nos.17 and 73 Squadrons, essentially forming a Debden Wing, had agreed that 73 would go for the bombers while 17 mixed it with any escorting fighters. Having met over the mouth of the Thames, both Hurricane squadrons orbited the estuary in vics line astern. At 16.09 hrs, off the Girdler Lightship, the Hurricane pilots sighted elements of the more northerly enemy force: twelve Me 110s flying east, in line astern.

As 73 Squadron made for the bombers, 17 Squadron's Flying Officer Count Manfred Czernin – who had been notified of his DFC award that morning – led Yellow Section (Sergeant Leonard Bartlett, Yellow 2, and Sergeant Clifford Chew, Yellow 3) to attack eight 'He 113s [*sic*]' seen above them. No.17 Squadron Intelligence Patrol Report:

> A He 113 [*sic*] dived on Yellow 2 as he was about to attack, and a cannon shell went into the fuselage of his aircraft, tearing away most of the fabric behind the pilot's seat, and denting, but not piercing, the armour plating. Machine-gun bullets also entered port mainplane and fuselage. Yellow 1 fired a 2-seconds burst in a beam attack on one of the Me 110s which dived into cloud with black smoke pouring from it. Yellow 1 followed E/A below cloud, and as he did so saw an Me 110 which had been attacked by Blue 1 [Flight Lieutenant Bayne] dive into the sea between Girdler Lightship and Margate Sands.

> Yellow 1 continued to chase the Me 110 he had previously attacked in and out of cloud, and in a clear gap got within 400 yards, and gave it a 7 to 8 seconds burst from dead astern. The E/A dived into the sea about ten miles East of Margate. A large yellow stain was seen to spread over the sea where the E/A went in. Yellow 3 attacked another of the Me 110s but did not observe the result.
>
> Blue 1 also led his Section, consisting of Polish pilots Flying Officer Niemiec, Blue 2, and Pilot Officer Kumiega, Blue 3, to attack the Me 110s. Blue 1 gave a four-second burst at one Me 110 from astern at 250 yards range and saw E/A dive for cloud with white smoke coming from the starboard engine, but was unable to observe results owing to low cloud.
>
> In breaking away he became separated from his Section, and coming out below cloud saw another Me 110 approaching him head-on. He gave the E/A five-seconds burst at a slight angle from the head-on position and saw it going down in a spiral dive. The E/A was seen to crash into the sea by Yellow 1. The remainder of the Squadron stayed above as escort and were not engaged in the combat.

With just one Hurricane suffering Category 2 damage and repairable, it was a good result for 17 Squadron. At the same time, 73 Squadron also engaged the Me 110s over the Isle of Sheppey. The CO, Squadron Leader Maurice Robinson, destroyed a 110:

> the tail and rear portion falling off some five miles East of Herne Bay, and Flying Officer Smith destroyed another 110, one engine being in flames, the other only windmilling. Pilot Officer Marchand got a probable 110, and Flying Officer Smith, Sergeant Scott and Flight Lieutenant Breytagh a damaged 110 each. [ORB]

Sergeant Herbert Webster, however, was shot down by an Me 110, baling out over Detling and landing unhurt. Sergeant John Ellis's Hurricane was also hit and damaged, although the pilot returned safely to base. The Me 110s belonged to ZG 26, which lost five aircraft in this afternoon's air battle, while another returned to Calais-Marck badly damaged and with a dead *Bordfunker*.

At 16.40 hrs, the South African Flying Officer Brian van Mentz was leading the Spitfires of 222 Squadron on patrol, 28,000ft south-west of Maidstone:

> I saw a formation of bombers. I manoeuvred and led an attack from out of the sun. My first attack was too fast and I had to break after firing only a short burst. I then shadowed the formation to the coast and carried out another attack. I saw the Ju 88 [*sic*] break formation and dive into the sea about ten miles SE of Hastings. On my way back I attacked a yellow-nosed Me 109, which I last saw diving towards the French coast with a stream of smoke pouring out.

This, however, was not a 'Ju 88' but a He 111 of 5/KG 26 which ditched off Hastings; three crewmen were brought ashore by a fishing boat and captured, the fourth man was killed. Sergeant Sidney Baxter also claimed a 'Ju 88' destroyed, and Pilot Officer John Broadhurst a probable. Baxter, and Sergeant Ernest Scott, also claimed He 111s destroyed, and Sergeant Iain Hutchinson a probable. In addition to the Me 109 damaged by van Mentz, one was also claimed as damaged by Arthur Spears.

While attacking a He 111, Scott was hit by a 109, returning to Hornchurch unhurt but with a shattered cockpit hood. Pilot Officer William Assheton was shot down, making a successful forced-landing at Fletching, and was also unscathed.

No.41 Squadron also reported Ju 88s south of London at 16.40 hrs. Pilot Officer John MacKenzie dived on a formation of bombers but was too fast and in too steep a dive to aim accurately; breaking away he climbed to 30,000ft:

> I watched for an opportunity to attack from the sun and spotted a He 111 behind the main formation, going for the coast. I came down in a shallow dive and attacked from dead astern. The E/A dived and the rear gunner fired from top gun of E/A. Gave very long burst as I was short of petrol and would have no further chance of attacking E/A. As I broke away I noticed smoke from port engine. Dived to ground level as I thought Me 109 on my tail (it was Pilot Officer Lock in a Spitfire). Pilot Officer Lock watched E/A continue to glide down and forced-land. Also, workmen at West Malling aerodrome saw E/A

> gliding down with smoke from port engine, below trees. I landed at West Malling aerodrome with seven gallons of petrol.

An Me 110 was damaged by Pilot Officer George Bennions, who was in turn shot-up, returning to base with a damaged Spitfire and slightly wounded, and Sergeant Isaac Howitt also returned to base with a damaged aircraft. A 'Ju 88' was claimed as damaged by Pilot Officer Gerald Langley – but he was then shot down himself, baling out over Sevenoaks.

On this occasion, North Weald's Station Commander, that indomitable Irishman Wing Commander Victor Beamish DSO, was flying with 249 Squadron, which was first ordered to patrol base at 15,000ft, then Maidstone to Mayfield at 10,000ft. Two miles south of London, 249 sighted the He 111s flying west, with only a small fighter escort apparent of Me 109s – this being because faulty routing had led to the majority of the escorting fighters burning up too much fuel and having to return early: the He 111s suffered accordingly.

The squadron attacked the bombers head-on, which, upon being attacked, turned north, dropping bombs of London Docks before turning south for the coast. As the German fighters were 10,000ft higher than the bombers, 249 Squadron, according to the Intelligence Patrol Report, 'was more or less unmolested in their first attack'. They attacked from ahead and at least four bombers were seen to drop behind, streaming glycol. These are claimed as damaged by the squadron as a whole.

A 3/KG 1 He 111 was shared between Pilot Officer Tom Neil, Flight Lieutenant Denis Parnall and Pilot Officer William Pattullo, which forced-landed at Hildenborough, where the crew was captured. Wing Commander Beamish claimed a He 111 probable before being engaged himself by Me 109s, but extricated himself and returned safely to base. Only Sergeant William Davis failed to return – having been hit by return fire he baled out over Benenden, his wounds sufficiently serious to prevent him returning to operations until December 1940.

For Squadron Leader John Sample's 504 Squadron at Hendon, the afternoon sortie did not begin well: an undercarriage leg of Flight Lieutenant Michael Rook's Hurricane collapsed, the aircraft swerving off the airfield and 'into the rough, on its nose [ORB]'. Then, shortly after take-off, Pilot Officer John Gurteen's aircraft developed oil trouble, compelling him to make a forced-landing back at base 'with some skill [ORB]'; fortunately, both pilots were unhurt. The squadron's remaining Hurricanes were first vectored to North Weald, then sent first to Maidstone and then Dover, to intercept the more southerly German force.

At 15.45 hrs, 504 Squadron reported incoming bombers over Lympne, flying north, the escorting Me 109s and 110s spread out, some level with, others above and behind the bombers. Squadron Leader Sample led Red Section into the bombers, hitting a Do 17 himself while his Red 2, Flying Officer Michael Royce, set a bomber's starboard engine ablaze. Yellow and Blue Sections went for the leading bombers, the enemy formation immediately breaking up.

Flight Lieutenant William Royce (brother of Flying Officer Michael Royce) saw:

> two bombers dive straight down, apparently out of control, and a third, with petrol streaming from starboard wing, turned homewards. This machine was immediately joined by six Me 109s which broke from the leading escort formation and escorted the lame machine. Green Section took no part in the combat having separated from the remainder of the squadron while weaving. [Intelligence Patrol Report]

One of the 'weavers', Pilot Officer Arthur 'Bill' Clarke, was shot down by an Me 109, most likely by *Hauptmann* Edu Neumann, *Kommandeur* of I/JG 27, who claimed a Hurricane over Dungeness at 16.05 hrs (BST).

No news, however, would be received by 504 Squadron concerning Clarke's fate; as fellow 504 Squadron pilot Sergeant Ray Holmes said at the time, 'I don't think anyone knew what had happened to him. I certainly didn't. Pilot Officer Clarke simply disappeared.' All Squadron Leader Sample could suggest to the pilot's grieving parents was that their son must have baled out over the sea, but was not rescued.

In 1971, though, the Hawkinge-based Kent Battle of Britain Museum excavated the crash-site of a Hurricane on Romney Marsh, which a local resident, Miss Homewood of Wills Farm, had noted in her wartime diary had 'crashed at Newchurch, burying itself deep in the ground'. During that dig at Rookelands Farm, certain personal effects were found, including a handkerchief named 'Clarke': Pilot Officer Clarke was the only pilot missing of that name. Beyond reasonable doubt, this was his crash-site, and although no human remains were apparently reported it seems clear that Pilot Officer Clarke perished in the crash but was never recovered. The MoD's post-war policy has been one of non-disturbance, and as Pilot Officer Clarke's sister decided against disturbing her brother's remains, it is assumed that 'Bill' remains buried with his Hurricane – remembered today by a roadside memorial.

No.504 was in company with Stapleford's 46 Squadron – for whom the day had also started badly; at 11.00 hrs that morning, Sergeant Stanley Andrew – a survivor of the Norwegian campaign and sinking of the aircraft carrier HMS *Glorious* – broke away from the squadron formation while returning from an otherwise uneventful patrol, and performed a steep-turn too close to the ground; the Hurricane stalled and hit the airfield, throwing Andrew out, who was killed.

Now, at 15.47 hrs, ten miles north of Dungeness, 46 Squadron attacked the same formation intercepted by 504. In the ensuing combat, Sergeant Richard Earp claimed a 'Do 215 [*sic*]' destroyed, and Pilot Officer Allan Johnson damaged an Me 110. The Belgian Sergeant Roger Emile de Cannert d'Hamale was shot down in the action, baling out with an injured forehead and landing at Hurst Green, Sussex, and Flying Officer Peter McGregor was shot-up and wounded, crash-landing at Staplecross. Of Sergeant William Peacock, sadly, nothing was ever seen again.

As the southerly Germans fought their way inland, the Spitfires of 72 Squadron entered the fray at 15.50 hrs over Maidstone, claiming three Do 17s, one He 111 and an Me 109 destroyed, in addition to three Do 17 probables and a 109 damaged. The squadron's only casualty in this skirmish was Sergeant Basil Douthwaite who was wounded, returning his badly damaged Spitfire to Croydon.

The somewhat intellectual Flight Lieutenant Minden Blake, a New Zealander, former physics lecturer at Canterbury University and 1936 RAF University Entrant, was commanding 'B' Flight of 238 Squadron and leading the 10 Group unit on this sortie:

> at approx … 16.06 hrs sighted formation of Ju 88 bombers [*sic*] escorted by Me 109s and Me 110s between Brooklands and Croydon, flying North. Squadron was split up and one of the bombers was slightly

> further away from the main formation. I did a quarter attack, developing into astern from 150 yards, fired one long burst of 7–8 seconds and the starboard engine caught fire, and I changed over to the port engine.
>
> The E/A started to lose height and went into a spiral slide. As I broke away, several Hurricanes and Spitfires also attacked it and two persons jumped and descended by parachute – one Ju 88 destroyed. I returned to base and landed at 16.48 hrs.

This was actually the He 111 of 3/KG 26 engaged by numerous defending fighters and which crashed at Dormansland. Indeed, it was also attacked and claimed separately by 238 Squadron's Polish Pilot Officer Wladyslaw Rozycki (illustrating again how one enemy casualty could be multiplied many times on the balance sheet); after the engagement Rozycki was so short of fuel that he was unable to regain Middle Wallop, instead landing at Old Alesford. Pilot Officer William Towers-Perkins, though, was shot down and baled out south of Tunbridge Wells and admitted to the hospital there – badly burnt (he received treatment at East Grinstead and became a founder member and secretary of the Guinea Pig Club). Two pilots were missing, however.

Flight Lieutenant David Hughes, a vicar's son, former army cooperation pilot and commanding 'A' Flight, was shot down and was never seen or heard of again. The other missing pilot was a Pole, Sergeant Stanislaw Duszinski, of whom nothing was heard until 1971, when the crash-site of his Hurricane was located near Lydd by aviation archaeology enthusiasts. Although the aircraft was identified and reported to the authorities, little or no effort was made to excavate the difficult site on Romney Marsh – and the soft, running sand at the site led to an unsuccessful attempt by enthusiasts in 1996, acting in contravention of the Protection of Military Remains Act, 1986. Consequently, Sergeant Duszinski remains missing, and very likely always will be.

No.238 Squadron was commanded by Squadron Leader Harry Fenton:

> We had a daily routine: rise before first light, at about 0330 hours, have a coffee and then go to dispersal, spending the day there and being scrambled in either section or squadron strength. We shared Middle Wallop with 609 Squadron, with whom we took it in turns to spend every

third day down at Warmwell, undertaking convoy protection patrols. That was during the early days, but I was shot down and wounded on 8 August 1940, returning to the Squadron on 12 September 1940.

By that time 238 had been back at Middle Wallop for two days but had already lost two pilots, both missing from action over 11 Group: David Hughes, an able flight commander, and Duszynski, a Pole whom I had not even met. The tempo of combat had completely changed.

At 16.15 hrs on 11 September 1940, Squadron Leader Eric McNab's Canadians of 1(RCAF) Squadron intercepted the retiring He 111 force, 'South and East of Gatwick', flying south at 14,000ft; Flying Officer Hartland de Montarville Molson:

> I was Red 3 and attack the enemy bombers behind my Nos 1 and 2, coming in from the starboard quarter. I got in a two-second burst but observed no result. After breaking away I circled around at 10,000ft and saw a single bomber. At the same time another Hurricane attacked it and a short burst of light smoke came from the starboard engine. I followed in immediately from astern on the port side and got in a good burst. The E/A was a He 111. It lost height quickly in a right-hand turn and I got in a short deflection shot. His turn increased and he went down, bursting into flames as he hit the ground.

Again, this was the 3/KG 26 He 111 which exploded at Dormansland. Flight Lieutenant Gordon McGregor was also credited with a He 111, although this too was the Dormansland Heinkel, as was the 'Ju 88 [*sic*]' claimed destroyed by Flying Officer Arthur 'Art' Yuile. Squadron Leader McNab and Flying Officer Beverley Christmas each damaged He 111s, but these successes were not without loss: Flying Officer Thomas Little was shot down by a He 111's return fire, baling out and landing at Rotherfield with burns to his face and body, and Flying Officer Peter Lochnan was similarly shot down, crash-landing near Romney, fortunately unhurt.

From Kenley, Pilot Officer Arthur Watkinson, a South African, took off a few minutes after the ten Spitfires of 66 Squadron owing to an oil leak, requiring him to jump into another aircraft. Patrolling alone thereafter, he soon sighted a 'Do 17 [*sic*]' flying south over Tunbridge Wells and 2,000ft below.

Watkinson attacked, hitting and stopping both engines, the enemy aircraft gliding down harassed by AA fire. The Spitfire pilot watched as the bomber forced-landed on Walland Marsh, inland of Dungeness, circling overhead as three crew-men climbed out and were taken into custody by the army. This was in reality the *Stab* KG 1 He 111, also attacked and claimed by Pilot Officer Crelin 'Bogle' Bodie of the same squadron, and possibly Flight Lieutenant John Freeborn of 74, which crashed at Camber.

Meanwhile, the remainder of 66 Squadron had sighted the retiring enemy but were broken up when attacked by the fighter escorts. Thereafter two sections successfully re-formed, which the CO, Squadron Leader Rupert 'Lucky' Leigh led towards Dungeness at 8,000ft. Ten miles north of Rye, according to the Intelligence Patrol Report, an 'enemy bomber of unknown type was seen proceeding due south'. Leigh led the Spitfires into the attack, whereupon the bomber dived steeply and turned to port.

Pilot Officer Bob 'Oxo' Oxspring overshot but attacked with full deflection, while Sergeant Douggie Hunt opened fire when the enemy aircraft was flying just 50ft off the ground, which also crashed near Camber – this being the 6/KG 1 He 111 also attacked by Pilot Officer Allan Wright of 92 Squadron. No.66 Squadron's only casualty was Pilot Officer Ian Cruikshanks, who was shot-up and slightly injured when he forced-landed north-east of Ashford.

By 17.15 hrs, the sky over London and Kent was clear of the enemy – who had achieved little. Bombs were again dropped on London Docks, but the He 111s responsible suffered badly owing to the majority of escorting fighters having had to turn about owing to lack of fuel. Bombs also fell on the London districts of Woolwich, Lewisham, Deptford, Bermondsey, Islington and Paddington – but this was nothing like the highly successful and intense attack of 7 September 1940. The action arising from this London raid was not quite over, however. Five Coastal Command Blenheims of 53 and six of 59 Squadron provided escort to nine FAA Albacore biplanes of 826 Squadron attacking invasion shipping off Calais; unfortunately these aircraft ran into a large number of JG 52 and JG 53 Me 109s: five Albacores and four Blenheims were claimed destroyed by the Me 109 pilots, although this was over-optimistic: two Blenheims of 235 Squadron and their crews were shot down into the Channel and reported missing, and one Albacore ditched in the Channel, two of the crew being rescued by a MTB while the third man was killed.

There was also action further west that afternoon, directed against Southampton.

The Reverend Dagger, RAF Exeter's Chaplain, recalled that day:

> A fine and warm August had passed into an equally fine September – but during this month, our Station Commander, Wing Commander John Dewar DSO DFC, came to the end as many had foretold, I remember that morning well, I was then, quite illegally and unsuitably, President of the Mess Committee, and was summoned to the Station Commander's office at 10.00 hrs.
>
> The Adjutant, to whom I applied for information before-hand, told me that, 'Sam, a most unpleasant Bull Terrier, possibly belonging to 87 Squadron, had bitten the CO.'
>
> Said CO, as usual, was about to fly, so my interview was short: dogs had to be banished from the mess for good and all.
>
> The CO talked about my work, expressing regret that he had been unable to attend any services. 'You know padre that I am a busy man, but I intend to come along one day', then added, 'and you can rely on me to give you all possible help.'
>
> I saluted and left the office with a new affection for the CO and the RAF. Wing Commander Dewar then followed me out on the way to his waiting Hurricane.

At 15.00 hrs that afternoon, Wing Commander Dewar took-off in Hurricane V7306 and before doing so was advised of enemy activity over Selsey Bill. The route to be flown was from Exeter, via Winchester, then to Tangmere, thus avoiding the balloon barrage over Southampton. The flight expected to take some forty minutes in duration and ETA being about 16.00 hrs: a routine flight.

That morning, the German precision bombing unit *Erprobungsgruppe* 210 had arrived at Cherbourg-Ost airfield, tasked with destroying Southampton's Spitfire production capacity. The famous Vickers Supermarine Aviation Works was located at Woolston – just sixty miles from France and virtually on the coast, the factory was extremely vulnerable to air attack.

At that time, the Woolston factory, was the main centre for Spitfire production. The busy factory was located on the Itchen's East bank, immediately north of the 'floating bridge', which ferried passengers to and from across the estuary which divided Southampton in two. A few hundred yards to the north was the company's 'Itchen Works'. Both factories fronted the Itchen, a 15ft high railway embankment rising up across the road behind them. Beyond the railway, to the east, was the open land of Peartree Green, and built-up area of Woolston. Completed Spitfire major sub-assemblies were transported by road to the company's hangars at Eastleigh airport for final assembly and test flying, so to a degree production was dispersed.

In terms of protection for the workforce, three surface shelters had been constructed along the Itchen Work's boundary, but the main shelters were constructed in rows on the railway's far side, access gained via a tunnel just 10ft wide, burrowed through the embankment. While these principal shelters were adjacent and close-by the Itchen Works, the main workforce was located at the Woolston Works, so had a fair distance to cover in the event of a raid. What made Woolston personnel especially vulnerable was that warnings were sounded at the last possible minute, so that raids only disrupted production for the minimum length of time. Two practices indicated that it took too long for Woolston workers to reach the shelters, and indeed that the narrow tunnel created a dangerous bottleneck, for which reason some staff never used the company shelters. In the days ahead, these factors would prove fatal for many 'Supermariners'.

At 15.30 hrs, the *Erprobungsgruppe* 210's Me 110 and Me 109 Jabos took off from Cherbourg-Ost, bound for Eastleigh, escorted by Me 110s of ZG 76, and Me 109s of JG 2.

At 15.40 hrs, 213 Squadron scrambled from Tangmere and were vectored to Selsey Bill, followed over the next ten minutes by 602 from Westhampnett, and 607 Squadron, also from Tangmere. While the latter patrolled base, the Spitfires of 602 Squadron headed out to sea, the Hurricanes of 213 following slightly below and behind.

At 16.05 hrs, according to the Intelligence Patrol Report of 213 Squadron, twenty Me 110s were engaged at 15,000ft over Selsey Bill, the Me 110s immediately forming a defensive circle while the Hurricanes attacked by section. Red Leader, Flight Lieutenant John 'Jackie' Sing, commanding 'A'

Flight, damaged a 110 but was then hit and forced to bale out – as the CO, Squadron Leader Duncan MacDonald, recalled:

> On 11 September 1940, one of my flight commanders, Flight Lieutenant Jackie Sing, was shot down over the sea and rescued by an American oil tanker. You can imagine his feelings when informed by the Captain that the cargo consisted of 100 octane aviation fuel for Fighter Command! The tanker made landfall at Shoreham, Sussex, and I motored down from Tangmere in the early evening to recover this valuable member of my Squadron who was a bit shaken but fortunately uninjured. He was in the air again next day and none the worse for this most frightening experience.

Red 3, Sergeant Reginald Llewellyn, hit an Me 110 which 'immediately dived vertically into the sea', then attacked the rearmost Me 110 of a formation inland of Portsmouth, leaving this enemy machine 'burning furiously'. Yellow 1, Flying Officer Raymond Kellow, also claimed to have hit a 110, which he watched 'dive into the sea', as did the Polish Pilot Officer Marian Duryasz and Sergeant Mike Croskell; Flight Lieutenant James Strickland, Pilot Officer Hubert Cottam and Sergeant Raymond Dunscombe all claimed Me 110s damaged. Considering that only one Me 110, of II/ZG 76, actually crashed into the sea, these claims were somewhat exaggerated. In addition to Sing being shot down, 213 also had a pilot missing: Sergeant Antoni Wojcicki, who vanished without trace.

In this action, 602 Squadron fielded all eight of its now serviceable Spitfires, engaging the enemy with 213 Squadron, reportedly at 16.10 hrs, Me 110s, again rather optimistically, being subsequently destroyed by Sergeants Cyril Babbage, Andrew McDowell and Jack Proctor, the later also claiming one damaged; Flight Lieutenant Finlay Boyd tackled the Me 109s, claiming one destroyed and another damaged. Two Spitfires, were shot-up and damaged, both Pilot Officer Nigel Rose, who was slightly wounded, and Sergeant Babbage, who was unhurt, returning to base safely. Sergeant Mervyn Sprague was shot down over the sea and killed, his body washing ashore at Brighton a month later.

Although both RAF squadrons attacked before the Germans reached their target, bombs fell on Eastleigh at 16.13 hrs – not, though, as intended, on the Spitfire Final Assembly and Flight Hangars, but on the Cunliffe-Owen Aircraft factory – just 400 yards away – where Lockheed Hudsons from America were assembled and parts made for the new Stirling bomber. Spitfire production was, therefore, unaffected by this raid, but forty-nine civilians were killed, thirty-eight badly injured, and fifty-four more slightly so.

At RAF Exeter, some-time after Wing Commander Dewar had taken-off, Reverend Dagger met 213 Squadron's Adjutant:

> passing through the Mess … 'I hope the CO is alright' he said. He told me that the Station Commander was flying to Tangmere and then possibly to London 'to see what it looks like after the Blitz, but hundreds of Jerries are passing over Tangmere' I knew only too well what he meant – and when some hours later the CO was reported missing, I was scarcely surprised. In my imagination then and since, I pictured hundreds of German bombers like evil vultures crossing the coast in the bright sunlight, screened over beneath and on the flanks by many fighters. Then faraway a tiny spec – a solitary Hurricane on its way to London.

On 12 September 1940, the 87 Squadron ORB recorded the following:

> Wing Commander Dewar set out from Exeter for a visit to Tangmere and was not heard of again. He had been informed of enemy activity on the route over which he was to pass, and no doubt must have run into more trouble than he could cope with by himself. A very sad loss to 87 Squadron.

On 12 September, the following telegram was sent to Wing Commander Dewar's wife, Kay:

> Regret to inform you that your husband, Acting Wing Commander John Scatliff Dewar DSO DFC, is reported missing as the result of air operations on September 12th 1940. Letter follows. Any further information received will be immediately communicated to you. Should news of him reach you from any other source, please inform this department. His father has been informed.

Mr Dewar, however, was puzzled, and wrote to the Air Ministry on 21 September:

> With reference to your telephone P702 of Sept. 13th stating that my son, Acting Wing Commander John Dewar DSO DFC is reported missing as the result of air operations on 12 September 1940, I beg to state that according to official reports none of our fighter aircraft was brought down by enemy action that day. This being so, I shall take it as a favour if you will kindly let us know the circumstances in which he and his aircraft came to be missing.
>
> I have not written earlier because in your wire to my daughter-in-law … you stated you would be writing to her, but when I last heard from her she had received no letter from you.

Mr Dewar was quite correct: on 12 September 1940, enemy air activity was much reduced, and not one RAF fighter was lost in combat.

So, what had happened to Wing Commander Dewar, and when?

On 27 September 1940, the Air Ministry responded to Mr Dewar, confirming that in fact: 'He took off from Exeter Aerodrome at 3 pm on the 11th September 1940, and proceeded to Tangmere, since when nothing has been heard of him.'

A more detailed explanation is preserved at The National Archives in Wing Commander Dewar's Casualty File. In this report, by Squadron Leader R.S. Mills at RAF Exeter, dated 23 October 1940:

> A/W/C J.S. Dewar on 11 September 1940, gave orders that he would be flying to Tangmere and the normal procedure for advising Operations at this station was carried out.
>
> This officer took off at 15.00 hrs in Hurricane V7306 and before doing so was advised of enemy activity over Selsey Bill. The route, however, to be flown was from Exeter, via Winchester, then to Tangmere, thus avoiding the balloon barrage over Southampton.
>
> The flight expected to take some forty minutes in duration and ETA being about 16.00 hrs.
>
> At 16.00 hrs, intense enemy air activity developed over the Southampton area and it is presumed that A/W/C Dewar decided to

engage the enemy, although there is no definite evidence to support this supposition. A pilot of a rear protective section later reported that he noticed a lone Hurricane had followed his Squadron just before enemy aircraft were engaged.

S/Ldr R.S. Mills, acting Station Commander of RAF Exeter, examined the Raid Tracings of Sector Station Tangmere, and formed the opinion that in view of anti-aircraft gunfire over Southampton and intense aircraft activity North of Southampton, that A/W/C Dewar followed one of the operating squadrons and definitely sought engagements as he would have been in the operational area at about that time.

Ignoring battle was not in Johnny Dewar's nature, so Squadron Leader Mills' assessment was doubtless correct, albeit based upon circumstantial evidence. The confusion over the date of his death, however, may have arisen because Johnny's was really an unofficial flight, to visit his wife at Thorney Island. RAF Exeter, therefore, waited as long as possible in the hope that he would turn up safe from some remote place, before coming clean on 12 September 1940 that their Station Commander was missing.

Frustratingly, the details of German combat reports available are incomplete, in many cases simply relating the unit, pilot, type of enemy aircraft claimed, time and location. Frequently, however, certain of these essential details are missing from the record, owing to the vast number of documents destroyed during the death-throws of Nazi Germany in 1945.

What we do know regarding the action with which we are now concerned, is that the following claims exist (continental time):

Leutnant Kurt Votel	3/JG 2	Hurricane	16.46 hrs
Oberfelwebel Hans Tilly	3/JG 2	Spitfire	16.50 hrs
Oberleutnant Hans Hahn	4/JG 2	Hurricane	16.15 hrs
Unteroffizier Kurt Bühligen	6/JG 2	Hurricane	16.35 hrs
Leutnant Heinz Bolze	4/JG 2	Spitfire	17.00 hrs
Oberfeldwebel Siegfried Schnell	4/JG 2	Spitfire	17.05 hrs
Oberfeldwebel Siegfried Schnell	4/JG 2	Spitfire	17.12 hrs
Oberfeldwebel Franz Willinger	8/JG 2	Hurricane	17.27 hrs
Oberleutnant Wilhelm Herget	6/ZG 76	Hurricane	17.00 hrs

The only known location is for Herget's claim, which is recorded as five to ten kilometres east of the Isle of Wight, and at 5,000 metres. Without doubt, Wing Commander Dewar was en route from Exeter to Tangmere, when he joined in this air battle near Selsey Bill. The likelihood is that one of the Jagdfliegern listed shot down Hurricane V7306, which crashed into the sea.

According to Wing Commander Ian 'Widge' Gleed, who had succeeded Dewar in command of 87 Squadron:

> Then one afternoon we lost our Station Commander, Johnny. He borrowed one of our machines to fly to Tangmere for a conference. He was in excellent spirits when he took-off. Just after he had left, Ops told us that there was a *blitz* in that sector. They warned Johnny on the R/T. He gave the usual answer, 'Message received and understood.' Then nothing more.

Nothing further was heard of Wing Commander Dewar, in fact, until 30 September 1940, when, according to Squadron Leader Mills,

> a body clothed in a shirt was washed up on the beach at Kingston Gorse, Sussex, and subsequently identified as A/W/Cdr J.S. Dewar by means of laundry marks. A tunic was also found near the body, marked JSD and had the ribbons of DSO and DFC … It was established that this officer was killed by machine-gun fire, there being bullet wounds in the back and head.

This was final, irrefutable, confirmation that Johnny Dewar had lost his life in action on 11 September 1940. As Gleed also wrote, 'We lost a grand Station Commander, and our friend.'

On 2 October 1940, Kay Dewar received a further telegram from the Air Ministry confirming that her husband was no longer missing but confirmed to have lost his life on '12 September 1940'.

According to the artist Sir William Rothenstein, who knew Dewar personally, his friend's body was 'riddled with shot'. Whether Johnny Dewar baled out, badly wounded, discarded his parachute but was not rescued, or, either badly wounded or already dead, had been thrown clear of his Hurricane upon impact, will never be known. At the time, a rumour circulated that

Johnny had been machine-gunned while descending by parachute, but there is no evidence to support such an allegation; it is also contrary to a file note of 8 October 1940, stating that the pilot had 'failed to bale out'.

Pilot Officer (later Group Captain) Denis David was a pilot on 87 Squadron, and wrote of Dewar: 'A man of his calibre, leadership and character cannot be replaced – and all who knew him felt this.'

Another distinguished 87 Squadron pilot, Wing Commander Roland Beamont remembered that Johnny was:

> a super chap, a marvellous commander and leader who inspired us all with his calm, totally unflappable, manner – he seemed to take the view that it was all rather a joke and certainly not good form for any of us to be in any way concerned about it!

Wing Commander John Scatliff Dewar DSO DFC was 33 years old and the highest-ranking officer to lose his life in the Battle of Britain. Today, his grave can be found in the quiet churchyard at St John the Baptist – where sadly Johnny had joined his brother-in-law, Pilot Officer Richard Bowyer, who had lost his life in a training accident at Hullavington on 18 September 1939. Kay, therefore, had lost both her brother and husband in less than a year (evidence provided to the CWGC by this author led to the date of death being accepted as 11 September 1940, and the headstone corrected accordingly).

Down at Tangmere, Pilot Officer Alexander Osmand was not flying on this day, on which he took the opportunity to write again to his wife, Marjorie:

> Wow!!! We have just been machine-gunned by a German plane! The weather is pretty foul at the moment, and it came over the drome very low. Golly, you should have seen us all dive under the beds! There was no time to get into the shelters; we just scrambled for what protection we could find. It's gone now, but we are wondering if it's going to return and present us with bombs. Needless to say, we are on alert, and hoping we don't suddenly have to dive under the beds again.

It would be the young Hurricane pilot's last day at Tangmere; he had done enough, and on this day was rested and posted to 3 Squadron at the somewhat quieter sector of Castletown in Scotland.

The daylight fighting on 11 September 1940 had seen the Germans fail to inflict heavy damage on London, as was their intention, and miss the Spitfire works; twenty-three Luftwaffe aircraft were lost and seventeen more damaged on these operations. Air Vice-Marshal Park had met the enemy in strength, reinforced by 10 and 12 Groups, but, even so, twenty-four Hurricanes and Spitfires had been lost and three more damaged: eight of their pilots were dead, four missing, and six wounded; it had been another hard-fought day.

Squadron Leader 'Sailor' Malan DFC, CO of 74 Squadron, graphically described the period:

> How did we feel? Of course we had our tails up. At that time the Luftwaffe seemed to be running on an endless belt – the fellow you knocked down yesterday seemed to be back next day, asking for another wallop. We were not without fear. The fellow who wasn't didn't live long. And taking a Spitfire into the sky in September 1940 often corresponded to entering a dark room with a madman weaving a knife behind your back. We could see behind us and the Hun was everywhere, ready to spit his guns.

Across the Channel, at Caffiers near Calais, III/JG 26 had cause to celebrate: their *Kommandeur*, *Hauptmann* Gerhard Schöpfel, had been awarded the Ritterkreuz, the coveted Knight's Cross, having achieved the necessary total of twenty aerial victories. This was only the second award of this decoration throughout the whole of JG 26 and richly deserved.

On 18 August 1940, Schöpfel had performed an unprecedented feat of arms in destroying four Hurricanes over Canterbury in half as many minutes, and only two days before his award had shot down three Spitfires in a single action. Without a doubt, Schöpfel was among the most experienced and dangerous *experten* on the *Kanalfront*, as many more Allied fighter pilots would discover to their cost.

Daily Home Intelligence Report:

> Reports now received make it possible to assess critically the effects of continued bombing in the East End. Morale is rather more strained than the newspapers suggest, whereas the damage to property seems to be less than is reported by them. The pictures of devastation and accounts of destruction weaken the resolve of people to stay put.

Thursday, 12 September 1940

Poor weather saw a day of vastly reduced aerial activity, although enemy reconnaissance bombers remained active over England, and lone nuisance raiders used cloud cover to reach such targets as Air Ministry buildings in Harrogate, the aluminium-producing factory in Banbury, and the railway at Reading.

At 11.10 hrs, 213 Squadron's Sergeant Ernest Snowden was up from Tangmere and claimed a Ju 88 damaged ten miles north-east of base, and at 19.00 hrs 238 Squadron's Pilot Officers Carl Davis and Vernon Simmonds, on patrol from Middle Wallop, damaged another over Boscombe Down. Westhampnett's 602 Squadron also intercepted one of the raiders, Flying Officer Christopher Mount, and Pilot Officers Archibald Lyall and Osgood 'Pedro' Hanbury sharing a 'Do 17' off Beachy Head at 16.30 hrs – although more likely this was the Ju 88 of 1(F)/121 which failed to return from operations over England and believed to have crashed into the Channel, although equally this could have been the 'Do 215' claimed destroyed off Hastings and shared by 605 Squadron's Croydon-based Pilot Officers Christopher 'Bunny' Currant and Thomas Cooper-Slipper, and Sergeant Eric Wright.

Similarly, the bad weather reduced both Coastal and Bomber Command operations. Nonetheless, the former escorted seventeen convoys, and 59 Squadron hit a tanker off Cap de la Hague, and a 206 Squadron Hudson engaged shipping off the Maas Light. PRU aircraft were active despite the cloud cover, returning with information on enemy shipping activity between Dunkirk and Cherbourg. There were no offensive daylight operations by 2 Group's Blenheims, and the weather also led to the scrubbing of night operations, although the Wellington force successfully bombed rail facilities at Flushing and Emden.

Across the Channel, the divide between the OKM and OKL was widening once more over Operation *Seelöwe*, the former complaining to the OKW that the air war was now 'being conducted as an absolute air war without regard to the present requirements of naval war and outside the framework of *Seelöwe*.' Indeed, the *Kriegsmarine* further charged that 'In its present form the air war cannot assist preparations for *Seelöwe*.' One great naval concern was that with London and other inland targets now being the Luftwaffe's apparently exclusive focus, the Royal Navy was no longer under duress and able to operate 'unmolested' in the Channel – a scenario far removed from the Kanalkampf, which had seen Dover closed down as a naval base.

Such was the 'interference caused by the enemy air force, long-range artillery and light naval forces' that this activity had, the HQ Naval Group West charged, for the first time 'assumed capital importance'. In truth, such was the effect that Coastal and Bomber Command were having on the 'Battle of the Barges' that the ports of Ostend, Dunkirk, Calais and Boulogne were no longer safe nocturnal anchorages – because that was when these attacks were largely made. Howsoever frustrated the OKM was, though, this doubtless paled into comparative insignificance considering the Luftwaffe's angst at still not forcing the required decision. And time really was running out now.

Friday, 13 September 1940

Further poor flying weather saw another day with little activity. At 11.10 hrs, King George VI was at Buckingham Palace, in a small sitting room overlooking the Quadrangle:

> All of a sudden we heard the zooming noise of a diving aircraft getting louder and louder, and then saw two bombs falling past the opposite side of Buckingham Palace into the Quadrangle. We saw the flashes and heard the detonations as they burst about eighty yards away. The blast blew in the windows opposite to us, and two great craters had appeared in the Quadrangle. From one of these craters water from a burst main was pouring out and flowing into the passage through the broken windows. The whole thing happened in a matter of seconds and we were very quickly out into the passage.

In addition to the Quadrangle, the forecourt and Chapel were also slightly damaged, and three Palace staff and an ARP warden were injured. To their great credit, the King and Queen were recently returned to London from their safer residence at Windsor Castle, twenty miles to the west, and on the afternoon 'Buck House' was hit, their Majesties visited the devastated East End. As Her Majesty said, 'I'm glad we have been bombed. Now I feel we can look the East End in the face.'

Indeed, ARP Regional Commissioner Euan Wallace wrote that 'The fact that they had had such a narrow escape in the morning made their reception even more enthusiastic.' The American journalist Ed Murrow was less convinced, however, remarking that 'Minds have been hardened and calloused. It didn't require a bombing of Buckingham Palace to convince these people that they are all in this together.'

Daily Home Intelligence Report:

> Public opinion on the bombing of Buckingham Palace is divided: most people feel a fresh bond with their leaders, others think that 'the King and Queen ought not to be exposed to such danger.

Whatever an individual's opinion on the matter, there was now no doubting that this was a shared peril from which their Majesties would not shy away from or abandon London.

Over Maidstone, at 12.40 hrs, Sergeant James 'Ginger' Lacey of 501 Squadron, destined to become one of Fighter Command's top scoring fighter pilots in the Battle of Britain, claimed a He 111 destroyed but was shot down himself by return fire. Taking to his parachute, the Hurricane pilot suffered slight burns, but fortunately survived the experience. No He 111 crashed in England, although one returned badly damaged and crashed at Etretat, near Le Havre, killing the crew, and another crash-landed at Montdidier with two dead crewmen aboard and two wounded.

At 12.50 hrs, ten minutes after Lacey took to his parachute, 607 Squadron's Flight Lieutenant Francis Blackadder damaged a Ju 88 off Beachy Head, and at 14.40 hrs 605 Squadron's Sergeant Eric Wright 'damaged a Ju 88 in a chase from Tunbridge Wells to Hastings [ORB]'. The final daylight claim was made by 253 Squadron's Pilot Officer Tadeuz Nowak, who damaged a He 111 between Henfield and Croydon.

Pilot Officer Richard Jones, 19 Squadron:

> When we returned from a sortie, anyone who had been successful in shooting down an enemy aircraft might do a victory roll over the airfield, but these were not encouraged because you didn't know whether your aircraft had some unseen damage to the flying controls. Immediately we landed the Intelligence Officer took full details from

each pilot regarding what had happened, while the groundcrew, who were absolutely marvellous, did a fantastic job of rapidly preparing the aircraft for another immediate take-off.

Sergeant Tony Pickering, 501 Squadron:

One day I came across a lone Ju 88 somewhere over Kent, heading back to sea. I thought that it would be no problem to catch up the Hun, press the gun button and that would be it. Suddenly he just pulled away from me, just left me standing, had at least an extra 50 mph on me, and that was the last I saw of him. The Hurricane just wasn't fast enough. We even used to bend the throttle levers in flight, trying to squeeze a bit more boost out of the Merlin. A Spitfire would have caught that Ju 88. In the Hurricane's favour was that it could take a terrific amount of punishment but still keep flying, whereas the Spitfire couldn't take quite as much.

I was eighteen during the Battle of Britain. I came from a small village where everyone knew everyone else, we went to school, did our homework in the evenings and went to church on Sundays. We were innocents, really, the RAF was a bit of a shock, all these chaps who were going around nightclubs and girls, it was something to touch a girl's arm at a dance in those days, not like it is now!

During the afternoon, 53 and 59 Squadrons of Coastal Command attacked a German convoy off Boulogne, and another, hauling barges, off Cap Gris-Nez. Again, PRU aircraft returned with details of barge concentrations and that night, doubtless to the OKM's displeasure, Bomber Command attacked barges all along the enemy-held coast between Antwerp and Calais. All these raids were successful with eighty barges claimed sunk at Ostend by the Hampden force. A Blenheim of 15 Squadron, engaged on these operations, failed to return, its crew reported missing, and one of 15 Squadron similarly disappeared, while a Hampden of 61 Squadron also crashed into the sea, members of the crew being either killed or still missing.

The bad weather also reduced German night operations, the focus of which remained London and the south-east. *Hauptmann* Hermann Kell was a He 111 pilot decorated with the Iron Cross 2nd Class during the Polish campaign, and who had participated in the major attack against London on 7 September 1940; Kell would have occasion to especially recall the night of 13/14 September 1940:

> On Friday 13 September 1940, all night missions were cancelled. An unusually bad weather front covered northern France, the Netherlands and Germany. There was thunder and lightning in every direction.
>
> At about 21.00 hrs, I received an order for a crew of volunteers to fly a nuisance raid against Victoria Station in London. This came from a high level of authority, which was apparently unaware that there are limits to such bad weather! I was the *Staffelkapitän*, the Squadron Leader, of 3/KG4, so I did not ask anyone else to volunteer and flew the mission myself. However, I excluded a trainee pilot from our crew, although he felt somewhat aggrieved.
>
> I was concerned about where I could land upon return, due to the weather, but the Meteorologist was unable to provide the answer. At about 23.00 hrs I switched on the plane's lights while I started up, and saw a car approaching from the left. It was the *Geschwaderkommodore* himself, *Oberstleutnant* Rath, who had come out in the heavy rain to salute our crew. I had never seen this before.
>
> I had hardly lifted the He 111 from the runway when I was in turbulent clouds. I had difficulty holding the plane on its course. Strong up and down winds played with our plane at their leisure. Frequently, I was unsure whether the plane was flying straight and level, the instrument needles going haywire.
>
> When a bolt of lightning illuminated the cockpit, I saw my good old navigator staring at me, the question of whether I could actually maintain control of the aircraft written all over his face. Sometimes I was unsure myself! When bolts of lightning hit the plane I often had no answer regarding what to do. Although I had previously flown many times at night and in bad weather, this flight taught me that in addition to ability and experience, sometimes you also need a little luck.
>
> We finally emerged from the clouds at 600 metres, to find a cloudless, moonlit night above the Thames Estuary, exactly where we were supposed to be. It was so peaceful and quiet that it was hard to believe that we were engaged on a war flight. The relaxation was rapidly

terminated when we were coned by searchlights. I took evasive action, which shook them off momentarily, but after a while I had to accept that it was futile – I did not know then that London's searchlights were guided by radar and not acoustics.

Orientation above blacked-out London was easy due to the recent heavy rain – the wet railway tracks reflected the bright moonlight. Where the glittering tracks joined many others but then suddenly disappeared was obviously Victoria Station. My navigator had actually guided me to this location with his homing device.

Suddenly an endless stream of bullets smashed into our aircraft. It was a Blenheim which attacked from fifty closing to twenty-metres, using all his ammunition in one continuous burst. I later learned that the pilot was a New Zealander, Pilot Officer Michael Herrick of 25 Squadron, who had already destroyed two Heinkels and after shooting us down received the DFC (sadly, he was later killed in action over Denmark, so I never got to meet this excellent and courageous young pilot after the war).

Considering the weather, it was a remarkable interception by Herrick. Kell continues:

After Herrick's attack the oil pressure of both engines rapidly dropped to zero. I knew that we had no chance. I immediately shut down both motors to avoid both fire or an explosion, but my actions were in vain. Flames spurted out of both engines and engulfed the plane. I called to the flight engineer and radio operator in the rear of the plane, telling them to bale out. There was no answer. I sent the navigator back to check them on them. He came back with news that both Kameraden were dead.

By now I had changed to a northerly course and we glided down at as shallow an angle as possible, hoping to clear the outskirts of London before hitting the ground. The flames blocked all view of the outside, and prevented use of all escape hatches, except the small one above my seat. I was unsure whether the hatch was big enough to get through with my parachute on, but I had no option.

> My navigator stood silently beside me, calmly awaiting my decision. At 2,000 metres I guessed that we should be over open countryside. As the hatch was above my seat I had to jump first to allow my navigator to climb up on my empty seat and out of the hatch. I trimmed the plane for the last time into a steady glide. My navigator and I shook hands and wished each other good luck.
>
> I dived onto the left wing to avoid being hit by the tailplane, and fell into space. As I pulled the ripcord, I saw our burning plane continue its downward glide until exploding on impact with our dead comrades aboard. Beneath me I saw a parachute, but although I called out several times to my navigator I received no response.
>
> Suddenly a Blenheim emerged from the night and circled me, uncomfortably close, stood up on a wing tip. Obviously, there was a master at the controls. I pulled some strings of my parachute to drop faster. I hit the ground hard and found myself lying in a field. With the parachute beneath my arm, I hastened to get away from where I had landed. I climbed over several walls, but then the pain from my broken leg caused me to hide beneath some bushes on the banks of a stream. It gave me chance to rest and think. At first light I saw to AA guns about 300 yards away, so decided to surrender.

Already in custody was Kell's navigator, *Feldwebel* Werner Hobe; *Unteroffiziers* Müller-Wernscheid and Töpfer were both killed when their aircraft crashed at Downs Hall, Newman's End, near Sheering, at 01.55 hrs GMT.

Saturday, 14 September 1940

By now, the British autumn was a fortnight old – and with the increasingly unpredictable weather likely to disrupt both air operations and a seaborne crossing, the Battle of Britain, certainly from a German perspective, was now at the tipping point: a decision had to be forced, or Operation *Seelöwe* abandoned. For the sake of prestige, Hitler could not risk a failed invasion attempt – and hence his continued indecision. Nonetheless, that time was now rapidly running out was inescapable.

On 10 September 1940, *Generalfeldmarschall* Water von Brauchitsch, chief of the German army, had reported to Hitler that his troops were keen to set sail, and *Grossadmiral* Erich Raeder's *Kriegsmarine*, while not over-enthusiastic at the prospect, was ready to go. On 13 September 1940, *Reichsmarschall* Göring had met with Hitler at the Reich Chancellery, the Luftwaffe chief astonishingly believed that Fighter Command was by now reduced to a mere handful of fighters, and persisted that all he required to finish the job was four of five days of unbroken weather – and the weather, Göring claimed, was what had delayed the decision. Still, then, the future of the whole *Seelöwe* enterprise lay with the Luftwaffe. After this meeting, the *Reichsmarschall* returned to the Pas-de-Calais to continue personally commanding the great aerial assault.

If Brauchitsch and Raeder had been reasonably optimistic on 10 September 1940, just four days later, on 14 September, the mood of high commanders had apparently changed: the OKH Chief of Staff, General Franz Halder, noted in the War Diary that the *Heer* and *Kriegsmarine* chiefs now no longer believed a successful landing in England could be achieved. Indeed, at 15.00 hrs on this day, Hitler met with Raeder, Brauchitsch and the Luftwaffe Chief of Staff, General Hans Jeschonnek, Raeder stating that 'the present air situation' prevented *Seelöwe* proceeding – contrary to Göring's ever-optimistic claims regarding the Luftwaffe's erosion of the RAF.

Raeder then added to Hitler's dilemma, however, by concluding that the prospect of an invasion must not be abandoned. Hitler knew full-well that occupying Britain – which had failed to attract Russian support – and with America still neutral, was the surest means of effecting a swift victory; the *Kriegsmarine*, the *Führer* also knew, had done everything possible to prepare for the invasion, and heavy artillery, ready to support a sea crossing, was in place along the Calais coast. According to Halder, Hitler considered that 'the operations of the Luftwaffe are beyond all praise', and reiterated Göring's belief that only a run of good weather was needed to achieve victory in the air.

Hitler did acknowledge that 'the enemy fighters have not been completely eliminated; our own reports of success do not give a completely reliable picture, although the enemy has been severely damaged'. Luftwaffe attacks to date, Hitler concluded,

> have had an enormous effect, though perhaps chiefly upon nerves. Part of that psychological effect is the fear of invasion, and the idea of its imminence must not cease. Even if air successes are only achieved in ten or twelve days-time, the English may yet be seized with mass hysteria.

Jeschonnek tendered the view that 'Material successes exceed our expectations', explaining that 'there has been no mass panic up to now because residential districts have not been attacked and destroyed'. Hitler refused Jeschonnek's request to deliberately target civilian populations, which was supported by Raeder, the *Führer* considering that 'attacks on military objectives are always the most important, because they destroy irreplaceable war potential'. Moreover, doubtless with concerns in mind regarding reprisal raids by Bomber Command on German civilians, Hitler made clear that bombing with the aim of achieving 'mass panic must be left to the last'. In truth, what Hitler was desperate for the air assault to finish Britain off, meaning that the invasion would be simply to take control of and occupy an already defeated country.

Helpfully, Raeder suggested that if it proved impossible to launch the invasion on 27 September 1940, which appeared the most favourable date owing to moon and tides, the next such date was 8 October 1940 – meaning that Hitler's decision could be delayed further still.

The *Führer*, however, was robust: come what may, his decision would be made on 17 September 1940. The conclusion of these deliberations on 14 September 1940, then, was Hitler refusing to abandon *Seelöwe* – yet – and ordering the Luftwaffe to continue attacking London, although, as a nod to Jeschonnek, the targets involved were to include railway and power stations, and objectives outside Central London.

The period 14–17 September 1940 inclusive, therefore, was critical – if *Seelöwe* was to become reality.

On 14 September 1940, the weather was better than the previous two days, although cloud persisted between 5,000 and 10,000ft. Such conditions were not ideal for mass bombing, but across the Channel, the pressure was on. An interesting feature of the enemy's tactics would be the reintroduction of *Freie Hunt* fighter sweeps, the Me 109s being allowed to roam freely, instead of being closely shackled to the bombers. Inevitably, however, the Luftwaffe's first sorties over England were by reconnaissance aircraft and nuisance raiders.

Up at Coltishall in 12 Group, at 09.26 hrs 74 Squadron's Blue Section was scrambled to orbit base at 10,000ft. Flight Lieutenant John Mungo-Park was Blue Leader, and on this occasion his Nos.2 and 3 were two former 142 Squadron Battle pilots who had volunteered to serve with Fighter Command, namely Flying Officer Alan Ricalton and Pilot Officer Roger Boulding. The section was soon ordered to 22,000ft and sent in pursuit of a bandit – an Me 110 being sighted ten minutes later at 23,000ft, ten miles north of Happisburgh (although more likely this was a Do 171/KGr 606).

Mungo-Park opened fire, black smoke immediately pouring from one of the 110's engines, the aircraft going into a dive. Ricalton then fired from 400 yards and broke away, enabling his section leader to attack again, leaving the 'E/A's starboard engine well on fire, as E/A dived steeply into cloud'. The damaged German then escaped back to France, the Spitfires returning to base at 10.15 hrs.

At 10.55 hrs, Blue Section of 72 Squadron, comprising Flying Officer John 'Pancho' Villa, Blue 1, and his No.2, Sergeant John White, were scrambled from Biggin Hill to patrol base. While climbing, the Spitfire pilots sighted a He 111 at 14,000ft, flying South. Villa 'climbed at full throttle', telling Blue 2 to 'keep up as much as possible'.

Over Hailsham the Spitfires finally caught the raider, both pilots attacking an expending their ammunition before leaving the bomber streaming white smoke and descending rapidly some ten to fifteen miles off Eastbourne. Back at base, Villa received conformation 'from Ops' that the raider had crashed in flames. This aircraft belonged to *Stab* KG 55 and had been engaged on a reconnaissance of, or nuisance raid on, London; the crew were all wounded but rescued by the ever-watchful *Seenotdienst*.

At 13.00 hrs Flight Lieutenant Francis Blackadder of 607 Squadron scrambled with Red Section, Flying Officers William Gore and Maurice Irving, from Tangmere to patrol Selsey Bill. At 16,000ft the Hurricane pilots sighted a 'Ju 88 [*sic*]' flying South at 9,000ft. Blackadder ordered the Section into line astern, each pilot attacking before the enemy escaped in cloud. As the plot disappeared from the radar screen thereafter, 11 Group Operations Room confirmed the aircraft as destroyed.

Similarly, at 13.15 hrs, Yellow Section of 253 Squadron, Pilot Officers Leonard Murch and the Polish Tadeusz Nowak, scrambled from Kenley with orders to intercept lone raiders. Off Hastings, a 'Ju 88' was seen approaching from the south, which Murch duly attacked. By the time the raider also disappeared in cloud, it was 'completely enveloped in smoke'.

Having landed at 13.45 hrs from the earlier patrol, Flight Lieutenant Blackadder scrambled from Tangmere again at 14.20 hrs, leading 607 Squadron's Yellow and Red Sections. At 15.20 hrs, when ten to fifteen miles south-west of Selsey Bill, the Hurricane pilots sighted a 'Ju 88' flying South between Selsey Bill and the Isle of White, which was being engaged by AA fire. Both sections attacked, this raider also disappearing into cloud, its port engine streaming black and white smoke.

In reality, however, more likely the aircraft attacked by both 607 and 253 Squadrons were not Ju 88s as reported but He 111s or Do 17s, aircraft of which types were lost or damaged on operations – among them the 4/KG 55 crew of *Leutnant* Hansen's He 111, who had welcomed a change from bombing London that day when tasked with attacking Brighton; the German pilot later recalled:

> The closer we got to the English coast, the sparser the cloud became. We orientated ourselves in a hole in the cloud and realised that Brighton was a few kilometres in front of us, to our left. The oil storage tanks were clearly visible and when three kilometres from the target I ordered preparations to drop our bombs – which hit the target, as indicated by rising black smoke visible as we turned for home.
>
> I was surprised that we had achieved this unmolested by RAF fighters, but then I saw three British fighters climbing to our right, in front of me, over the Channel. I immediately warned the crew and turned left, to reduce our target profile. I then heard a large number of hits on our plane, in between the loud barking of our own machine-guns.
>
> I searched for a cloud to hide in but there were none, but then I saw a fighter approaching from the left, aiming straight at me. At the same moment I felt a blow to the left side of my face, like being slapped. My head was jerked to the side and I started bleeding, although my observer successfully stemmed the flow of blood. Finally I found a bank of clouds below me, so inverted the aircraft and headed for the clouds at 400 kmh.
>
> Our relief was short-lived, however, because no sooner than we entered the cloud we were out again and the fighters were still after us. The radio

> operator, flight engineer and gunner all returned fire at these savages. My radio operator, *Unteroffizier* Kauder deserves special praise as he fired the contents of an ammunition drum into the cockpit of a British fighter, having held his fire and nerve until the enemy came within 100m. My crew was able to watch closely as the Spitfire, leaving a thick trail of smoke behind it suddenly tipped over its left wing and disappeared into the sea. The other two fighters then continued attacking us until I found and disappeared into another blanket of cloud.
>
> My flying controls were damaged, one elevator being jammed and the trim control unresponsive, but we returned safely to France – where forty-five bullet holes were counted in the horizontal stabiliser in an area of just one square metre.

Hansen and crew had a lucky escape, although it is more likely that they had been attacked by Hurricanes, and no Spitfires or Hurricanes were lost in these engagements.

As the afternoon wore on, two more lone raiders were intercepted and destroyed: at 16.15 hrs, Flight Sergeant Frederick 'Taffy' Higginson DFM of 56 Squadron sent a Do 17 into the Channel a long way off Bournemouth – forty miles – and at 16.30 hrs 501 Squadron's Sergeant Paul Farnes damaged a 'Do 215 [*sic*]' off Hastings.

The main afternoon action, however, chiefly concerned German fighter sweeps over Kent and Essex, the first of which was met by the Spitfires of 222 and 603 Squadrons, which scrambled from Hornchurch at 13.20 hrs and 13.25 hrs respectively to operate together. According to the former's Intelligence Patrol Report, the two squadrons co-joined over Rochford, 222 Squadron leading, and,

> intercepted a large concentration of Me 109s over Canterbury district at about 21,000ft. The 109s were apparently spying out the land and looking out for any of our machines which may be separated from the Squadron. On sighting our Spitfires, the enemy formed into the usual circle and it was difficult to single out any particular machine to attack.
>
> However, Sergeant Hutchinson managed to get within 250 yards, at which range he opened fire, closing to 100 yards and two more bursts, while following him in his dive. The E/A was seen by Detling Controller

> to dive straight down, after only pulling out very slightly … Sergeant Marland also damaged a 109 and observed pieces flying off it.

Several of 603 Squadron's pilots peeled off from the Spitfires' defensive circle to attack stray Me 109s: Flying Officer Brian Carbury claimed one destroyed over the sea, Flying Officer Brian MacNamara one which 'crashed in field North of Maidstone', and Flying Officer John Boulter one 'crashed south-west of Maidstone'. The second of these was most likely the 1/JG 77 aircraft also attacked by 222's Sergeant Iain Hutchinson and which crashed at Long Barn Farm, Boxley Hill, near Detling, where the pilot, *Feldwebel* H. Ettler, set his machine alight before being captured.

While 603 Squadron suffered no loss, 222 Squadron fared not so well: Sergeant Hutchinson was shot up and landed his damaged Spitfire, unhurt, at Detling, and Sergeant Reg Johnson was shot down, baling out over Aveley (the pilot told this author) with shrapnel wounds to his legs. Sergeant Sidney Baxter was also shot down but was killed when crash-landing near Rochford.

From 15.00 hrs onwards, RDF indicated strong enemy forces assembling over Calais. The first enemy force crossed the South Kent coast at 15.30 hrs, and by 15.45 hrs four more came in between Dover and Ramsgate, while another two passed over Beachy Head. Just before 16.00 hrs, two of these formations had reached London, dropping bombs on Camberwell, Battersea Power Station and a gasometer there, and the railway between Victoria and Clapham Junction was also damaged.

At 15.30 hrs, 73 Squadron was scrambled from Castle Camps with orders to link up with Debden's 17 Squadron and patrol North Weald at Angels 15. According to 17 Squadron, however, it patrolled 'Gravesend – Biggin Hill from 1530–16.45 hrs' but 'No E/A were seen [ORB]'. No.73 Squadron, therefore, was alone over Tilbury when bounced by Me 109s of JG 77, four Hurricanes being hit.

Green Section, comprising Sergeants Robert Plenderleith, Herbert Webster and Geoffrey Garton, 'reported that their formation had been attacked and broken up by a section of Spitfires diving on them at 16,000ft near Tilbury [ORB]', and Flying Officer James Smith, a Canadian, 'reported having seen a Hurricane shot down by a Spitfire South of Tilbury [ORB]'. There are no corresponding claims by Spitfire pilots, however, but Hurricanes were claimed in this area and at this time by *Oberleutnants* Hubert Mütherich and Franz Hahn, and *Feldwebel* Franz Barten, all of 2/JG 77, and two by *Unteroffizier* Rudolf Meixner of 3/JG 77. A subsequent 73 Squadron ORB entry states:

> The Squadron Intelligence Officer sent in a report and Group has called for a further report on the matter. It is possible that the 'Spitfires' which attacked Green and Blue Sections were He 111s [*sic*] [means He 113s] and it is to be hoped that investigation will prove this possibility to be correct.

There is no doubt that it was not Spitfires which caused these losses, as 73 Squadron reported, but Me 109s.

In this clash over Tilbury, Pilot Officer Roy Marchand's Hurricane was hit and he returned to base with 'a bullet through his port main tank, another through the port aileron and main spar, and another clean through the top of the W/T mast [ORB]'. Flight Lieutenant Michael Beytagh forced-landed at West Malling with a damaged radiator, while Sergeant Alfred Marshall 'was shot down by an Me 109 [ORB]' and forced-landed at the Air Ministry Experimental Station, Dover. Sergeant Maurice Leng was also shot down, landing his very badly damaged Hurricane back at base; fortunately none of these pilots were injured.

As the Germans withdrew, the battle ebbed south – where 73 Squadron suffered more casualties, *Hauptmann* Dieter Hrabak and *Oberleutnent* Heinz Stegmann of *Stab* II/JG 54 claiming Hurricanes destroyed south-east of London. Over Tonbridge, 73's CO, Squadron Leader Maurice Robinson, was shot down and baled out, wounded; the surgeon at Kent and Sussex Hospital was unable to save his right eye.

Sergeant John Brimble, however, was also lost over Tonbridge and reported missing in action – which he would remain until 1980, when discovered still in the wreckage of his Hurricane at Chart House Farm, Park Sutton. In response, 73 Squadron made no combat claims, only six of the squadron's Hurricanes surviving the engagement.

Squadron Leader Gerry Edge had led seven 253 Squadron Hurricanes off from Kenley at 15.24 hrs to first patrol Tenterden before being vectored to Maidstone with orders to intercept enemy bombers at 15,000ft. Instead of bombers, however, 253 Squadron, which was flying sections in vic formation with a weaver at 18,000ft, encountered twelve Me 109s flying between 20,000 and 22,000ft. Five miles west of Faversham, Edge turned south-west, towards the sun, but while turning, at 16.30 hrs, the Hurricanes were jumped by yellow-nosed Me 109s over the Isle of Sheppey.

Within seconds, two Hurricanes were shot down by *Hauptmann* Rolf Pingel, *Kommandeur* of I/JG 26 (who received the coveted Knight's Cross on this day), and the Adjutant of I/JG 26, *Oberleutnant* Kurt Dähne. Sergeant William Higgins crashed in flames at Swanton Bridge, Bredgar, and was killed, and Sergeant John Anderson baled out with severe burns, observed by Sergeant Allan Dredge to land safely in a field near Faversham, his Hurricane crashing into the corner of a wood. When the 109s attacked, Dredge saw a 109 diving and as the enemy fighter broke left, slightly above the Hurricanes, he throttled back, did a semi-stall turn and opened fire. Sergeant Ernest Kee saw the 109 hit by Dredge explode in mid-air – this being *Oberleutnant* Dähne, whose success was short-lived as he was killed, the main wreckage of his fighter crashing to earth at Beacon Hill, Stone.

By 16.30 hrs the operation was over, but at 16.45 hrs, Flight Lieutenant Gordon MacGregor was leading 1RCAF 'Caribou' Squadron, up from Northolt, on patrol South of Biggin Hill, when the Canadian Hurricanes became separated in cloud; Pilot Officer Peter Lochnan, Green 3, came out of the cloud with Blue Section – finding a lone 'Do 215 [*sic*]', at 4,000ft. Blue Section attacked from astern, followed by Lochnan: 'Rear gun not firing, bits flew off.' The reconnaissance bomber escaped into cloud, however, and was accredited as 'damaged' to the squadron as a whole.

For 12 Group's 'Big Wing', there had been no action that afternoon, however.

At 15.50 hrs, Squadron Leader Douglas Bader led his Duxford Wing over London, the formation now including the Polish Hurricanes of 302 Squadron. During the evening, the wing went off on another uneventful patrol, but astonishingly – and in complete contravention of orders – instead of patrolling north of the Thames, Bader led the Duxford squadrons on a fighter sweep of Kent and, according to the 19 Squadron ORB, 'almost France'. Pilots putting themselves at unnecessary risk by flying over the sea had already been the subject of a rebuke from Air Vice-Marshal Park, and, furthermore, what would have happened if a raid had come in from the east while Bader was swanning around over the Channel?

Pilot Officer 'Teddy' Morten, Ops 'B', Duxford:

> On one of the many occasions Bader tackled me in the Mess regarding the 'Hun in the sun' etc, he said, 'Morty, you know that yesterday you told the wing to patrol North Weald at Angels 20?'
>
> 'Yes', I said.
>
> 'Well, d'ya know where we were upon reaching required height?'
>
> 'No', I said.
>
> 'Over Reading! We were looking down on the patrol area, up sun and all eyes skinned!'
>
> I thought that this was a bit too buccaneerish and bound to cause trouble eventually.

Another eye witness was Group Captain (then Wing Commander) Thomas Long, who had been one of three officers selected by Park to control the air component of the Dunkirk evacuation, after which he had served as an 11 Group Controller; writing in 1961, he recalled:

> On one occasion I had specifically asked 12 Group to have their Balbo patrol over London, from North Weald to Kenley … Knowing that we had no operational control over it, as 'LM' simply refused to allow us to give a single order to his favourite Balbo, I asked the Observer Corps to plot this Balbo on this occasion. The WAAF and RAF plotters were amazed to see what transpired. From Duxford … the plots took them right out to Lowestoft then turned South and entered the Thames Estuary East of Southend! By then, they were in the midst of a small ragged formation of German enemy aircraft beating it to France. I told the AOC, Keith Park, who took due note. What happened about it, I don't know.

Nonetheless, on this day Squadron Leader Bader was appointed to the DSO.

The enemy's next attack was a strong high-flying fighter sweep at 20,000ft and above, five separate formations which separated over south-east Kent, three advancing to Biggin Hill and Chatham, one to the west of Kenley, and another to London.

At 18.00 hrs, nine Spitfires of 72 Squadron – once more operating from Biggin Hill – scrambled to patrol Ashford, over which, at 18.35 hrs, seventy Me 109s were encountered. Pilot Officer Ernest Males:

> I was flying Blue 2 in the leading section at 20,000ft when I was attacked from the left by an Me 109 doing a quarter attack, developing into an astern. He overshot badly and appeared on my starboard side, diving steeply. I followed him down at about 400–500 mph, and opened fire at 3,000–4,000ft above sea-level. He reduced height to 100ft and turned back over the land. Smoke came back from underneath the engine, and I saw tracer hit the cockpit, and the aircraft burst into flames from the cockpit backwards. The E/A did a steep left-hand turn and dived into the ground from about 50ft at about 200 mph. The position of the crash was five miles south-west of Lympne airport. The E/A hit a hedge and the wings broke away. No sign of the pilot could be seen.

Strangely, no wreck on the ground, of either side, appears corresponds to this location.

Sergeant William Rolls, Blue 3, attacked a 109 which was firing at a Spitfire, watching his bullets 'sweep down the side of the Me 109', which went into a spin, streaming glycol. Another Spitfire then attacked the stricken 109, which Rolls saw crash 'in flames near Bethersden after the other pilot had put a burst into it'. The other pilot was Pilot Officer John Lloyd, who watched the pilot – *Unteroffizier* Viktor Blazejewski of 6/LG 2, bale out; the 109 crashed at Great Chart, the enemy pilot captured unhurt.

This Me 109 may also have been one of two claimed destroyed at an unspecified time by 41 Squadron's Pilot Officer Eric 'Sawn-off' Lock, who was flying alone, between Dungeness and Ramsgate:

> I was out on patrol to the South coast to give information. I was flying at 31,000–33,000ft when I saw a formation of twelve Me 109s travelling East of the coast, between Dover and Deal. I attacked the last section of the formation; they were flying a diamond formation. I was just about to close in when I was attacked from above by some Me 109s. They peeled off from about 3,000ft above me and carried out a head-on attack on me.
>
> I waited until he was in range and gave him a long burst. He passed a few feet above me. I carried out a sharp turn to the right and saw him in flames. Just then I was attacked again from head-on. I waited until he was at point-blank range. I saw my bullets go into the enemy

aircraft, and as he went past underneath me, I gave him a very long burst. I saw some more E/A coming down on me, so I half-rolled and dived through the clouds. I had just passed through the clouds when I saw someone who had baled out.

I followed him to the ground. I am pretty certain it was an Me 109 pilot, as I saw him wearing a tin hat. I saw the troops rush up to him and he appeared to be holding up his arms. I flew low over the field and he waved back. This was afterwards confirmed by the police.

At 18.15 hrs, 222 Squadron left Rochford, and 603 Squadron took-off from Hornchurch to patrol Gravesend together at 20,000ft. No.603 Squadron took no part in the subsequent engagement, but 222 Squadron reported encountering 'large forces of Me 109s, principally in the Dungeness area'.

Upon sighting the Spitfires, the 109s went into a circle, German pilots occasionally diving to try and lure a Spitfire to attack, so it could be set upon by other 109s. Sensibly, the Spitfire pilots remained together, although Flying Officer Des McMullen, 'finding himself over Calais, dived in a northerly direction onto a 109, which crashed in flames. He then continued on his course, going all out.'

Up from Biggin Hill, Flight Lieutenant Brian Kingcome was leading 92 Squadron over Canterbury when at 18.30 hrs, while still climbing, the Spitfires were vectored into the path of advancing Me 109s:

I saw several formations of Me 109s passing directly over us in the opposite direction, about 5,000ft above us … I turned about and was climbing after the Me 109s when I noticed another formation of 109s diving onto another squadron of Spitfires, which was following us and about 2,000ft below us on our right. The Spitfires apparently did not notice them, as I turned and dived into the 109s. I gave the first one a 2-second burst ¾ deflection and it turned away in a gentle spiral glide to the right, into some cloud below. I gave another one a 2-second full deflection shot and it pulled up practically on its back and fell away. I was then attacked by several 109s and escaped into a cloud. When I climbed back again I could not find any more bandits, so eventually returned to base.

Kingcome was credited with two Me 109s damaged, Flying Officer Allan Wright and Pilot Officer Tony Bartley both also damaging 109s.

No.92 Squadron's Pilot Officer Robert McGowan, however, was shot down in the skirmish over Canterbury, baling out wounded, and Sergeant Jack Mann was shot-up and also wounded, although he returned to base safely and was admitted to Orpington Hospital.

Meanwhile, 46 Squadron, up from Stapleford, had rendezvoused as ordered with Hendon's 504 Squadron, the wing being vectored to Maidstone, with orders to patrol there at 15,000ft. The Hurricanes, however, somewhat sensibly, climbed higher, to 18,000ft and when over Headcorn saw some forty Me 109s higher still, at 21,000ft, flying north-west. These enemy fighters continued on their way, but twenty other 109s, joined by six more, attacked the British fighters from above and astern, breaking up the wing.

The two squadrons then became separated, fortunately suffering no casualties. Ten aircraft of 504 Squadron re-formed, then saw AA fire bursting; upon investigation, the gunners' target was found to be seventy more Me 109s at 18,000ft, a formation of twenty of which 504 attacked from abeam in sections line-astern. The enemy, however, now had the height advantage and as 504 attacked, other 109s countered and a second combat ensued, which became so confused that, according to 504's Fighter Command Form 'F', 'our pilots were unable to see clearly the results of their fire, though several E/A are believed to have been hit'. Pilot Officer Blair 'Crasher' White, though, did claim a 109 damaged, having seen 'white smoke … pouring from the tail after hits'.

Having disengaged, 504 Squadron returned to Hendon intact. No.46 Squadron's experience was virtually identical, with Flight Lieutenant Alexander Rabagliati (somewhat optimistically) claiming a 109 destroyed, which 'turned over and went down with smoke coming out and flame below the fuselage', and Pilot Officer Robert Reid one damaged, which 'dived vertically through the clouds … No flames were seen.' All of 46 Squadron returned safely to Stapleford.

At 18.10 hrs, Flight Lieutenant Ken Gillies led 'B' Flight of 66 Squadron up from Gravesend, engaging Me 109s overhead at approximately 18.45 hrs. Sergeant Douglas Corfe subsequently claimed an Me 109 destroyed, but Sergeant Robert Robbins was shot down over Maidstone and admitted to Leeds Castle Military Hospital seriously wounded and suffering from shock.

Squadron Leader Robert Lister DFC, a Cranwellian and former army cooperation pilot who earned his decoration for gallantry in Waziristan in 1937, had taken temporary command of 41 Squadron at Hornchurch on 8 September 1940, and on this particular evening was among ten of the squadron's pilots who left Hornchurch at 18.10 hrs, flying at the squadron's rear, to patrol Kent.

Official documents are lacking in specific details but it is known that Lister was ambushed and shot down in flames, baling out slightly wounded – although exactly at what time and where is unknown. *Oberleutnant* Gerhard Ködderitzsch of 1/JG 54, however, claimed a Spitfire destroyed at 18.45 hrs (BST) 20km east of Sevenoaks; whether or not this was Lister is impossible to say, but the wounded pilot was admitted to hospital and replaced in command of 41 Squadron by the Olympian Squadron Leader Don Finlay. No.41 Squadron suffered no other casualties in the action, and made no combat claims.

Shortly after 19.00 hrs, the sky was clear of German fighters. The day's raids had involved minimal bombing of London and largely involved high altitude fighter sweeps – which would become the prominent feature of the following month's fighting. RDF, of course, was unable to distinguish between fighters and bombers, so these threats had to be reacted to – when the mass fighter formations actually presented little or no danger to land targets, and could, therefore, have been left just to waste petrol over south-east England.

During the skirmishing arising, eleven RAF fighters had been destroyed, six pilots wounded and three killed (plus the Czechoslovak Sergeant Frantisek Marek of 19 Squadron, who was killed owing to oxygen failure on a routine patrol). The German fighters, operating at heights of up to over 30,000ft, enjoyed the advantage of height and numbers, and it showed: only three Me 109s were destroyed and two damaged, with one pilot killed and two captured. So far as the enemy bombers were concerned, two He 111s had been destroyed and another damaged, and four Do 17 reconnaissance raiders returned to France shot-up by RAF fighters.

In addition to these two main incursions over Kent and to London, nuisance raiders had operated far and wide by day: a cinema was hit in Brighton, killing thirty-five people and injuring eighty-two more, and a low-level attack by another solo bomber hit a works' canteen at a Warrington factory, killing fourteen workers and injuring many more. By night, enemy activity was reduced – for reasons soon to become all too apparent – but nonetheless, some 27 Londoners were killed and 108 injured, and across the counties were 67 more deaths and 318 people injured.

Squadron Leader 'Sailor' Malan DFC, 74 Squadron:

> Many of us were tired. We had been pulled out for a second breather. Older sweats like Mungo-Park, Steve (Stephen) and Johnny Freeborn and I were using a few hours' rest to train new pilots and snatch an odd half pint of the local brew at Coltishall, on the East coast. Sharing our airfield was 242, a Canadian squadron commanded by Douglas Bader. As far as I remember – I don't believe in diaries – it was a quiet day [14 September 1940].
>
> Bader and I, and, for that matter, all the fellows in the squadrons at Coltishall, knew that Göring's nut still had to be cracked. The fact that at that moment the Luftwaffe was being assembled for its greatest bid only a hundred or so miles from us across the Channel, was unknown to us as we played our game of billiards, drank a glass of beer or lay on our beds in the dispersal huts at readiness.

At Hornchurch, 222 Squadron's Pilot Officer Laurie Whitbread wrote to his mother – giving no indication of the danger he faced on a daily basis:

> Dear Mother,
>
> Thank you for your letter, received this morning. How nice to have Rex and Doris and Colin at home together. I am disappointed that I won't be there too. Fancy Ludlow having some bombs!
>
> Everything is going fine down here. We get far less to do now that the weather has broken. There is no sign of leaving this station yet, so I doubt that I will get any leave until things quieten down again.
>
> I am keeping fit – except that I got a touch of frostbite in the left-hand last week. Its better now, except for a large blister on the thumb.
>
> Mother, would you see if I've left my RAF navy blue blazer at home. I don't want it but can't find it here. Please tell me in the next letter, I do hope that I haven't lost it.
>
> Love to all, Cheerio, Laurie.

For Coastal Command, it was an unremarkable day, although various reconnaissance sorties were flown and twenty-one all-important convoys escorted. Owing to the lack of cloud over the Continent, however, 2 Group's Blenheims abandoned their proposed daylight attacks, just one Blenheim bombing the airfield at Haamstede. Bomber Command's primary nocturnal targets were again the Channel ports and marshalling yards. Four Blenheims attacked the Ostend barges, five those at Calais, three the invasion preparations at Dunkirk, while Boulogne received the unwelcome attention of twelve Battles and five Blenheims hit the heavy artillery battery at Cap Gris-Nez.

The Wellington and Hampden forces reported successful raids on marshalling yards in Germany and Belgium, the Whitleys attacking shipping at Antwerp and Flushing – losing two aircraft, one ditching in the North Sea, the crew being rescued, but a 78 Squadron machine and its crew disappeared without trace. The Heston-based PRU lost two Spitfires: Flying Officer Anthony Parker, who was shot down by *Feldwebel* Kurt Goltsch of 8/JG 2 while on a sortie to photograph the ports of Boulogne and Le Havre, and reported missing, and Flying Officer Peter Dakeyne, who was hit by flak over the Belgian coast, baling out to become a prisoner.

Daily Home Intelligence Report:

> People in London are slightly less cheerful today. The decline in the activity of the AA barrage has caused comment, and there are many questions about the effect of cloud and rain on the barrage.

Southern Region (Reading):

> Although the public is alive to the possibility of invasion, there is a general feeling that it can only be a disaster for the Germans.

South-eastern (Tunbridge Wells):

> Tunbridge Wells suffered considerable damage on Thursday as a result of a lightning raid. No siren was sounded but members of the Civil Defence behaved splendidly, but soon after the streets became full of curious sightseers who interfered with the work of the Fire Service. If the raider had returned, there might have been many casualties.

Another day had passed, but the absence of massed bomber raids was ominous. Prophetically, the 19 Squadron diarist commented on this current lack of activity, observing that the enemy must be 'Saving up for "der Tag", evidently'.

The anonymous scribe was right.

Sunday, 15 September 1940

At Hitler's Reich Chancellery conference of the previous day, the *Führer* had made clear that although the Luftwaffe had yet to destroy the RAF, air attacks on Britain had been effective and Fighter Command was mortally wounded. With better weather now forecast, it was necessary, he believed, to maintain both heavy attacks on London and the threat of invasion.

Things, however, had changed since the Germans' aerial devastation of Guernica, Warsaw and Rotterdam – and, unlike the Danes, who had capitulated at the threat of bombing – the civilian population of Britain was proving infinitely more robust and stoic to air attacks.

Before the war, especially after Guernica, the fear of bombing was endemic. The prophecies of the Italian air strategist, General Giulio Douhet – that a civilian population could be bombed into submission – appeared believable, so much so that this theory underpinned the air power doctrines of the day. Indeed, the public's imagination ran riot due to scaremongering films like the previously mentioned H.G. Wells' *Things to Come*. For the British now, though, bombing was no longer an unknown entity – it was real. Very real indeed. But despite the bombing to date, the capital remained an effective economic and administrative hub, the docks still functioned, and there was no rioting or mass panic.

Mark Benney, London factory worker:

> There was little absenteeism caused by the raids; in part because we felt that the raids gave added importance to our work, but much more because we knew that if we didn't turn up our mates would be worrying. You would see men staggering at their work from lack of sleep, snatching a ten-minute doze in the canteen over their food, and still, when knocking off time came, going off with a cheerful 'See yer in the morning, boys!'

West End restaurants remained open, some – including the famous 'Savoy' – offering all-night shelter; the band of 'Snake-hips Johnson' played on at the Café de Paris, the lurid 'Windmill' theatre remained open, and so too did cinemas; the people adapted to 'shelter life', many choosing to take deep cover in London's underground tube network; shop windows were blown out, with signs declaring 'More open than usual'. A damaged public house advertised 'Our windows are gone but our spirits are excellent. Come in and try them.' Life went on: 'London can take it' became the catchphrase – and if London could take it, so too could other cities.

Already, the British public's reaction to bombing had confounded Douhet. Hitler, though, still refused to authorise the indiscriminate bombing of London's civilian population, reserving this as the ultimate reprisal. Nonetheless, the *Führer* still expected a wearing down of British civilian morale through continued bombing and the ongoing threat of invasion. As the autumn had worn on, however, the British public had begun to consider invasion unlikely – although, Hitler would have been gratified to know, Ministers, the press and radio were working hard to keep the prospect alive and fixed in people's minds, to avoid complacency.

The *Sunday Chronicle* of 15 September 1940, stated that, 'If and when the invasion comes, there will be no secrecy. The news will be given by the BBC and the newspapers.'

London, therefore, remained the Luftwaffe's primary target for the forthcoming action on '*Der Tag*' – which, as Churchill wrote, would see 'the greatest concentrated effort in a resumed daylight attack on London'. This was not, though, just because of the effect such raids would have on civilians. There were other reasons too, foremost among them the Germans' mistaken belief that *Loge* was still the only target Air Chief Marshal Dowding would commit his entire force to defend – and therein lay the crux of the Luftwaffe's problem: inaccurate intelligence.

As we have seen, on 16 July 1940 the Luftwaffe intelligence chief, General Joseph 'Beppo' Schmid, a close friend of *Reichsmarschall* Göring, produced an incompetent assessment of Fighter Command, inaccurately summarising aircraft strength and performance, declaring both the Spitfire and Hurricane inferior to the Me 109, and the Hurricane inferior to the Me 110, and the capacity of British aircraft manufacturing.

According to Schmid, the Britain's factories were only capable of producing between 180 and 300 fighters per month, which, he predicted, would decrease owing to the effect of German air attacks and blockade. According to Schmid's figures, therefore, Fighter Command should have been destroyed by now, if German combat claims were to be accepted as accurate – but between July and September 1940, Lord Beaverbrook's MAP actually provided 450–500 fighters. Moreover, Schmid was completely unaware of the Civilian Repair Organisation and its units, which contributed enormously to repairing and maintaining the flow of fighters – and it was really, so far as the daylight battle went, Spitfires and Hurricanes that were most important.

In any case, it was not aircraft Fighter Command lacked – pilots were the critical commodity, especially those with combat experience, and yet Schmid's *Abteilung* 5 report opined that there were 'no difficulties regarding the supply of men'. In truth, by mid-September 1940, Fighter Command was short of pilots by 10 per cent, having only 1,492 against a requirement of 1,662 – and the replacements provided by the OTUs, which had reduced courses and were working at full-stretch, lacked combat experience.

Schmid also completely failed to grasp how Fighter Command was structured and controlled, believing:

> The command at high-level is inflexible in its organisation and strategy. As formations are rigidly attached to their home bases, command at medium level suffers mainly from operations being controlled in most cases by officers no longer accustomed to flying. Command at low-level is generally energetic but lacks tactical skill.

In truth, Air Vice-Marshal Park was the only group commander who could fly a modern fighter, but we now know (see Volume 2) that he flew his personal Hurricane, OK-1, on at least two operational sorties during the Battle of Britain and is now recognised as a legitimate holder of the coveted Battle of Britain Clasp. Furthermore, at least seven station commanders flew occasional operational sorties with squadrons on their bases – the same could not be said of the Luftwaffe. Schmid was also wrong about Fighter Command being inflexible – which he had reiterated in a memorandum to all *Luftflotten* and *Fliegerkorps* on 8 August 1940:

> As the British fighters are controlled from the ground by R/T their forces are tied to their respective ground stations and are thereby restricted in their mobility … Consequently the assembly of strong fighter forces at determined points and at short notice is not to be expected. A massed German attack on a target area can therefore count on the same conditions of light fighter opposition as in attacks on widely scattered targets.

Schmid made no reference whatsoever to RDF, concluding that the defences would simply be overwhelmed by mass raids – the reality of which being that it was easier for RDF to detect and forewarn of large formations assembling and approaching.

Luftwaffe intelligence also grossly over-estimated the damage to Fighter Command's airfields and its fighter losses. During the period 12–19 August 1940, for example, Luftwaffe intelligence reported that 644 RAF fighters had been destroyed – the actual figure was 141. Going forward, it was the same story: ninety-three RAF fighters were claimed destroyed on 7 September 1940, the true number being twenty-five. Indeed, earlier in September 1940, *Generalfeldmarschall* Kesselring, having done the maths according to Schmid's figures of RAF strength and aircraft losses, felt sure at the Hague conference that Fighter Command was on its knees – *Generalfeldmarschall* Sperrle was less optimistic and gave a more accurate prediction that Fighter Command still had around 1,000 aircraft.

Although Kesselring's optimistic view found favour with the deluded Göring, Sperrle was right: on 14 September 1940, Fighter Command's strength was 943 serviceable fighters – of which 533 were Hurricanes and 261 Spitfires. Of those, all but 128 Hurricanes and 44 Spitfires were in 10, 11 and 12 Groups – with 218 Hurricanes and 92 Spitfires available in Air Vice-Marshal Park's 11 Group. Any notion, therefore, that London's defences would be swamped, and that the attackers would be met by a handful of RAF fighters, was pure fantasy.

After Hitler's decision that London was to be subjected to another major attack, Kesselring's Luftflotte 2 HQ in Brussels became a hive of activity, as staff officers prepared plans for this huge raid. During the Battle of Britain to date, the Germans had employed various tactics: lone bombers, small formations of bombers, pure fighter sweeps and escorted mass raids, attacks often being made simultaneously on different targets by formations which separated into several smaller groups of aircraft, each bound for different targets.

Because the Me 109 was now operating at the extremity of its limited range, however, there was no such luxury of feints and subterfuge – the route to the target had to be the minimal distance from the French assembly areas – and therefore direct. Given the Germans' previous mass attack on London, the likely target of these newly proposed raids would be obvious to Fighter Command. Anticipating being met by a minimal force of fighters, this was of no concern to Kesselring's planners. Clearly, they had not spoken to the Jagdflieger engaged on 14 September 1940, who would have known full-well that there were still plenty of Spitfires and Hurricanes available.

In those days, railways were much more important than today, being before the advent of the first British motorways (1958) and conveyance of supplies via Heavy Goods Vehicles. Being also before the automobile became affordable and in wide use, railways were an essential and common form of public transport too. Being the nation's hub, London's railway network was vitally important – and these converged at Battersea, sometimes twelve tracks running alongside each other, connecting the capital with the rest of the country and London's other mainline overland stations.

If these tracks could be destroyed, chaos would visit London's transport network. This important target was chosen for the morning raid. The plan entailed an attack on London at 11.50 hrs by twenty-one high-flying Me 109 fighter-bombers of II/LG 2, followed, at 12.10 hrs, by the Battersea bombing by twenty-five Do 17s of I and III/KG 76. The bombers were to be heavily escorted, needless to say, by Me 109s, including those of JGs 2, 3, 26, 27, 51, 52, 53 and 77.

For a larger attack in the afternoon, the intention was that London's East End docklands, Victoria, Royal Albert and King George V, would again be battered, as would the Surrey Commercial Docks, south of the Thames. This was to be carried out in four waves: at 14.45 hrs, twenty He 111s were to bomb the Royal Victoria Dock, followed three minutes later by the second wave, eleven Do 17s of II/KG 3; at 14.50 hrs, twenty-seven He 111s of I and II/KG 26 were to attack the West India Dock, and finally, five minutes later, an even larger force, forty-two Do 17s of II and III/KG 2, would hit the Surrey Commercial Docks. Again, these bombers would have a heavy escort of Me 109s, JGs 3, 77 and LG 2 all contributing, and on this occasion Me 110s of V(Z)/LG 1 and I/ZG 26 would provide close escort.

At his Parisian HQ, *Generalfeldmarschall* Sperrle's staff officers were also busy; after Luftflotte 2's second and major attack on London, at 15.30 hrs, Luftflotte 3 was to attack further west. The plan entailed eight He 111s of I/KG 55 targeting the Royal Navy installations at Portland, and eighteen of III/KG 55 hitting the fuel storage depot at Portland harbour. Then, at 17.30 hrs, three Me 109 and ten Me 110 fighter-bombers of *Erprobungsgruppe* 210 were to attack the Supermarine factory at Woolston, Southampton – the experimental unit now operating from Cherbourg-Ost to specifically target the all-important Spitfire factory.

In the belief that Luftwaffe intelligence was correct, the enemy plan had a fourfold objective: cause chaos to London's railway network, destroy essential supplies imported from overseas and stored at dockland warehouses, reduce civilian morale, and – most important of all so far as the future of Operation *Seelöwe* was concerned – finish Fighter Command as an effective defending force. Moreover, by also attacking Portland and Southampton it was hoped that the defences would be overwhelmed, and that on this occasion Spitfire production at Woolston would be grievously hurt. Schmid's faulty intelligence, however, unduly informed and influenced German plans and strategy at this critical moment. Had Schmid's intelligence been correct, conversely so too would the German strategy have been. It was now, more than ever, that the Luftwaffe would pay the price for over-confidence and having neglected the importance of accurate air intelligence.

After dark on 14/15 September 1940, London was bombed for the eighth consecutive night – but understandably, given preparations being made to hopefully overwhelm the defences by day, this was on a reduced scale.

Sunday, 15 September 1940 dawned clear and fine, but according to the HQ Fighter Command Intelligence Officer, the weather became 'fair to cloudy during the morning with some showers mainly in the North and West, and with cloud at 2,000 to 3,000ft lowering to 1,000 to 2,000ft and showers'. From first light onwards, standing patrols of RAF fighters were up over the coast between Land's End and Harwich. In addition, each sector station kept at least one squadron at readiness, to scramble at a moment's notice.

Typically, the first combat of the day involved a German reconnaissance aircraft, a He 111 of *Wetterkundungs Staffel* 51, which was caught at 08.45 hrs some five miles south-west of Bolt Head by a section of 10 Group's Exeter-based 87 Squadron. In cloud, Pilot Officers Dennis David and Trevor Jay attacked but lost the bomber, which turned seawards; the Heinkel would not make it home and the crew of five remain missing.

Further east, at 10.00 hrs RDF indicated an increase in German patrols over the Dover Strait, two formations of these fighters sweeping in over Dover and Ramsgate at 10.40 hrs and leaving eastwards virtually straightaway.

That historic morning, Churchill was at Chequers – the British Prime Minister's country residence in Buckinghamshire, twenty-five miles north-west of Air Vice-Marshal Park's 11 Group HQ at Uxbridge, which the great man had already visited,

> on several occasions … to witness the conduct of an air battle, when not much had happened. The weather on this day seemed suitable to the enemy, and accordingly I drove over to Uxbridge and arrived at the Group Headquarters … Air Vice-Marshal Park had for six months commanded this Group, on which our fate largely depended … all his arrangements and apparatus had been brought to the highest perfection.

No doubt, however, Park and his staff could have done without a visit from the PM on this particular day, although the AOC 11 Group later recalled that Churchill:

> came down a number of times … he must have come down more than half a dozen times. He sat in my Operations Room at Uxbridge for hours watching, waiting for the battle to start and watching what happened and listening to my orders. He was excellent. He never interfered or made any attempt to interfere in the conduct of operations. Of course, I think he was intensely interested and I'm sure he knew that what the consequences were of winning or losing this battle; it was vital to the Allied cause that we should win.

Churchill's description of the 11 Group Operations Room that morning, before the air battles began, provides a unique and indelible first-hand impression:

My wife and I were taken down to the bomb-proof underground Operations Room, fifty feet below ground. All the ascendency of the Hurricanes and Spitfires would have been fruitless but for this system of underground control centres and telephone cables, which had ben built before the war under Dowding's advice and impulse.

Lasting credit is due to all concerned. In the South of England there was at this time 11 Group HQ and six subordinate fighter station centres. All these were ... under heavy stress. The Supreme Command was exercised from Fighter HQ at Stanmore, but the actual handling of the direction of the squadrons was wisely left to 11 Group, which controlled the units through its fighter stations located in each county.

The Group Operations Room was like a small theatre, about sixty feet across and with two stories. We took our seats in the Dress Circle. Below us was a large-scale map table, around which perhaps twenty highly-trained young men and women, with their telephone assistants, were assembled.

Opposite to us, covering the entire wall, where the theatre curtain would be, was a gigantic blackboard divided into six columns with electric bulbs, for the six fighter stations, each of their squadrons having a sub-column of its own, and also divided by lateral lines. Thus the lowest row of bulbs showed as they were lighted the squadrons which were 'Standing-By', at two minutes' notice, the next row those at 'Readiness', five minutes, then at 'Available', twenty minutes, then those which had taken off, the next row those which had reported seeing the enemy, the next – with red lights – those which were in action, and the top row those which were returning home.

On the left-hand side, in a kind of glass storage box, were the four or five officers whose duty it was to weigh and measure the information received from our Observer Corps, which at this time numbered upwards of 50,000 men, women and youths. Radar was still in its infancy, but it gave warning of raids approaching our coast, and the observers, with field-glasses and portable telephones, were our main source of information about raiders flying overland. Thousands of messages were therefore received during an action.

Several roomfuls of experienced people in other parts of the underground headquarters sifted them with great rapidity, and

> transmitted the results from minute to minute directly to the plotters seated around the table on the floor and to the officer supervising from the glass stage-box.
>
> On the right-hand side was another glass storage-box containing Army officers who reported the action of our anti-aircraft batteries, of which, at this time in the Command there were 200. At night it was of vital importance to stop those batteries firing over certain areas in which our fighters would be closing with the enemy. I was not unacquainted with the general outlines of this system, having had it explained to me a year before the war by Dowding when I visited him at Stanmore. It had been shaped and refined in constant action, and all was now fused together into a most elaborate instrument of war, the like of which existed nowhere else in the world.
>
> 'I don't know', said Park, as we went down, 'whether anything will happen today. At present all is quiet.'

Near Amiens, the Do 17s of the depleted I and III/KG 76 formed up, climbed to their allotted attack altitude and headed for Cap Gris-Nez to meet their fighter escorts. During the bombers' climb, however, at 10.40 hrs, the formation became split up in thick cloud, necessitating in the lead aircraft orbiting above the cloud to enable the formation to re-form. This caused a ten-minute delay – a serious problem considering that the Me 109 escorts only had fuel for twenty minutes over London. The Me 109s of JG 3 circled Cap Gris-Nez, but the Dorniers were nowhere to be seen. The fighters continued their orbits, but with every minute precious fuel was wasted until, at 11.04 hrs, the Dorniers finally appeared and the raid set off across the Channel.

The rendezvous of bombers and fighters over the French coast had not gone unnoticed by the ever-open but invisible eye of RDF, this information being communicated to HQ Fighter Command and HQ 11 Group. At Hendon, 504 Squadron was 'released' but with these new threats impending called to readiness at 11.00 hrs: 'At this moment a party of American generals and an admiral complete with cine camera arrived from the Air Ministry to see the life of a fighter squadron. After being introduced to pilots at dispersal a real flap occurred [ORB].'

Air Vice-Marshal Park's 'quiet' morning was about to transform into one of the most bitterly contested days of the entire sixteen-week-long battle

– and the Prime Minister would not be disappointed with the high drama and outcome. Without delay, squadrons were scrambled:

11.00–11.05 hrs:	Spitfires of 72 (three of which were already patrolling Canterbury) scrambled from Croydon, and 92 Squadron from Biggin Hill, to patrol Canterbury together at 25,000ft.
11.15 hrs:	Hurricanes of 229 and 303 (Polish) Squadrons from Northolt to patrol Biggin Hill at 15,000ft; 17 and 73 Squadrons went from Debden to patrol over Chelmsford at 15,000ft, and 253 and 501 Squadrons together from Kenley to intercept the enemy over Maidstone.
11.20 hrs:	No.504 Squadron scrambled from Hendon to rendezvous with Martlesham's 257 Squadron to patrol North Weald at 15,000ft, and then Maidstone. At the same time, 603 Squadron left Hornchurch to patrol Dover at 25,000ft, and 10 Group's Middle Wallop-based 609 Squadron took-off and headed for the Brooklands-Windsor line at 15,000ft.

Clearly, Air Vice-Marshal Park's intention was for the Spitfires of 72, 92 and 603 Squadrons to provide an element of top cover at 25,000ft, while the remaining six squadrons patrolled at 15,000ft in order to intercept the German bombers.

Still watching proceedings expectantly in Air Vice-Marshal Park's 11 Group Operations Room, the Prime Minister recalled these opening events:

> One after another signals came in. '40+', '60+'; there was even an '80+'. On the floor-table below us the movement of all waves of attack was marked by pushing discs forward from minute to minute along different lines of approach, whilst on the blackboard facing us rising lights showed our fighter squadrons getting into the air, until there were only four or five left at 'Readiness' … Park spoke to Dowding at Stanmore, asking for three squadrons from 12 Group to be put at his disposal …

> This was done. They were especially needed to patrol London and our fighter aerodromes.

At 11.30 hrs the Duxford Wing, comprising 19, 242, 302 and 310 Squadrons, was therefore scrambled; 12 Group's 611 Squadron, which was flying into Fowlmere from Digby, joining the wing over Duxford a minute later.

At 11.33 hrs, an enemy formation crossed the coast between Dover and Folkestone, followed three minutes later by two more, incoming over Dover and the South Foreland. The enemy then flew a 'dog-leg' course, first northwards towards the Thames Estuary, then turning south or south-west before reaching the north coast of Kent, then west to Maidstone before finally spreading out to fly over the entire London area. To meet this attack, Air Vice-Marshal Park scrambled even more squadrons:

11.35 hrs: Nos.249 and 46 Squadrons from North Weald, vectored to South London.
11.40 hrs: No.1 (RCAF) Squadron from Northolt and Croydon's 605 to meet over and patrol Kenley at 15,000ft, and 41 from Gravesend to patrol base at 20,000ft.
11.42 hrs: No.66 Squadron, also from Gravesend, to intercept the approaching raid.

At midday 72 Squadron, led by Flight Lieutenant John 'Pancho' Villa, 'Tennis Leader', sighted the formation of Me 109s and Do 215s [*sic*] incoming over Dungeness.

As planned, 72 was in company with 92 Squadron, the former leading. Villa ordered 72 Squadron – which for once had the advantage of height and sun – into line astern, changing to echelon starboard while diving to attack Me 109s below:

> The Me 109 I attacked half-rolled as I opened fire and before he could dive away he caught fire and exploded. I was then attacked by five other Me 109s. I did a steep turn to starboard and continued turning until I out-turned one Me 109 which was on my tail. I gave him two short bursts and he burst into flames. I then span down to get away from more Me 109s which dived down on me.

In this clash with the Me 109s, 72 Squadron's Sergeant William Rolls claimed a 109 damaged; 72 Squadron suffered no loss. No.92 Squadron also became embroiled with the escorting fighters as the enemy advanced, two Me 109s being claimed as probably destroyed and two damaged, although both Pilot Officer Tony Bartley and Sergeant Ronald Fokes managed to penetrate the fighter screen and damage Do 17s.

No.603 Squadron also barred the raiders' way at 12.00 hrs; Squadron Leader George Denholm:

> When between Dungeness and Dover I saw an Me 109 and gave it a short burst from astern. It emitted glycol steam and dived into the cloud. I followed it but lost it in the cloud. On coming out I saw an Me 109 in difficulties which I took to be the E/A at which I had previously fired, and I fired a short burst. The E/A did a gentle dive, landing on the sea within fifty yards of Dover outer harbour.

Pilot Officer James MacPhail also claimed a 109 destroyed, and Pilot Officer Ronald 'Raz' Berry a probable. Only Pilot Officer Bill Read managed to attack the bombers, damaging a Do 17. The Hornchurch-based Spitfires suffered no loss.

The incoming enemy was also met by 253 and 501 Squadron. Pilot Officer Anthony Barton of the former found a Dornier straggling 2,000ft below and five miles to starboard of the main formation. The Hurricane pilot attacked, head-on – three times. The bomber turned south, losing height, its starboard engine ablaze: 'After the third attack he appeared to have lost control … he circled and lost height. About eight minutes after my having ceased fire, he crashed in the sea about four miles NW of Herne Bay.' This Do 17, the crew of which were all killed, belonged to 8/KG 76.

Flight Lieutenant Raymond Duke-Woolley and Robert Innes, also of 253 Squadron, shared a Dornier damaged near Beachy Head; the squadron suffered no casualties.

No.501 Squadron reported that having been vectored to Ramsgate, the enemy bombers and their escorts were sighted 'coming straight towards them'. Squadron Leader Harry Hogan's Hurricanes were at Angels 15, the bombers 2,000ft higher and the German fighters higher still. Hogan climbed 501 Squadron towards the bombers, which also began climbing.

The initial attack was made at 17,000ft, after which 501 broke up and individual dogfights ensued.

Flight Sergeant Peter Morfill and Pilot Officer Everett Rogers both claimed Do 17s destroyed, while the rest of the squadron mixed it with the Me 109s; Sergeants James 'Ginger' Lacey DFM and Eddie Egan each claimed a 109 destroyed, and Lacey another damaged. Squadron Leader Hogan's Hurricane was hit by a cannon shell from a 109, the CO forced-landing near Sundridge with a damaged radiator. The Belgian Pilot Officer Albert van den Hove d'Ertsenrijk, however, was shot down by a 109, an eye witness reporting that the pilot attempted to effect a forced-landing near Chilham, but then baled out, very low, and was killed.

When the enemy reached Ashford, the Spitfires of 41 Squadron were at 20,000ft – but the 109s were, as ever, higher still. Pilot Officer George Bennions:

> Leading Blue Section I was attacked by Me 109s. After a steep right-hand climbing turn the Me 109, with a yellow nose, fell out of the turn and I turned on his tail. He rolled over and went vertically downwards and pulled out, heading south-east as soon as he straightened up. I gave him three short bursts. He burst into flames and after knocking off his roof, baled out. The E/A hit the ground alongside a wood North of the railway line running West from Ashford. The pilot was still floating down when I left to pick up the enemy again.

The vanquished German pilot was *Leutnant* Hans Bartel of *Stab* I/JG 52, who was captured unhurt. Flying Officer Tony Lovell also destroyed a 109, of 1/JG 53, the pilot of which, *Feldwebel* Tzchoppe baled out over Bekesbourne, near Canterbury, and was badly burned. Again, though, the escorts had done their job well, only Sergeant Edward Darling damaging a Do 17. Thirty minutes later, 41 Squadron lost a pilot, Pilot Officer Gerald Langley, who was shot down and killed north of the Thames, at Bulphan, near Thorrock, Essex.

As the Do 17s approached London, 229 Squadron also intercepted over Maidstone, led by 'Keta Leader', namely Flight Lieutenant Frank Rimmer, who first evaded Me 109s before finding the Do 17 near Maidstone – which he attacked and watch crash 'near a dummy airfield South of Sevenoaks'.

Two Hurricanes were shot down, however, in the action occurring over Sevenoaks: Pilot Officer Robert Smith, a Canadian, baled out with leg wounds, but the Belgian Pilot Officer Georges Doutrepont was killed, his Hurricane crashing onto Staplehurst Station, killing Charles Ashdown, a Southern Railway employee.

Following 229 Squadron were the Poles of 303 Squadron, led by the Canadian Flight Lieutenant Johnny Kent. Watching the enemy turn for home, the Poles gave chase, catching some Me 109s near Folkestone, individual combats then taking place. Pilot Officer Marian Pisarek attacked a 109, descending to 400ft and at which point the enemy fighter 'burst into flames and fell into the sea'. Sergeant Miroslaw Wojciechowski chased a 109 towards France, hitting it from 'very close range' and noting the 'Me burst into flames'.

The Pole then chased another 109, which was trailing smoke and losing height, which he watched crash to earth and saw the 'pilot arrested' (very likely *Unteroffizier* Anton Walburger of 2/JG 27, who was shot down by Sergeant David Cox of 19 Squadron and forced-landed at Uckfield). Wojciechowski then joined up with Sergeant Tadeuz Andruszkow, the pair attacking a Do 17 which 'crashed to earth and burst into flames'. Flying Officer Ludwick Paszkiewicz engaged Me 109s over Folkestone – attacked by four of the enemy fighters he shot one down 'which fell in flames into the sea, and the other three fled to France'.

Flying Officer Zdzislaw Henneberg 'after a lengthy chase of Me 109s' was ordered to attack the Dorniers approaching London, attacking one before being chased off by Me 109s; looking round, Henneberg noticed that 'the right engine and petrol tank of the Do 215 [*sic*] was in flames'. Flying south, he then chased three Me 109s heading for the Channel, firing at one from 300 yards which went into a spin, smoking; Henneberg attacked again, having closed to 150 yards, the 109 then crashing into the sea some five miles off the Kentish coast and 'disappeared'. Earlier, when Henneberg was attacked by a 109, Pilot Officer Jan Zumbach fired at his assailant, which 'began to smoke and draw away'. Zumbach pursued the damaged fighter, attacking again from fifty yards and setting the 109 alight.

Together with another Hurricane, Zumbach then engaged twelve Me 109s heading back to France, 'but scarcely had I begun to fire than my ammunition ran out'. Over Dungeness, Pilot Officer Miroslaw Ferric was attacked by two Me 109s, which were reinforced by three more, one of which the Pole shot down, confirmed by Flight Lieutenant Kent, who 'saw the E/A burst into flames and fall to earth'. The Poles' only casualty in the fight was Pilot Officer Witold Lokuciewski, who was shot-up by a 109 after setting one alight, and returned to Northolt wounded in a leg.

Midday also saw the Dorniers attacked over Croydon by 605 Squadron, which did 'conspicuously well. Flight Lieutenant Currant destroyed two Do 17s and damaged another, Sergeant Wright and Sergeant Howes each destroying another, Flight Lieutenant MacKellar destroyed two Me 109s [ORB].' Pilot Officer Robert Jones was shot down by a 109, however, and baled out over West Malling, slightly wounded.

Still on course for the capital, the Dorniers were also attacked by 257 and 504 Squadrons. Flight Lieutenant Peter Brothers of 257 Squadron was leading, with both squadrons in line-astern, and attacked the bombers from the starboard side. Brothers ordered his Blue Section to concentrate their fire on one particular Do 17 – the gunners of which in turn focused on Brothers. Fortunately, only one enemy round hit the Hurricane, passing through the port ammunition tank and very nearly severing the aileron control cable. Brothers broke away, then attacked a lone 9/KG 76 Dornier, the crew of which baled out before their aircraft crashed at Underriver, near Sevenoaks.

The strain of this attack, though, caused Brothers' weakened aileron cable to snap, although the pilot reached Biggin Hill and landed safely. The destruction of the enemy bomber was shared by Brothers and Pilot Officers Alan Hedges and Percival Mortimer (and also attacked by various pilots of other squadrons). Pilot Officer Arthur Cochrane also claimed a Do 17 destroyed, shared with 'friendly fighters [ORB]', Sergeant Peter Robinson a probable, and Pilot Officer Gerald North one damaged.

Following 257 Squadron, Squadron Leader John Sample's 504 Squadron engaged the oncoming Dorniers at 12.10 hrs, first harrying the bombers over Fulham, then, after they turned about, to Gravesend. As Sample's men attacked in sections line astern from the starboard rear quarter, the bombers turned slightly to port, so the Hurricanes actually intercepted from dead astern. According to the squadron's Intelligence Patrol Report, 'About seventy Hurricanes and Spitfires joined in the battle' – leaving the German aircrews in no doubt as to the inaccuracy of Luftwaffe intelligence. Indeed, as Dornier pilot *Feldwebel* Wilhelm Raab remembered, 'yet more

British fighters' were 'closing rapidly'. The German counted ten, then gave up because there were so many.

Worse, owing to the fuel wasted by the bombers' forty-minute delay in rendezvousing with their fighter escort, the Me 109s were already being forced to break away and return home, leaving the bombers to their fate. From now on, the air battle was a chaotic mass of aircraft, with multiple pilots and squadrons engaged simultaneously – a total of 312 RAF fighters.

It was now, at 12.05 hrs, that the bomb-carrying LG 2 Me 109s of *Hauptmann* Otto Weiss, flying at 23,000ft, overtook the Dorniers, flying above the bombers at twice their speed. Over London, Weiss selected a railway station, pitching his aircraft into a 45° dive towards the target. Having lost 3,000ft, Weiss released his single bomb, as did his pilots. From the height involved and method of aiming, this was essentially indiscriminate bombing, after which Weiss turned about and made off home.

Four minutes later, Squadron Leader Douglas Bader and the Duxford Wing arrived over London, 242 Squadron leading with all sections in line astern. It had previously been agreed that the Spitfires of 19 and 611 Squadrons would attack the enemy fighter escort, while the Hurricanes of 242, 302 (Polish) and 310 (Czech) Squadrons would go for the bombers.

Having escorted the Dorniers to London without losing any of their charges, none of the Me 109 pilots could linger any longer and had to turn for home – leaving the bombers to their fate. Bader later recalled that the Dorniers were 'without a single fighter to escort them'. His combat report reads:

> Saw two squadrons pass underneath us in formation, travelling NW in purposeful manner, then saw AA bursts so turned 12 Group wing and saw E/A 3,000ft below to the NW. Managed perfect approach with 19 and 611 between our Hurricanes and sun, and E/A below and down-sun. Arrived over E/A formation of twenty-forty Do 17. Noticed Me 109 dive out of sun and warned our Spitfires to look out. Me 109 broke away and climbed SE.
>
> About to attack E/A which were turning left-handed, i.e. to West and South, when I noticed Spitfires and Hurricanes (11 Group?) chasing them. Was compelled to wait for friendly fighters and dived down with leading Section in formation onto last section of three E/A. Pilot Officer

Campbell took left-handed Do 17, I took middle one, Sub-Lieutenant Cork the right-hand one, which had lost ground on outside of turn.

Opened fire at 100 yards in steep dive and saw a large flash behind starboard motor of Dornier as wing caught fire. Must have hit petrol pipe or tank. Pulled up, overshot and pulled up steeply. Then carried on and attacked another Do 17 but had to break away to avoid Spitfire. The sky was then full of Spitfires and Hurricanes, queuing up and pushing each other out of the way to get at the Dorniers, which for once were outnumbered.

I squirted at odd Dorniers at close-range as they came into my sights but could not hold them in my sights for fear of collision with other Spitfires and Hurricanes.

Saw collision between Spitfire and Do 17, which wrecked both aeroplanes. Finally ran out of ammunition chasing crippled and smoking Do 17 into cloud.

Bader later wrote:

This time, for a change, we outnumbered the Hun, and, believe me, no more than eight got home from that party. At one time you could see planes going down on fire all over the place, and the sky seemed full of parachutes. It was sudden death that morning, for our fighters shot them to blazes.

One unfortunate German rear-gunner baled out of the Do 17 I attacked, but his parachute caught on the tail. There he was, swinging helplessly, with the aircraft swooping and diving and staggering all over the sky, being pulled about by the man hanging by his parachute from the tail. That bomber went crashing into the Thames Estuary, with the swinging gunner still there.

Just about the same time, one of my boys saw a similar thing in another Do 17, though this time the gunner who tried to bale out had his parachute caught before it opened. It caught in the hood, and our pilot saw the other two members of the crew crawl up to set him free. He was swinging from his packed parachute until they pushed him clear. Then they jumped after him, and their plane went into the water with a terrific smack. I've always thought it was a pretty stout effort

> on the part of those two Huns who refused to leave their pal fastened to the doomed aircraft.

One of KG 76's Dorniers was flown by *Feldwebel* Wilhelm Raab, a veteran of the campaigns in both Poland and France, in addition to numerous sorties over England. High above Brixton, Raab's bomber was attacked by numerous RAF fighter pilots: first Sergeant Edward Tyrer of 46 Squadron, then Flight Lieutenant Frank Rimmer of 229 Squadron, and both Flight Lieutenant Peter Brothers and Pilot Officer Percival Mortimer of 257 Squadron.

As the Dornier dived for cloud cover, Flight Lieutenant George Powell-Sheddon and Pilot Officer Hugh Tamblyn of 242 Squadron attacked next. The CO of 19 Squadron, Squadron Leader Brian Lane DFC, then also saw and attacked the Dornier, at first unaware of the attack in progress by the Hurricanes; realising that he had 'jumped the queue', he followed the Hurricanes and took his turn to fire. Lane was unable to tell, however, whether he or the two 242 Squadron Hurricanes were responsible for the hits he could see on Raab's aircraft. Descending at 100ft per minute, the Dornier dropped out of the cloud and, after being attacked by even more fighters, Raab ordered his crew to bale out before tumbling into space himself.

At 12.30 hrs, Squadron Leader Lane watched the pilotless bomber narrowly miss a house, and explode on impact at Underriver, south of Sevenoaks in Kent. This aircraft was also attacked by Flight Lieutenant Stan Turner, commander of 242 Squadron's 'B' Flight, who reported that 'three people jumped by parachute and the E/A crashed into a field and blew up'. The bomber would also feature in various other pilots' reports, Raab's fate confirming 310 Squadron statement that on this day 'no individual pilot could claim one bird as his own [ORB]'.

No.72 Squadron's Flight Lieutenant Jon 'Pancho' Villa, after the initial clash:

> returned to base and was informed that E/A were over base at Angels 14. I climbed up and saw a formation of Dorniers in front of me. I chased them and attacked the outside one on the starboard side. I gave him two short bursts from dead astern and his port engine stopped and he dropped out of position, losing height. I attacked this Do 215 [*sic*] again and white vapour poured out from his starboard engine. Five or

> six friendly fighters then came up and started attacking him. He crashed into a wood and exploded.

This was also the Underriver Dornier.

Many RAF fighters also attacked *Oberleutnant* Robert Zehbe's Beauvais-Tille-based 1/KG 76 Do 17, which, as the bombers reached London, was suffering engine trouble and straggling behind the main formation. First attacked by Pilot Officers Arthur Cochrane and Gerald North of 257 Squadron, Flying Officer Michael Rook and Pilot Officer Michael Royce of 504 Squadron next hit the Dornier, along with Flight Lieutenant Jerrard Jefferies, and Sergeants Raimond Puda, Jan Kaucky and Josef Hubacek of 310 Squadron, and 609 Squadron's Pilot Officers John Curchin and Keith 'Skeets' Ogilvie, a Canadian.

The bomber was shot to pieces; within, the gunner, *Unteroffizier* Gustav Hubel, and observer, *Unteroffizier* Hans Goschenhofer, were both dead, and Zehbe had no choice but to order his two other crewmen, *Obergefreiter* Ludwig Armbruster and *Unteroffizier* Leo Hammermeister, to bale out over London. Having engaged the auto-pilot, Zehbe followed them.

Having already damaged one of the bombers, Sergeant Ray Holmes of 504 Squadron also attacked Zehbe, making two quarter attacks and knocking pieces off the bomber before his windscreen became covered in oil from the damaged aircraft:

> I attacked a third time and a member of the crew baled out. On my fourth attack from the port beam a jar shook my starboard wing as I passed over the E/A and I went into an uncontrollable spin. I think the E/A must have exploded beneath me. I baled out and as I landed I saw the Dornier hit the ground by Victoria Station, half a mile away.

The foregoing is Holmes' official combat report, which strangely does not mention that, as claimed post-war, he had deliberately rammed the Dornier. Holmes' Hurricane crashed into the crossroads of Buckingham Palace, Pimlico and Ebury Bridge roads, the pilot alighting on an apartment building, his parachute catching on the guttering, suspending him above a dustbin. None the worse for wear, Holmes was taken to see his aircraft's crash-site before being entertained in the Mess at Chelsea Barracks and returning to Hendon.

Having lost its tail and wings outboard of both engines, Zehbe's Dornier had gone into an uncontrollable spin, centrifugal force punching the bombs through the fuselage, some of which fell on Buckingham Palace: one 110-pounder went through the roof, smashing through several floors before coming to a stop in a bathroom; another of the same size landed in the grounds – neither detonated. A cannister of incendiaries also landed in the grounds, some of which ignited, but these were swiftly dealt with by the palace's fire watchers. Unlike the previous incident, their Majesties were not at home.

The main wreckage of Zehbe's Dornier fell on the corner of Wilton Road and Terminus Place, with debris scattered over a wide area of the central West End. As for the Dornier's crew, Armbruster landed safely by parachute and was captured at Wells Park Road, Sydenham, and Hammermeister, who was wounded, was similarly taken into custody when he landed in Dulwich.

From the evidence available, exactly what befell the 27-year-old Zehbe, however, is unclear. His parachute snagged a telegraph pole at the Kennington Oval so, like Holmes, the German pilot was left dangling there; according to the popular narrative, Zehbe was attacked by an angry crowd, including women armed with knives and pokers, who mortally wounded the enemy pilot. No primary source, though, can be found supporting this version of events, which, if true, was murder. Some oral accounts state that Zehbe was taken away by the military, but, as confirmed by the Metropolitan Police Museum, he was, in fact, taken into custody by a Superintendent Gillies from nearby Kennington Police Station.

Admitted to the Queen Alexandra Military Hospital, Millbank, Zehbe died there the next day, in the presence, according to his Death Certificate, of a 'J. Marsland', the stated cause of death being 'Due to War Operations'. Whether Zehbe's injuries were sustained in combat, at the hands of an angry mob, or perhaps even both, it is impossible to say. Whatever happened, Zehbe's Do 17 undoubtedly became the most famous German aircraft casualty of the entire Battle of Britain.

Returning to the action high over the capital, 504 Squadron's Flying Officer Michael Jebb was shot-up and crashed at Dartford; badly burned, he would die of his injuries four days later; Pilot Officer John Gurteen was also shot down, and killed when his Hurricane smashed at full throttle onto a house at Hartley, near Longfield. Flying Officer Michael Royce, however, was somewhat more fortunate, returning safely to Hendon with a damaged oil cooler.

Over Croydon, 46 Squadron engaged the oncoming Germans, the Hurricane pilots immediately becoming embroiled in the confused fighting between the capital and Dover, as the enemy withdrew. After the initial charge, Sergeant Charles Hurry became detached from the squadron but at 12.30 hrs found a lone Do 17 over the Thames Estuary, heading south,

> and carried out deflection attacks from the quarter until my ammunition was expended. Another Hurricane joined me and carried out similar attacks. He glided down through the cloud and was again attacked by five or six fighters. The rear-gunner attempted to bale out but his parachute opened in the cockpit and streamed over the tailplane. Shortly afterwards the aircraft crashed into some trees and burst into flame on impact. My aircraft had four bullet holes in the starboard wing through the gun compartment. The E/A crashed approximately fifteen miles North of Dungeness.

The other Hurricane pilot was Sergeant George Jeffreys, the bomber being the 9/KG 76 aircraft also attacked by pilots of 229 and 310 Squadrons and which crashed at Rotherfield; the crew were all killed.

Flight Sergeant Edward Tyrer also claimed a Dornier destroyed, Pilot Officer John Crossman, an Australian, claiming a probable, and Pilot Officer Peter Gunning one damaged. 'All our aircraft returned safely [ORB].'

No.249 Squadron, operating with 46, also attacked the bombers, Pilot Officer George Barclay claiming a Do 17 probably destroyed over South London.

Also engaged with the Duxford Wing at midday was the Czech Flight Sergeant Josef Kominek, who attacked the leading section of Do 17s with his Section Leader, Flight Lieutenant Jerrard Jefferies, with whom contact was then lost owing to the sheer number of fighters in the sky. Kominek then found a bomber:

> trying to escape. When I carried out the attack on this aircraft, three Hurricanes joined me and the E/A tried to disappear in clouds. Above

> the clouds the Hurricanes broke away and I followed the E/A beneath the clouds and made three more attacks. After the third attack at 200 yards some sheets started to fall off and smoke was pouring from the starboard engine. The crew dropped the bombs and baled out (three men). The E/A crashed about three miles SW of Tunbridge Wells.

For no loss, in total the Czechoslovak squadron claimed four of the bombers destroyed.

As the Me 109s withdraw back to the coast, some of 19 Squadron's Spitfires managed to attack some at 12.10 hrs over Westerham, Flight Sergeant George 'Grumpy' Unwin engaged 3/JG 53's *Staffelkapitän*, *Oberleutnant* Julius Haase, in a dogfight:

> I was Red Three with Flight Lieutenant Lawson. We sighted the enemy aircraft which were flying in vics of three. The escorts dived singly onto us and I engaged an Me 109 with a yellow nose. I gave one burst of six seconds and it burst into flames. The pilot baled out and the enemy aircraft crashed between Redhill and Westerham.

Haase was killed as his parachute failed to open. As other Me 109s dived on 19 Squadron, Sergeant David 'Little Boy' Cox climbed and flew south. A few minutes later he found six 109s of 2/JG 27 flying in the same direction. Simultaneously, the Germans saw the Spitfire, and so Cox, Green 1, attacked from astern. Cox's target immediately half-rolled and dived away.

Four of the German fighters then broke off and continued south, being low on fuel, but the sixth attacked Cox head-on. As his assailant reared up to pass over the fleeting Spitfire, Cox climbed and turned sharply, attacking from below. The 109 dived through cloud, pursued by Cox, who, upon emerging, saw his victim's wreckage burning in a field. This was at Lodge Wood, near Uckfield, and the pilot, *Unteroffizier* Walburger, was captured unhurt.

The ORB of 611 Squadron, another Duxford Wing unit, provides a dramatic account of the action:

> 611 Squadron joined wing of Hurricanes over Duxford at 15,000 feet at 1131 hours then climbed to 27,000 feet to the left and above the wing which was at 22,000 feet. When SW of London, 50 enemy bombers

and 30 Me 109s escorting above were sighted coming from south. The wing went into attack the bombers and escort turning south-east. No.611 Squadron kept beside the Me 109s which were to the west and above. After the wing attack had broken up bomber formation, the Me 109s did not come down.

After waiting for about seven minutes, S/Ldr McComb informed Wing Leader that he was coming down, and gave order echelon port. The Squadron proceeding at the time south-east and up sun of the enemy. The Squadron in line astern, three sections of four aircraft executed a head-on attack down onto a formation of about 10 Do 215s and Do 17s. Then flying at 18,000 feet in a south easterly direction. S/Ldr McComb attacked Do 215 head on, hits observed, no results. Pulling up he made a beam attack on an Me 110 which turned in its back and went down.

The Squadron formation then broke up. S/Ldr McComb chased an Me 109 which was in a dogfight with a Hurricane, but could not catch up with them as he was too far behind. He then proceeded to the coast in the hope of attacking homing lame ducks before returning to base. P/O Williams after making his attack with the Squadron but without any observed results, saw a Do 215 attacked by six fighters crash into a wood near BISHOPSBOURNE, KENT. Two of the crew baling out. P/O Lund dived into initial attack but enemy aircraft passed through his sights before he could fire. P/O O'Neill attacked six or seven times a Do 215 which had fallen behind the enemy formation.

Four Hurricanes also attacked at same time. He chased this enemy aircraft as far as DUNGENESS where three other Spitfires carried on the attack. He then returned to base, being short of petrol and ammunition. F/Lt Leather carried out a head on attack on three Do 215s. No results observed. He then attacked a Do 215 at rear of large formation using up remainder of his ammunition. The port engine exploded and stopped. A number of other fighters also attacked this enemy aircraft and Red 2 reports seeing two crew bale out and machine crashed near B1SHOPSBOURNE, KENT.

Yet again, it was Raab's Dornier featuring in the combat reports of two pilots from 611 Squadron.

The 611 Squadron report continues:

> P/O Pollard, after firing a short burst in the initial dive attack, chased, in company with one other Spitfire and a Hurricane, a Do 215. Between Rochester and Herne Bay, enemy aircraft lost height, smoke coming from port engine. Crew of two baled out and aircraft crashed on edge of a wood about four miles south of Herne Bay. He landed at Detling at 1305 hours having lost his bearings, later returned to Gl.

This was a 3/KG 76 Do 17Z which was also engaged by Pilot Officer James Meaker of 249 Squadron, and both Flight Lieutenant Ken Gillies and Pilot Officer Crelin 'Bogle' Bodie of 66 Squadron. The Dornier crashed in flames and exploded at Slurry.

The very detailed 611 Squadron account continues:

> Yellow Three, P/O Brown after initial dive attack on pulling out saw no enemy aircraft. After circling for about 10 minutes he returned to home base. P/O Walker after initial dive attack on pulling out saw no enemy aircraft. He developed engine trouble and had to force land at West Malling at 1235 hours.
>
> F/Lt Stoddart fired one quick burst in initial dive attack, and then had to take evasive action in order to avoid attack from Me 109s. He circled for some time and then returned to base.
>
> F/Sgt Sadler after initial dive saw 12 Do 215s going south east so executed two frontal attacks on leader. Enemy aircraft believed hit but no results were seen. Abandoned chase at Lympne being short of ammunition and petrol.
>
> P/O Dewey fired a short burst at a Do 215 but observed no results. After circling for some time returned base.
>
> Sgt Levenson broke formation to attack an Me 109 but enemy aircraft got away. He then flew towards large formation of Do 215s flying at 18,000 feet. After sighting one Do 215 by itself at 14,000 feet he rolled over and carried out an old astern attack diving onto the enemy. Got in a long burst and both enemy aircraft motors were smoking when he broke away. Climbing again, he carried out the same attack. He broke

> away when both engines and both mainplanes immediately behind them were on fire.

The Duxford Wing's 302 (Polish) Squadron also engaged the Dorniers over South London at 12.10 hrs. 'A' Flight's Flight Lieutenant Tadeusz Chlopik attacked the rearmost section of Dorniers from abeam, developing into an astern attack as the bombers turned. With both engines smoking the bomber rolled over and dived, inverted, Chlopik reporting that 'three of the crew baled out', suggesting, therefore, that this was the 9/KG 76 machine down at Underriver and which appeared in multiple pilots' reports – including that of 302's Flight Lieutenant Franciszek Jastrzebski, with the two pilots sharing the kill. Chlopik then turned his attentions to another Do 17, which was attacked in turn 'by a large number of Hurricanes and two Spitfires'. In total, 302 Squadron claimed four bombers destroyed and an Me 109 probable, all for no loss.

Bader's Canadian 242 Squadron, leading the Duxford Wing, claimed five Do 17s and an Me 109 destroyed, and two Do 17s damaged, against just Flight Lieutenant Eric Ball being shot-up and forced-landing, unhurt.

In addition to Bader's Canadians, those of Squadron Leader Eric McNab's 1(RCAF) Squadron were also up and defending the capital. Unfortunately the Northolt Hurricanes were patrolling Biggin Hill at 12.10 hrs when bounced by high-flying Me 109s, which pounced from out of the sun. The German pilots flew to their machine's best technical advantage, making a single high-speed diving pass, firing as they went. So swift was the encounter that only McNab and Flying Officer Dean Nesbitt managed to open fire, as recounted by the Intelligence Patrol Report:

> Flying Officer Nesbitt got in a good burst at close range, observing his fire hitting the E/A, then he was himself attacked and his aircraft badly damaged, the cockpit filling with smoke and going into a vertical dive. He was unable to see, or right his machine, so he baled out, coming down in a field where some LDVs picked him up with a wrenched neck and back. They reported seeing his fight and that the Me 109 he was attacking came down in flames on land.

Both McNab and Flight Lieutenant Gordon MacGregor witnessed this combat, Nesbitt being credited with the kill – very likely being 3/JG 53's

Oberleutnant Julius Haase, also attacked by 19 Squadron's Flight Sergeant George Unwin and who crashed at Mullard Wood, Northend Farm, Biggin Hill. Nesbitt was admitted to Pembury Hospital, but Pilot Officer Ross Smither was missing, later reported killed when shot down over Tunbridge Wells.

At 12.15 hrs, 66 Squadron sighted the Dorniers still flying north, over London. Led by Flight Lieutenant Ken Gillies, Green 1, as they turned to attack, the ten Spitfires were bounced from above and behind by Me 109s. Although the enemy fighters' fire was ineffective, the British formation was broken up and scattered, only Sergeant Douglas Corfe, Red 3, getting off a quick burst at the fleeting 109s. Pilot Officer Crelin 'Bogle' Bodie lost the squadron but found the bombers again, attacking them twice.

Other fighters were also attacking, but Bodie noted that the enemy fighter escort had now disappeared. After dropping their payloads, the Dorniers wheeled about, turning south, Bodie being joined by Gillies and a Hurricane to attack and damage one of their number. According to the Intelligence Patrol Report:

> The E/A was already riddled with MG fire; the port engine then stopped, the cowling and cabin top both flew off and the starboard engine was smoking. Two of the crew baled out, the rear-gunner attempted to do so, but stuck, hanging from the lower escape hatch. The pilot remained at the controls, but was possibly wounded. The plane eventually crashed on the edge of a wood, ten miles East of Canterbury and exploded.

This was the 3/KG 76 Do 17 down at Sturry, also attacked by pilots of at least three other squadrons.

Green 3, Sergeant Claude Parsons, chased a retreating bomber in and out of cloud, which he last saw 'going down slowly at about 3,000ft somewhere South of Gatwick, its starboard engine smoking badly. He was forced to break off on being attacked himself by an Me 109.'

All of 66 Squadron's Spitfires returned safely to Gravesend.

No.609 Squadron was also in action over the capital at 12.15 hrs, the Canadian Pilot Officer Keith 'Skeets' Ogilvie having a hand in the destruction of Zehbe's Dornier. This action was witnessed by the exiled Queen of the

Netherlands, who 'conveyed her thanks to the Squadron and to the successful pilot ... One portion of this Dornier is reported to have reached the ground just outside a Pimlico public house, to the great joy of the patrons [ORB].'

Other Dorniers were also claimed destroyed by Flight Lieutenant Frank Howell and the American volunteer Pilot Officer Eugene 'Red' Tobin, and Pilot Officer John Curchin one which was also 'attacked by Hurricanes'. Both Flight Lieutenant James McArthur and Flying Officer John Dundas damaged Do 17s, and Pilot Officer Michael Appleby 'also claimed a share in the damage or destruction of one of the Dorniers'.

The 10 Group auxiliary squadron, however, suffered a sad loss: over the capital, Pilot Officer Geoffrey Gaunt was hacked down by a 109 and killed when his Spitfire crashed in flames near Kenley; he was 24.

When scrambled, the Debden Sector's 73 Squadron was at fifteen-minutes availability – but nonetheless the ten Hurricanes were airborne in just five minutes, taking off at 11.10 hrs and joining with 17 Squadron to patrol Chelmsford:

> Blue and Green Sections ('B' Flight) kept in formation while Flying Officer Smith, in command, and Sergeant Leng kept a look-out on one side and Pilot Officer Scott and Pilot Officer Marchand on the other. Near Maidstone [at 12.20 hrs] interception was made, Flying Officer Smith destroying an Me 109 and Pilot Officer McGaw getting another 'destroyed'. Sergeant Webster damaged another 109, Pilot Officer Scott had trouble with his cooling system and left for base by himself. On his way home near Blackwater Estuary he espied a 109 by itself, hopping from cloud to cloud, going south-east, and having stalked it out of the sun, shot it down. Pilot Officer McGaw landed and re-fuelled at Rochford, and Sergeant Leng did likewise at Hawkinge before returning to base. [ORB]

Like 609 Squadron, however, 73 Squadron had suffered a particularly sad loss in Pilot Officer Roy Marchand:

> News came that another pilot of 73 Squadron had landed at Biggin Hill uninjured and as he was the only one missing, we assumed that it was Pilot Officer Marchand, so no one worried about him until the evening

> when we were astounded to be told that he had crashed at Tynham, near Sittingbourne, and was killed. Much sympathy felt for his very young wife who lives in the neighbouring village and it was a horrible task undertaken by the CO, Flying Officer Beytagh, in company with Pilot Officer Hoole, to break the news to her at Dispersal, where she had gone to seek news of her husband. Pilot Officer Marchand was an excellent pilot and a charming, unassuming, boy who was never ruffled by anyone or anything. We will sorely miss him. [ORB]

Marchand, a 22-year-old former medical student, was buried at Bromley.

After 249 Squadron's initial charge over South London, Pilot Officer James Meaker climbed again and at 12.20–12.30 hrs found the bombers heading east, towards Chatham – by which time the Me 109s had deserted them. Meaker targeted the left-hand Dornier of the rearmost formation, executing a quarter attack which stopped the bomber's port engine.

As the Hurricane pilot broke away, he noticed that the bomber had dropped out of formation, and was therefore vulnerable to further attack. Concentrating on the starboard engine, Meaker 'was then joined by Spitfires who also fired at E/A. Large pieces fell off and two crew baled out. E/A crashed about five miles South of Margate.'

By 12.45 hrs the enemy had retired, the RAF fighters then urgently rearming and refuelling in anticipation of another attack. At Air Vice-Marshal Park's underground Operations Room, the Prime Minister had watched the tense proceedings in awe – Park had reacted in strength, with twenty-two of the twenty-three squadrons scrambled engaging the enemy. The defenders had been assisted by the length of time it took the enemy to assemble, owing to the Dorniers being disrupted by cloud and meeting their escorts late – enabling Fighter Command to be airborne, ready and waiting. The late rendezvous of enemy bombers and fighters also worked very much to the defenders' advantage, dictating that the Me 109s had no choice but to turn back early, leaving the Dorniers unescorted – with obvious consequences.

Inevitably however, with so very many fighters engaged simultaneously, combat claims were wildly exaggerated, however, along with the usual misidentification of aircraft types. Some fifty-three bombers were claimed as destroyed, in addition to six probables and nineteen damaged, along with twenty-seven Me 109s destroyed, three probably so and six more damaged.

In reality, KG 76 had lost seven Do 17s destroyed, their crews either dead, missing or prisoners, with four more returning to France damaged. Of the fighter escorts, just nine were lost, and two damaged. Because times are unavailable for all German combat claims involved, it is impossible to say exactly how many Spitfires and Hurricanes were claimed destroyed, but that figure is at least eighteen. Indeed, the after-action report by *Hauptmann* Hans-Karl Mayer, *Kommandeur* of I/JG 53 is telling:

> There are no certain witnesses for the victories because in the air fighting this day the escorts had to break up into individual combats in the face of superior numbers of English fighters.
>
> A large number of aircraft were observed going down in flames by several members of the *Gruppe*. In no case was it possible to observe precisely by whom and how these were shot down.

Two Spitfires and eleven Hurricanes had, in fact, been destroyed, plus two Spitfires and nine Hurricanes damaged; seven RAF pilots had been killed, and eight more wounded (one of whom later died of his injuries).

There can be no doubt that the number of RAF fighters from all 3 groups engaged over the capital – 312 – was a fearsome shock to the enemy – not least when Squadron Leader Bader's 5-squadron strong Duxford Wing appeared over London. Indeed, in the subsequent Luftwaffe report on the action, the size of this formation was over-estimated at 'up to eighty aircraft'. Clearly, this was very far from a defeated air force – and to 66 Squadron's Flight Lieutenant Bob Oxspring, who watched in awe as Bader arrived over London, thought 'this a great sight', which, he had no doubt, 'must have been devastating for the Germans to see that lot coming in all at once'. The Duxford Wing, therefore, for all its faults, did two things on this great day: crushed the enemy's morale while turbo-charging that of the hard-pressed defenders.

Considering the negative effect on Luftwaffe morale and losses, the raid achieved little in terms of damage. The Me 109s of LG 2, having bombed indiscriminately, caused minor damage in Penge, Dulwich, Streatham and Lambeth; railway lines were hit, though, stopping trains running between

Beckenham and Norwood Junctions, and Crystal Palace; a gas main was set alight at Brixton Hill, and unexploded bombs caused disruption. I and III/KG 76 did reach their target, severing the railway network in Battersea as intended. The Pouparts Viaduct had collapsed onto the track below, and further UXBs hampered rescue and repair work. In Battersea and Clapham, twenty-four deaths were reported and more than thirty people were injured.

The quiet that now descended enabled a shift change at the 11 Group Operations Room, the morning's plotters having received a congratulatory 'Well done!' from the happy Prime Minster – who now settled down to await the enemy's next move. The lull would last but an hour.

At 13.45 hrs, RDF forewarned that the Germans were again assembling over Calais and Boulogne. Based around Lille, I and II/KG 53's He 111s had taken-off and headed for the assembly point over the French coast, followed by the Do 17s of II and III/KG 2, flying from Cambrai and St Leger, the Do 17s of II/KG 3 from Antwerp, and the Gilze Rijen He 111s of I and II/KG 26 – 114 bombers in all. This raid, much bigger than the day's previous attack, would be preceded by Me 109s of III/JG 51 sweeping over Kent, while *Major* Adolf Galland led the whole of JG 26 on a *Freie Hunt* on the flanks. On this occasion, each bomber formation was to be closely escorted by a *Gruppe* of Me 109s, with Me 110s of V(Z)/LG 1 and I/ZG 26 also escorting the Heinkels of KG 26: target London's docklands.

At 10.35 hrs, 92 Squadron's Flight Lieutenant Allan Wright had flown from Biggin Hill to Hawkinge, where he was to remain for use as a 'spotter'. Now, he took off, climbing over the Channel, to see exactly and report upon what what the enemy was doing.

At 14.00 hrs, Air Vice-Marshal Park scrambled a number of squadrons in what would be the first deployments of another reaction in strength.

The Spitfires of 222 Squadron scrambled from Rochford, and 603 from Hornchurch, to patrol Sheerness together at 20,000ft.

Hurricanes of 17 and 257 Squadrons from Debden to rendezvous over Chelmsford at 15,000ft.

Hurricanes of Kenley's 501 Squadron to meet those of Croydon's 605 over Kenley – at 15,000ft.

Hurricanes of 249 Squadron from North Weald and 504 Squadron from Hendon, with instructions to rendezvous over Hornchurch at 15,000ft.

At 14.05 hrs, the Germans struck out across the Channel – and immediately Park scrambled more squadrons: Spitfires of 41 Squadron from Hornchurch to meet over that aerodrome those of Biggin Hill's 92 Squadron, to patrol at 20,000ft, and Hurricanes of 1(RCAF) and 229 Squadrons to patrol their Northolt base.

Again, the Spitfire, with its superior high-altitude performance, was being deployed as a shield to protect the Hurricanes positioned to attack the enemy bombers lower down.

At that time, 14.05 hrs, Flight Lieutenant Wright was high over the Channel on his 'spotter' patrol and reported German aircraft approaching – but too far distant to identity. This was a *Schwarm* of Me 109s, which approached the Spitfire pilot – who, having a height advantage of 2,000ft, dived upon the enemy fighters. He selected a 109 to attack, which turned north and dived vertically at great speed – the Spitfire struggling to keep up. Having neither time to trim his aircraft before plunging after the diving 109, or a hand free to do so, Wright's ailerons, at such a high speed and G force, locked up, pulling the aircraft sharply out of the dive, the pilot blacking out. Upon regaining consciousness, Wright was inverted at 7,000ft – straightening up, the vulnerable, lone, 'spotter' sped north and out of harm's way.

Continuing with his reaction in strength, at 14.10 hrs Air Vice-Marshal Park scrambled 41 Squadron's Spitfires from Hornchurch to patrol base at 25,000ft, and ordered 46 Squadron's Hurricanes from Stapleford Tawney to patrol London's dockland. The Spitfires of 66 Squadron left Gravesend, and those of 72 from Biggin Hill, to rendezvous over the latter at 20,000ft, and 'B' Flight of 73 Squadron from Castle Camps to patrol over Maidstone at 15,000ft.

At 14.15 hrs, 11 Group scrambled 253's Hurricanes from Kenley to patrol base at 15,000ft, and those of Tangmere's 213 and 607 Squadrons to patrol the Biggin Hill – Kenley Line, also at 15,000ft. At the same time, assistance having been requested by Air Vice-Marshal Park, 10 Group's 238 Squadron took-off, the Hurricanes first order to patrol their Middle Wallop base before vectored to the Brooklands – Kenley Line. Also at 14.15 hrs, Squadron Leader Douglas Bader led the five-squadron-strong 12 Group Wing, again comprising the Spitfires of 19 and 611 Squadrons, and the Hurricanes of 242, 302 (Polish) and 310 (Czech) Squadrons, off to patrol Hornchurch at 25,000ft.

Considering that only a relatively short time before 312 RAF fighters had been in action, it can only considered a great tribute to the ground personnel involved that so many aircraft were so rapidly 'turned around' and able to fight again so soon.

The enormity of what was happening was not lost on the Prime Minister, deep underground at Uxbridge:

> Hitherto, I had watched in silence. I now asked: 'What reserves have we?'
>
> 'There are none', said Air Vice-Marshal Park. In an account he wrote about it afterwards he said that at this I 'looked grave'. Well I might. What losses should we not suffer if our refuelling planes were caught on the ground by further raids of '40+' or '50+'! The odds were great; our margins small; the stakes infinite.

By this time, London's civil defenders were at readiness: Air-Raid Warning Yellow, then Red – attack imminent – the siren's banshee wail announcing the raiders' approach to frightened Londoners – who immediately scurried for shelter. It would be a saving grace, however, that the cloud over the capital and south-east England had increased: cloud-base was now 3,000ft, extending to 12,000ft, with a 7/10ths covering of cumulus. In the battle ahead, this would prove significant.

At 14.10 hrs, the German bomber force, occupying a front six miles wide and five deep, crossed the Kentish coast over Dungeness, turning north-west, to pass over Maidstone before continuing on that course until reaching the Thames just west of Gravesend, the intention being to then follow the river upstream to East London. In the lead, flying abreast at 22,000ft, were, from the left, III/KG 2's Do 17s, I and II/KG 53's He 111s, and on the right, II/KG 3. Bringing up the rear, also in Gruppen line abreast, were II/KG 2's Do 17s on the left, and I and II/KG 26 on the right. With Me 109s on both flanks and below, and Me 110s above, the steel-helmeted bomber crews felt confident and well-protected.

At 14.20 hrs, Air Vice-Marshal Park scrambled further squadrons: the Poles of 303 Squadron took-off from Northolt to patrol base at 20,000ft, and 602 Squadron was sent from Westhampnett to the line Kenley – Biggin Hill – Gravesend. Then, at 14.28 hrs, 10 Group's 609 Squadron headed to its usual patrol area over Brooklands.

Over Hornchurch, the Spitfires of 41 and 92 Squadron rendezvoused as ordered. Commanding the latter was Squadron Leader Phillip James 'Judy' Sanders – 'Ganic Leader', who sighted the most northerly enemy bombers at 14.30 hrs over Maidstone:

> I then turned and climbed steeply on a southerly course, watching enemy fighter smoke trails to the ESE. At about 20,000ft I saw a large formation of enemy bombers passing underneath us from the ESE. Enemy fighters seemed too far away to protect them so I ordered line astern and peeled off to the right, on top and behind them. I singled out the Do 17 on the right of the formation.
>
> I fired a long steady burst of 4 to 5 seconds, diving from the right. I closed to about 75 yards and saw large pieces coming adrift from the top of the fuselage and starboard engines. As I broke away downwards one of the crew, presumably the rear-gunner, baled out. The E/A was behaving in an erratic manner and leaving a heavy smoke trail from the starboard engine when I saw it last.

Unteroffizier K. Falke, who had taken to his parachute, was captured unhurt at Fawkham. This Do 17, of 5/KG 3, was that of the *Staffelkapitän*, *Hauptmann* E. Püttmann and crashed into the Thames Estuary, killing the remaining crew.

The day's killing had resumed.

Pilot Officer Howard Hill, a New Zealander, was Green 2, and together with his Section Leader, Pilot Officer Dennis Williams, carried out beam attacks on a 4/KG 3 Do 17 over Hornchurch. After several passes and short bursts from just 20–30 yards, the bomber began smoking and *Unteroffizier* G. Friebe baled out and was captured.

Attacked by various other RAF pilots, the Dornier eventually crashed and exploded in Gladstone Road, Billericay, killing all aboard. Hill then climbed and when at 10,000ft: 'I saw a He 111 heading East, just above cloud level. I carried out three beam attacks from slightly ahead and above, breaking away at about 50 yards, and below. This aircraft crashed in the edge of a wood South of the Estuary and exploded. Crew baled out.'

This Heinkel belonged to 3/KG 53 and crashed at Bourne Farm, Sandhurst, having also been attacked by various other pilots; two of the crew were killed, the other three captured.

Hill then attacked another He 111, 'which after two beam attacks landed undercarriage up on Maidstone aerodrome' – a 5/KG 53 aircraft which also featured in numerous pilots' combat reports, the pilot forced-landed on West Malling airfield; again, two of the crew were killed, three captured.

Still, however, Hill was not finished: 'I then climbed again and as I was about to enter cloud saw a He 111 coming through. I carried out two beam attacks, also one stern attack, and E/A finally crashed into a block of houses near Rochester.' This was not, however, a 'He 111' but an 8/KG 2 Do 17, also attacked by pilots of 253 and 66 Squadrons. The enemy pilot had actually tried to forced-land on Rochester airfield but as the aircraft passed over the North Downs at Bluebell Hill, the Burham-based 166 Battery of the 55th Heavy AA Regiment, RA, opened fire.

The Dornier was hit and broke in half, the crew wasting no time in baling out. The fuselage crashed into the garden of 13 The Chase, City Way, Chatham, and the tail ended up on the roof. The occupants were sheltering in the garden, and 18-year-old Ronald Seaborn was admitted to St Bart's Hospital with fatal injuries (of which he died on 21 November 1940). An LDV volunteer, Cyril 'Sandy' Le Gassick, had watched proceedings from his nearby garden and went off on his bicycle, rifle slung over his shoulder, in search of the parachutists. Finding one of the Germans dangling from a tree in his parachute, Le Gassick took the airman into custody, marching him to Walderslade Police Station.

Pilot Officer Dennis Williams, Green 1, attacked a straggling Do 17 together with 'two Hurricanes and one Spitfire. We shot him down and all the crew baled out.' This being the Gladstone Road Dornier – also attacked, among others, by Pilot Officer Hill. Williams then attacked another straggler, a He 111 of *Stab* II/KG 53 which eventually disappeared into cloud, on fire, over Hendon. Various other 92 Squadron pilots also attacked this bomber, which crashed near Staplehurst after being abandoned by five of the crew – all of whom including the *Gruppenkommandeur*, *Major* M. Gruber; a sixth man, *Feldwebel* A. Grassl, was killed during the Spitfires' attacks.

Other 92 Squadron pilots also claiming German bombers as destroyed, probably destroyed and damaged – but Pilot Officer Trevor Wade, Red 2, went for,

> a formation of Me 109s about 1,500ft above and a half a mile behind the bombers. I fired a short burst at about 150 yards head-on from starboard quarter. I saw it break away downwards with smoke coming out. I dived away myself as I was being attacked by numerous 109s.

Hauptmann Fritz Losigkeit, *Staffelkapitän* of 2/JG 26, recalled:

> After we crossed the coast, the British fighters came in from a great height, going very fast. They broke through to the He 111s ahead of us and below, to attack the rear of the formation. During the dive, some of the Spitfires became detached from the others. Using full throttle, my *Staffel* was able to catch them up and I got into an attacking position. I fired a long burst and pieces broke away from the Spitfire's wing and fuselage. The pilot slid back the canopy and jumped from the cockpit. Overtaking rapidly, I pulled to the Spitfire's left and saw his parachute open.

Losigkeit had shot down Pilot Officer Bob Holland of 92 Squadron, who baled out west of Ashford, wounded, and was admitted to East Grinstead Hospital. Pilot Officer Tony Bartley was also shot-up, but was unhurt and returned his badly damaged Spitfire to Biggin Hill.

The Spitfires of 41 Squadron, operating with 92, also went into action at the same time. Flying Officer John Boyle, a Canadian,

> was Blue 4, doing look-out for 'Mitor' Squadron … Three Me 109s came out of the sun and I turned towards them. Gave a continuous burst at an Me 109 which was attacking head-on – range opened at 500 yards and closed to avoid collision. Smoke and flames came out of the 109 and it spun down. I then drove straight at the bomber formation from 1,000ft above. I opened fire with full deflection and broke off to avoid collision. No damage done. I then noticed a lone Do 17 making for the clouds – I followed and gave a short burst. Mitor Leader [Flight Lieutenant Norman Ryder] attacked same Do 17. Two Hurricanes came in and attacked before I turned back for my-second burst. Do 17 came down on the Isle of Sheppey.

This Do 17 belonged to 4/KG 3, and also attacked by pilots of 310 and 603 Squadrons. The bomber forced-landed on the Isle of Grain, where the crew were captured.

Pilot Officer Eric 'Sawn Off' Lock, Red 3:

> We sighted a large formation of E/A. We were in line astern and peeled off to port. We delivered our attack and I broke away to starboard. I started to climb again and sighted a formation of three Do 17s escorted by three Me 109s just above the clouds. I saw a Hurricane attack the Me 109s so I joined him. He shot one down in flames as I was attacking. I attacked from behind and underneath, rather a long burst. He went into a vertical dive, on fire.
>
> The Hurricane pilot then beckoned me to attack the three Do 17s so we selected one each. We both delivered an astern attack, to stop the rear MG; this seemed rather effective. We then carried out quarter attacks. When I had delivered my second attack, the starboard engine burst into flames and [the E/A] dived into the sea.
>
> By now, the other two Do 17s had dived to sea-level. We carried out quarter and beam attacks on the remainder. After a while the starboard engine caught fire and he also landed in the sea, by a convoy, but this was shot down by Hurricanes 30–40 miles south-east of Clacton. I left the other Do 17 being chased by the Hurricane as I had no ammunition.

Both Dorniers belonged wo 8/KG 2.

Like 92 Squadron, 41 Squadron's pilots would make multiple combat claims, all for no loss.

As ordered, 222 and 603 Squadrons were patrolling Sheerness at 20,000ft when, the former's Intelligence Patrol Report describes:

> Enemy machines consisting of Do 17s, Ju 88 [*sic*], Me 110 and Me 109 were sighted in great numbers and spread over a wide area. Our fighters attacked the bombers and were themselves attacked in turn by superior numbers of Me 109s. The bombers were working in sections of three in a long narrow formation with 109s below and 110s about 4,000ft above, forming defensive circle of criss-cross. The bombers were

> at 22,000ft. The combats took place between Chatham-Canterbury- and Dungeness areas.

Flight Lieutenant Eric 'Tommy' Thomas – who had been among the very first Spitfire pilots when 19 Squadron received the Spitfire in 1938 – was commanding 222 Squadron's 'B' Flight, and reported that:

> Our formation having been broken up by enemy fighters, I dropped to 10,000ft and noticed black anti-aircraft fire about ten miles away at about 10,000ft in the direction of Chatham. By this time I was alone and saw a Do 17 flying alone, due East. I disregarded the AA fire and went in a beam attack out of the sun and managed to get in a short burst at long range, about 400 yards.
>
> The E/A then disappeared in a cloud bank. I set my course due East and kept above the clouds, and about four miles further on the Do 17 arrived, flying due East again. I did an astern attack and closed from 300 to 50 yards, firing all the time. I saw pieces of aircraft flying off and rear-gun fire stopped. Just then a yellow-nosed Me 109 got on my tail – I broke off the attack and took cover in cloud. The Do 17 had disappeared when I came up again to look for it.

Thomas's attack had been delivered between Chatham and Canterbury, in concert with Pilot Officer Ronald 'Raz' Berry of 603 Squadron, also based at Hornchurch. According to the latter Squadron's 'Fighter Command Form "F"', the Do 17 concerned 'crashed near Maidstone', the bomber's destruction shared between the two Spitfire pilots. This was the 4/KG 3 Do 17 down on the Isle of Grain. It was the first time 'Tommy' had fired his guns in anger.

No.222 Squadron's Flying Officer Des McMullen chased an Me 109 back across the Channel, which 'blew up in air over Calais', and also damaged an Me 110, setting its 'port engine on fire'. Pilot Officer John Broadhurst also damaged a 110, noting 'pieces flying off it', and Sergeant Arthur Spears hit an Me 109 which 'turned over and spun into clouds'. The South African Flying Officer Brian van Mentz claimed a 'Ju 88 [*sic*]' damaged, which he 'helped to bring it down, shared with a Hurricane'. All seven of the squadron's Spitfires returned safely to base, 'without suffering anything but very minor damage – mostly ricochets'.

Ten miles south-east of Chatham, the Spitfire pilots of Squadron Leader 'Uncle' George Denholm's 603 Squadron also sighted the vast enemy armada approaching. Pilot Officer Keith Lawrence, a New Zealander, was Yellow 2, and engaged south-east of Maidstone:

> I went in to attack with the Squadron a formation of approximately 30 Do 17s and He 111s 3,000ft below. Due to the awkward approach and excessive speed on reaching the bombers, I pulled up to engage the Me 109s coming down, one of which I chased and opened fire at 75 yards, and after about 6 seconds, and having closed to about 30 yards, it went up steeply and then fell away in a spin and was still spinning on entering cloud. 109 lost control about 18,000ft. I used the remainder of my ammunition on two Me 109s which dived into the clouds. Range in both cases approximately 30 yards.

Sergeant George Bailey also claimed a 109 destroyed, and Pilot Officer Ronald 'Raz' Berry a probable. Squadron Leader Denholm managed to get through to the bombers, damaging two Do 17s, but was hit by return fire and forced to bale out near Hastings; he landed unhurt near Guestling Lodge, Fairlight. Pilot Officers Berry and the South African Basil 'Stapme' Stapleton both claimed Do 17s destroyed, and Flying Officer Brian MacNamara damaged one. Back at Hornchurch, however, a pilot was missing: Pilot Officer Peter Pease.

Pease, an Old Etonian, was the son of Sir Richard and Lady Pease of Richmond, Yorkshire. While studying history at Trinity, Cambridge, he had joined the University Air Squadron, later becoming an army cooperation pilot. While training for that role at Old Sarum, he met and became a close friend of Pilot Officer Richard Hillary, with whom he would be posted to 603 Squadron on 6 July 1940. Hillary had been shot down and terribly burned on 3 September 1940 (see Volume 4) and, before perishing in a flying accident, later published the classic, soul-searching, memoir *The Last Enemy*. Within, Hillary described envisioning Pease's death in action while under anaesthetic, coming to and shouting 'Peter! For God's sake look out behind!' Pease had indeed been shot down and killed, crashing near Chartway Street in Kent; he was 22.

By 14.30 hrs, the sky was a mass of aircraft, as defending squadrons hastened to engage the enemy formations, which found themselves under attack from all sides.

No.605 Squadron, led by Flight Lieutenant Archie McKellar, had met as planned with 501 Squadron, and set off on various vectors, McKellar leading the formation, until meeting the incoming enemy at 14.15 hrs over Maidstone. No.501 Squadron was attacked by Me 109s and broken up, but suffered no losses; individual dogfights ensued, during which Sergeant James 'Ginger' Lacey DFM destroyed a He 111 and an Me 109. Flight Lieutenant McKellar reported that, after sighting the incoming Do 17s:

> I instructed Red Section to take the leading vic, whilst I, with my Section, would attack one of the outside and rearmost vics. Head-on, I did a slight diving head-on attack and allowing a 1/3 top deflection, bringing my sight up, and the starboard wing of the E/A fell off 1/3 from the tip. I broke downwards and into the direction of the sun and started to climb up again, endeavouring to get members of my Squadron to join up with me, and Blue 2 did so. I then saw tracer flying past my left wing and saw an Me 109 attack me.
>
> I turned quickly to the right and lost sight of him as he dived off. I then noticed tracer going past my right wing from another Me 109. I dodged him and continued climbing into the sun. By this time another bomber formation of 24 was approaching the capital with no obvious fighter escort. I informed 'Runic' [Kenley Control] and carried out a head-on attack on the leader of the formation [He 111s], and saw his Perspex burst and the E/A spun down. I broke off and dived down.
>
> I then again climbed up into the sun and joined up with another Hurricane squadron, whose lettering I could not see. They were going in the direction of the He 111s, who were by now going south-east. I then noticed another large formation, much larger than the previous two formations. I flew in front of the Hurricane squadron in an attempt to lead them onto this lot, but they continued to follow the retreating He 111s. I informed 'Runic' of this large formation and went off on my own to try and have a crack at them, as I could see no fighter escort. I again attacked the leader head-on but could see no result.

> I broke downwards and then noticed six Me 109s coming down on me. I therefore did a spin into the clouds and came out south-east of base, landing at 15.00 hrs.

McKellar was credited with a Do 17 and a He 111 probable, while his counterpart, Flight Lieutenant Christopher 'Bunny' Currant, claimed an Me 109 destroyed, and two Do 17s and a He 111 damaged. Another Do 17 was claimed destroyed by Sergeant Harold Howes, and one damaged by Pilot Officer Edward Watson. Pilot Officer Tom Cooper-Slipper destroyed a Do 17, and,

> had a remarkable escape. His control was shot away and his aircraft hit a Do 17 amidships. Pilot Officer Cooper-Slipper, aircraft, minus port wing, spiralled down and he baled out, landing unhurt, other than small bruises, near Marden. He returned to Croydon later in the evening, apparently unshaken, with two German Mae Wests and complete rubber boat, given to him by Maidstone Police! [ORB]

The Do 17 concerned belonged to 5/KG 3 and also crashed at Marden. One of the crew baled out too low and was killed, the remainder landing safely by parachute to become prisoners for the duration.

The Tangmere-based Hurricanes of 213 Squadron were south of Biggin Hill when these pilots also sighted the enemy approaching London. Flight Lieutenant John 'Jackie' Sing was leading the squadron and ordered a head-on attack on the Do 17s, the Intelligence Patrol Report describing the action:

> Flight Lieutenant Sing singled out one E/A and shot away the whole of the nose, including the pilot's cockpit. The aircraft went into a steep dive and a probable is claimed. Sub-Lieutenant Jeram, Green 2, and Flying Officer Duryasz [Polish], Red 3, both went right through the same formation and then, turning back, attacked astern an E/A each and both claim one Do 17 each destroyed, as they followed their opponents down and saw them blazing on the ground.
>
> Green 1, Flight Sergeant Grayson, carried out an astern attack on another and after several bursts saw it go down in an absolutely vertical dive, out of control, and claims a probable. Sergeant Bushell carried out

> astern attack on a Do 17 and damaged it. Blue 2 [Pilot Officer Cottam] dived vertically onto a Do 17, damaged it, and having lost it proceeded to Dungeness on the look-out for stragglers, and having found an Me 110 he attacked it, and using deflection, shot it down into the sea. The crew of this E/A was seen in the water.

The report states that 'one of our sergeant-pilots made a forced-landing at Detling', his aircraft being 'Category 2', meaning damaged but repairable, but who this was is unrecorded. Sergeant Michael Croskell was shot down, however, and baled out, wounded, and Sergeant Reginald Llewellyn, was also shot down and baled out with 'a bullet wound in one shoulder'.

Having left Kenley at 14.15 hrs, eight Hurricanes of 253 Squadron, Squadron Leader Gerry Edge, were at just 4,000ft when the massive enemy formation was sighted ten miles south-east of base, heading north-west. The squadron climbed and endeavoured to position for a head-on attack, but when fifteen Me 110s dived on the British fighters, Edge ordered a beam attack at very close range.

After the initial attack, 253's pilots engaged individually. Red 3, Sergeant Robert Innes pursued and caught a 'Do 215 [*sic*]' in cloud, and, according to the Intelligence Patrol Report, 'on opening fire saw three parachutes opening behind E/A, which crashed South of the river at Chatham'. Yellow 3, Sergeant Allan Dredge, attacked a Dornier three times, leaving it 'heading South, port engine stopped and starboard engine belching black smoke, and losing height'. The squadron's only casualty was Pilot Officer Anthony Barton, whose Hurricane was hit by a Dornier's return fire, forcing him to land at Hawkinge, fortunately unhurt.

As the Dorniers approached London's docklands, Wing Commander Victor Beamish, North Weald's Station Commander, was again patrolling with 249 Squadron. No.249 Squadron's main attack was against the incoming Do 17s, but Beamish went for the rearmost aircraft in a formation of He 111s, giving it a long burst which left an engine 'smoking badly', after which the bomber was 'attacked by a Spitfire'.

After a second attack by Beamish, both engines were 'pouring smoke, the undercarriage had dropped down, and the E/A was disappearing vertically for the ground'. Finishing off what little ammunition he had left on another He 111, without visible effect, Beamish, the highest-ranking RAF officer in action on this great day, returned to base. In total, 249 Squadron would claim eight Dorniers destroyed, four probables and one damaged, and two He 111s destroyed, three probables, and two Me 109s damaged. The squadron's only casualty was Flying Officer Keith Lofts, who was shot-up attacking a He 111 and crash-landed at West Malling, unhurt.

According to 504 Squadron's Intelligence Patrol Report, the enemy was met flying towards London near Gravesend at 14.30 hrs, the bombers 'well escorted in all directions by Me 109s', which, somewhat surprisingly, 'did not attack our aircraft'. Squadron Leader John Sample DFC put the Hurricanes into sections line astern and attacked the Do 17s from abeam, breaking up the formation. Sample engaged a 4/KG 3 Do 17 attempting to find refuge in clouds, the crew of which baled out, their bomber crashing into Perry Street, Dartford. Pilot Officer John Hardacre claimed a Do 17 destroyed, this being the 4/KG 3 machine also featuring in various other pilots' combat reports which crashed in flames onto Gladstone Road, Laindon Hills, Billericay – indicating the dangers of living below these aerial combats.

The He 111s were then seen following the first wave of Dorniers, Sample and Pilot Officer Trevor Parsons joining in the destruction of the 5/KG 53 He 111 which forced-landed on West Malling airfield. Pilot Officer Michael Jebb, however, was shot down and crashed near Dartford, 504 Squadron receiving news 'that he was in Dartford Hospital gravely burnt and wounded' – sadly, Jebb, the 22-year-old son of Brigadier General G.D. Jebb, would succumb to his injuries four days later.

The pilots of 46 Squadron had actually become separated while climbing through cloud, 'the main body of the Squadron never saw the enemy [ORB]'. Flying alone over the Thames Estuary, Pilot Officer William Pattullo was,

> attacked by six orange-nosed Me 109s. I evaded these and after losing them sighted a Do 17 on the fringe of cloud at 10,000ft. I attacked and put the rear gunners out of action and in the same burst set the starboard engine on fire. This aircraft promptly lost height and prepared to pancake in the Thames, East of the Isle of Sheppey. Whilst gliding down he released what appeared to be a very heavy calibre bomb at about 100ft. This bomb did not explode. Only the pilot left the aircraft on hitting the water, and the aircraft sank in roughly 30 seconds. A

> naval pinnacle proceeded to the point immediately and presumably took the pilot prisoner.

The 9/KG 2's Do 17 crashed into the water off Herne Bay and, in fact, two of crew were picked up by the Royal Navy.

Over Southend, 46 Squadron's Pilot Officer Allan Johnson claimed a 'Ju 8 [*sic*]' destroyed, the Stapleford-based Hurricanes suffering no loss during the engagement.

As the enormous 'Valhalla' reached Gravesend and turned NNW, following the Thames to London, the enemy was reportedly sighted at 14.30 hrs by 66 Squadron – and immediately engaged. Flight Lieutenant Bob Oxspring, commanding 'B' Flight, was leading the rearmost section, guarding the Spitfires' tails. A *Schwarm* of Me 109s 3,000ft above, however, did not attack as anticipated, so 'Oxo' led his Section in a gentle dive down-sun to attack the He 111s, concentrating his fire on the leading Heinkel as the fighters passed through the German bomber formation. No return fire was experienced, leading Oxspring to conclude that the interception 'had been a complete surprise'. He then saw,

> another He 111 sinking towards the clouds with its wheels down and several fighters attacking it. I got in a short burst just before it went into cloud, resulting in something flying off it. I followed it and continued attacks by other fighters until it landed at West Malling.

Attacked by multiple RAF fighter pilots, two of this 5/KG 53 crew were killed and two captured. Oxspring then evaded an Me 109 and saw,

> a Do 17 climbing quite rapidly towards the cloud, steering West, almost over Rochester aerodrome. I attacked from the beam, allowing full deflection, and closing round almost astern to about 35 yards. During the burst two people baled out and I wheeled around and started another attack whereupon one, whom I thought was the pilot, jumped. I think there were four in all. The E/A then did a spiral dive to the right until it got steeper and crashed in a garden about ¾ mile South of Chatham, hitting the house and bursting into flames.

This was, of course, the 8/KG 2 Do 17 which crashed on 13 The Chase.

Like the other squadrons, 66's combat claims were exaggerated: five Do 17s destroyed and one damaged, two He 111s destroyed, a probable, and two damaged along with two Me 109s probably destroyed. 'Clickety-Click' suffered no losses.

No.72 Squadron was operating as ordered with 66, engaging at the same time, subsequently claiming three He 111s destroyed, one probable and another damaged, noting that 'The enemy fighters did not appear to afford the bombers any protection [ORB].' All eight of 72's Spitfires landed safely at 15.15 hrs.

Led by its new CO, Squadron Leader Robert Stanford Tuck DFC, 257 Squadron had joined up with 17 Squadron over Chelmsford and also contacted the enemy at 14.30 hrs, near Gravesend. Tuck later recalled the engagement:

> This was the first time that I took my 257 'Burma' Squadron into action. We found a big bunch of mixed bombers, flying in formations of anything from 30 to 60, with escorting fighters above them. As I led my new Squadron in, I saw three of these parties nearing London. As the boys waded into the bombers, I went for some of the fighters. I picked off an Me 110 which I shot down over Barking, and one of his pals nearly got his own back when he put a bullet through my windscreen a few inches from my head.

The Me 110 destroyed by Tuck belonged to 1/LG 2 and crashed into Hartlip churchyard, near Rainham.

Pilot Officers Arthur Cochrane and Percival Mortimer, Blue 1 and 2, were initially forced to turn away from the bombers owing to AA fire, and were then bounced from out of the sun by Me 109s. Having successfully evaded the German fighters, the Hurricanes then found a He 111 which they attacked with another Hurricane and a Spitfire; they pursued it until the bomber 'landed wheels-down in the mud at Foulness Point', this being the 1/KG 26 aircraft featuring in many combat claims, the crew of which were captured. Pilot Officer Alan Hedges claimed a He 111 damaged, and an Me 109 probably destroyed by Tuck completed the squadron's 'bag'. It had been a successful 'first outing', 257 Squadron suffering no loss, Tuck recalling that 'there was quite a party of the Mess that night!'

The Canadians of 1(RCAF) Squadron were also among the defending squadrons in action at 14.30 hrs, Squadron Leader Eric McNab's men claiming two He 111s destroyed, two probables and three damaged, together with an Me 109 probable. The Northolt-based squadron's only casualty was Pilot Officer Arthur 'Art' Yuile being shot-up and wounded in the shoulder, 'but courageously brought his aircraft home safely. Squadron Leader Foss from RCAF HQ witnessed this action [ORB].'

Yet another Hurricane squadron sighting the enemy approaching London at 14.30 hrs was Squadron Leader Arthur Banham's 229 Squadron, also up from Northolt. Banham ordered his pilots into line-astern and turned to attack the He 111s from the sun, as 1(RCAF) Squadron turned east to attack the middle and rear of the formation. Banham saw his bullets striking the engines of a He 111, which disappeared into cloud, and another Heinkel was damaged by William Smith. Flight Lieutenant Frank Rimmer, and Pilot Officers Vernon Bright and Geoffrey Simpson then joined with Hurricanes of 1(RCAF) Squadron to attack a He 111, which was under fire from 'four Spitfires and three Hurricanes before he crash-landed on West Malling aerodrome', this being the 5/KG 53 aircraft. All of Banham's pilots returned safely to base.

At this time, some 276 RAF fighters were airborne, less than during the lunchtime engagement (312), and by now virtually all squadrons were engaged.

All of the red lights in Air Vice-Marshal Park's 11 Group HQ would again be illuminated on this day of high drama and derring-do. Churchill, still watching proceedings, observed:

> A subdued hum arose from the floor, where the busy plotters pushed their discs to and fro in accordance with the swiftly-changing situation. Air Vice-Marshal Park gave general directions for the dispositions of his fighter force, which were translated into detailed orders to each Fighter Station by a youngish officer in the centre of the Dress Circle, at whose side I sat. Some years after I asked his name. He was Lord Willoughby de Broke. He now gave orders for individual squadrons to ascend and patrol as the result of the final information which appeared on the map-table. The Air Marshal himself walked up and down behind,

> watching with vigilant eye every move in the game, supervising his junior executive hand, and only occasionally intervening with some decisive order, usually to reinforce a threatened area. In a little while all our squadrons were fighting, and some had already begun to return for fuel. There was not one squadron left in reserve.

As Squadron Leader Brian Lane DFC, the CO of 19 Squadron, later wrote, the Duxford Wing 'ran into the whole Luftwaffe over London. Wave after wave of bombers covered by several hundred fighters.' Unfortunately, the 'whole Luftwaffe' was some 4,000ft above the wing, and as the 12 Group fighters climbed, the Me 109s inevitably plunged down; Squadron Leader Douglas Bader, once more leading the five-squadron-strong wing, reported that:

> On being attacked from behind by Me 109, I ordered 'Break up!' and pulled up and round violently. Coming off my back partially blacked out, nearly collided with Yellow 2 [Pilot Officer Crowley-Milling]. Spun in his slipstream and straightened out at 5,000ft below without firing a shot. Climbed up again and saw E/A twin-engine aircraft flying westwards. Just got in range and fired a short burst (3 seconds) in a completely stalled position and then spun off again and lost more height.

Pilot Officer Denis Crowley-Milling was startled at so narrowly avoiding collision with his leader, but nonetheless latched on to the tail of a 109, remaining there in spite of the German's violent evasive manoeuvres; Yellow 2 fired a 'good burst', igniting his target's cockpit area before the pilot, *Oberfeldwebel* Hessel of 1/JG 3, baled out.

Yellow 1 of 242 Squadron, Pilot Officer Noel Stansfeld, joined two other Hurricanes attacking the 5/KG 53 He 111 which forced-landed on West Malling airfield.

Although 310 Squadron had intended to attack the bombers, the 109's intervention dictated otherwise; the Czechs were,

> themselves attacked by the Me 109s as the wing formation was broken up. F/Lt Jeffries ordered the squadron to climb to 24,000ft into the sun when another large formation of E/A were seen approaching from the

> South. The Squadron delayed the attack until they turned and when faced West, a head-on attack was launched out of the sun. [ORB]

The *Kommodore* of JG 26, *Major* Adolf Galland, singled out the Hurricane of 310 Squadron's Sergeant Josef Hubacek:

> With the *Stabstaffel* I attacked two Hurricanes, which were about 800 metres below us. Maintaining surprise, I closed on the wingman and opened fire from 120 metres, as he was in a gentle turn to the left. The enemy plane reeled as my rounds struck the nose from below, and pieces fell from the left wing and fuselage. The left side of the fuselage burst into flame.

Galland's Katchmarek, *Oberleutnant* Horten, had shot down the CO of 310 Squadron, Squadron Leader Sacha Hess: 'I had the impression that there was machine-gun fire behind me. I looked back several times but saw nothing. I re-trimmed the aircraft but at that moment I was hit – I do not know by what.'

Hess baled out, landing at Billericay 'little worse except for bruises'.

Some of 310 Squadron's pilots did manage to get through to the bombers; Sergeants Edward Prchal and Josef Rechka joined the queue of RAF fighters attacking the He 111 which crashed at Asplin's Head, and Sergeant Bohumir Furst, together with Flying Officer Blair Russell of 1(RCAF) Squadron destroyed a *Stab* KG 53 He 111 which crashed and exploded in the shell-filling area of Woolwich Arsenal. Pilot Officer Stanislav Fejfar claimed the Do 17 which forced-landed on the Isle of Grain, the same enemy bomber appearing in the combat reports of at least three Spitfire pilots from 41 and 603 Squadrons.

Squadron Leader Jack Satchell had climbed his 302 (Polish) Squadron hard after 242 and 310 Squadrons, but as he prepared to attack a formation of bombers, an Me 109 fired at his Hurricane, but overshot. Giving chase, Satchell fired, the 109 rolling inverted and diving earthwards. Some of Satchell's Poles reached the bombers: Flight Lieutenant Tadeusz Chlopik, Red Leader, attacked a Do 17 which other pilots later confirmed had 'disintegrated'.

In a subsequent combat, however, Chlopik was hit by another bomber's return fire and baled out – but was killed when his parachute failed. Pilot

Officer Stanislaw Lapka was also shot down attacking a Do 17, but baled out safely; Sergeant Julian Kowalski attacked a straggling bomber from just 30 yards, blowing its tail clean off. Later, a machine-gun panel of his Hurricane flapped open, negatively affecting the aircraft's flying qualities, forcing Kowalski to land in a nearby field.

The 611 Squadron ORB provides a stirring account of a Spitfire squadron engaged in this action:

> [No.]611 Squadron ran into several formations of bombers before sufficient height could be reached so ignored them, attempting to get height in Westerly direction to keep Me 109s off wing. The squadron consisted of 8 aircraft in three sections flying line astern. It was not possible to out climb the Me 109s and the wing appeared to be both attacking and being attacked.
>
> When at 20,000 feet over West London, the Squadron Leader sighted a formation of 25 Do 17s proceeding South unmolested and being by then separated from the wing, gave the order Sections Echelon Right. The Squadron dived down on the formation, coming out of the sun. At the end of the general attack, Me 110s came down. S/Ldr McComb attacked rear E/A. Rear gunner ceased firing and smoke appeared from port engine. He then pulled up into a loop and dived again in inverted position. Guns worked perfectly in this position and E/A went down in flames.
>
> Result of attack is confirmed by Yellow Two and Yellow Leader. S/Ldr McComb then blacked out badly and came to in the clouds. After looking around and seeing nothing he returned to base. P/O Williams carried out a No. 3 FC attack on an He 111. A-second burst at 80 yards was given but no result observed. E/A returned machine-gun fire. He was unable then to return to Squadron which had now broken up, but observing two enemy formations, he made an astern attack on No. 3 of the last section of the formation of Do 215.
>
> The formation turned north but Red 2's target fell out, losing height. He then carried out another attack finishing his ammunition. E/A descended into the clouds, one engine stopped, Red Two following. Cloud was 2,000 feet thick and on emerging no E/A was visible but two minutes later he saw enemy airman descending by parachute.

Latter landed on edge of wood corner of Hawkhurst Golf Club about 15 miles North of Hastings.

F/Lt Leather followed Red Leader into attack astern and took machine next to his as his target was already aflame. He fired all ammunition and when broke away the Do 17 was in flames. He then was forced to land at Croydon at 1540 hours, from where he later took-off to rejoin the Squadron.

P/O Brown had first to evade enemy fighters and then put one short burst into the Do 215 already attacked by Red Leader which had one engine out of action. Oil or glycol from E/A covered up windscreen and so he had to break away. Then he attacked one E/A which broke away from formation using deflection. E/A went into a steep spiral dive with escape hatch over pilot's seat open. No further results seen as large formation of Me 110s appeared and Yellow Two escaped into cloud.

P/O Lund attacked a Do 215 which was also being attacked by several other aircraft. He saw flashes of fire and smoke coming from E/A. While climbing back to main formation of bombers, one Me 110 came down on him so he fired one short burst before turning away and down. As the E/A passed his port side, black smoke was pouring from engine. No more E/A seen after this so he returned to base.

F/Sgt Sadler after attacking with Squadron, saw a Do 215 break away and begin losing height. He made two attacks on this E/A, his second attack being made at 50 yards. A Hurricane also attacked after him and the E/A apparently badly disabled disappeared below cloud.

P/O DH O'Neill lost touch with Blue Leader but after circling for about 6 minutes had to evade 8 Me 110s into cloud. Up again out of cloud saw Me 109s attacking one Hurricane and attacked one of these over Faversham without observing result although E/A took evasive action. After being attacked by another Me 109, he returned to base landing, however, by mistake first at Debden.

Sgt Levenson after attacking without visible result an Me 109 and a crippled Do 215 found himself at 10,000 feet over Brooklands aerodrome. He then saw about 50 Do 215s guarded by two Me 109s overhead. He climbed to 1,000 feet below formation and delivered a quarter frontal attack opening fire first at 100 yards, developing this into normal quarter attack at about 200 yards when all his ammunition was exhausted. He observed ammunition hitting leading E/A and the leading vie of 4 A/C broke away to port, smoke coming from engines of No.1 and No. 2. No further result was seen but he assumed that No.1 was out of action. F/Lt Stoddart and P/O Dewey, owing to refuelling, took off 15 minutes after the squadron. The weather above cloud was perfect with visibility good.

Squadron Leader Brian Lane, 19 Squadron:

At approximately 14.40 hrs, AA fire was sighted to the South and at the same time a formation of about thirty Do 215s was seen. I climbed up astern of the enemy aircraft to engage the fighter escort which could be seen above the bombers at about 30,000ft. Three Me 109s dived on our formation and I turned to starboard. A loose dogfight ensued with more Me 109s coming down. I could not get near to any enemy aircraft so I climbed up and engaged a formation of Me 110s without result.

I then sighted 10 Me 109s just above me and attacked one of them. I got on his tail and fired several bursts of about two seconds. The enemy aircraft was taking violent evasive action and made for cloud level. I managed to get in another burst of about five seconds before it flicked over inverted and entered cloud in a shallow dive, apparently out of control. I then flew south and attacked two further format ions of about thirty Do 215s from astern and head-on.

The enemy aircraft did not appear to like the head on attack as they jumped about a hit as I passed through. I observed no result from these attacks. Fire from the rear of the enemy aircraft was opened at 1,000 yards. Me 110s opened fire at similar range but appeared to have no idea of deflection shooting.

Squadron Leader Lane's combat was the only protracted dogfight between the opposing fighters on this day.

Flight Sergeant George Unwin was Lane's Red 3, and reported sighting 'thousands of 109s'. When the wing was attacked, at close range Red 3 fired a three-second burst at a 109 which half-rolled and dived steeply into the clouds. Although the Spitfire pilot pursued his prey, he lost the 109 at

6,000ft when his windscreen froze up. Climbing back up to 25,000ft, a *Rotte* of 109s appeared above him, flying south.

Unwin gave chase and caught both over Lydd. The first consequently burst into flames and went down vertically, the second crashing into the sea. It is likely that these two 109s were from I/JG 77: *Oberleutnant* Kunze, of the *Geschwaderstabschwarm*, was killed when his aircraft crashed at Lympne; *Unteroffizier* Meixner also lost his life when his 109 crashed into the sea off Dungeness at about 14.55 hrs. This brought Flight Sergeant Unwin's personal total of Me 109s definitely destroyed this day to three.

As the Me 109s rained down on 19 Squadron, Green 1, Flying Officer Leonard 'Ace' Haines, attacked a 3/LG 2 machine flown by *Unteroffizier* Klick. The enemy machine's radiator was badly damaged so Klick forced-landed at Shellness, where he was captured. Haines went on to engage an Me 110 which he also claimed as destroyed when he saw it crash on a French beach. Green Section's other two pilots, Flight Sergeant Harry Steere and Pilot Officer Arthur Vokes, were also successful; the latter wrote in his log book:

> 'B' Flight attacked six Do 17s, one breaking away chased by F/Sgt Steere and self. One Jerry baled out. One Me 110 surprised me and bored a hole in starboard wing. After two or three turns I got on his tail and gave him everything. Dived vertically into cloud, starboard engine smoking. One probable Me 110. Hundreds of Jerries!

Sub-Lieutenant 'Admiral' Blake, 19 Squadron's FAA pilot, noted the quantity of enemy aircraft engaged as 'innumerable', but nonetheless dived to attack six Dorniers detached from the main formation. He then attacked the 109s, which came down from above, firing at one particular machine twice, after which it 'burst into flames'. Blake next joined a queue of fighters attacking the Asplin's Head He 111, but was forced to land at Rochford because his Spitfire had been hit and was smoking badly. Pilot Officer Wallace 'Jock' Cunningham shot down a 7/JG 51 Me 109, which crashed at St Margaret's at Cliffe, near Dover, the pilot of which, *Leutnant* Bildau, baled out and was captured. Sergeant Jack Potter, however, ill-advisedly chased the enemy far out across the Channel and was himself shot down off Calais by *Feldwebel* Luders of 6/JG 26; the British pilot was captured.

After the engagement, the Duxford Wing pilots returned individually, landing at various times from 15.00 hrs onwards.

In both of these actions, the following claims were made by the Duxford Wing:

19 Squadron: 12 destroyed, 2 shared, 4 probables, 1 damaged.
242 Squadron: 11/0/0.
302 Squadron: 12/1/2.
310 Squadron: 4 and 1 shared/0/0.
611 Squadron: 6 and 1 shared/4/0.

Total: 45 destroyed and 5 shared/10/1.

Owing to the volume of fighting, however, it is impossible to cross-reference the majority of claims with actual German losses, but suffice it to say, the Duxford Wing substantially over-claimed.

The Duxford Wing's casualties were as follows:

19 Squadron: 1 Spitfire destroyed, pilot POW; 2 Spitfires damaged.
242 Squadron: 1 Hurricane lost, pilot baled out wounded; 2 Hurricanes damaged.
302 Squadron: 1 Hurricanes lost, pilot killed; 1 Hurricane damaged.
310 Squadron: 2 Hurricanes lost, 1 pilot wounded.
611 Squadron: 1 Spitfire damaged.

Total: 5 fighters destroyed, 6 damaged; 1 pilot killed, 1 POW, 2 wounded.

This, then, was 12 Group's not insignificant contribution to the defence of London on this historic day of days.

According to the ORB of 11 Group's 73 Squadron, this squadron took-off at '14.45 hrs', but that was not the case and as confirmed by the Intelligence Patrol Report: six Hurricanes of 'B' Flight, led by Flying Officer Donald Scott, scrambled from Castle Camps at 14.10 hrs. These Hurricanes also engaged the incoming enemy over Maidstone at around 14.30 hrs. The bombers were attacked, but Pilot Officer Neville Langham-Hobart was forced to break off his attack owing to heavy cross-fire from the German gunners.

Climbing, he saw three Me 110s in a circle, diving onto one and firing one continuous burst, exhausting his ammunition. One of the 110's engines caught fire but then the aircraft disappeared into cloud. Sergeant Geoffrey Garton attacked a vic of Do 17s, one of which began smoking from both engines and dropped out of formation, losing height. Sergeant John Ellis went for the Heinkels, out of the sun, leaving one falling away from the formation with an engine ablaze.

The squadron suffered no casualties, but noted 'that Do 17s looked exceptionally dirty and dilapidated'. The result of 73's attack was sufficient for the squadron to feel 'that to some extent the death of gallant Marchand today has been avenged by the day's good work [ORB]'.

According to the 607 Squadron ORB, the enemy was sighted flying north-west over Appledore at '14.45 hrs' – but, again, this must have been earlier. Led by Flight Lieutenant Jim Bazin, the Hurricanes attacked the Do 17s head-on, noting that the Me 109s and Me 110s following the bombers made no effort to engage them. No.607's pilots saw 'various E/A falling to pieces in the air, but owing to the head-on attacks it was difficult to see whether damaged E/A, other than those seen to break up in the air, were destroyed or probable'. In total, 607 Squadron claimed 'four Do 215s [*sic*] destroyed on land, one Do 215 probable, four Do 215 damaged, one Ju 88 [*sic*] damaged [ORB]'. The squadron's only casualty was Pilot Officer Patrick Stephenson, who baled out, slightly wounded, after colliding with a 5/KG 3 Do 17. This aircraft crashed into Combwell Wood, near Goudhurst, and exploded with such force that what little was found of its crew defied identification.

Despite the tenacity and numbers of RAF fighters, and a heavy AA barrage, the German bombers reached London at 14.45 hrs. West Ham was hit, the KG 26 He 111s devastating Bromley-by-Bow gas works, on which two huge 2,200lb bombs, among many others, were dropped. The new St Mary's Hospital was hit, and a train at Upton Park, causing casualties and blocking the line. An electricity sub-station was wrecked, cutting off power across a wide area, and great damage was caused to residential areas.

Five minutes later, the Do 17s arrived over their allotted target area – but were unable to locate the Surrey Commercial Docks which was covered in cloud. Consequently, the Dorniers turned about, dropping their bombs as they retreated through gaps in the cloud, hitting Penge, Bexley, Crayford, Dartford and Orpington. Few casualties arose, however, and the only significant damage was at Penge East railway station where both platforms were hit, and a tunnel on the line into central London was blocked.

There would, however, be no respite for the retiring raiders – yet more RAF fighters were now bearing down on the Germans to harry them back to the coast.

Having met 257 Squadron over Eastchurch, at 14.55 hrs 17 Squadron sighted the enemy over London: 'The Squadron attacked, but results were mostly not observed owing to 10/10ths cloud [ORB].' The Polish Pilot Officer Pawel Niemiec damaged a Do 17, and both Pilot Officers Harold 'Birdy' Bird-Wilson and Leonard Stevens claimed probables. The Hurricanes, however, were attacked by the fighter escort, as Bird-Wilson reported:

> I led my Section into the bombers and did a climbing frontal attack on a Do. I did not notice the effects of my attack as Me 110s came down on us. I climbed up to make another attack on some Me 110s but my oxygen had given out and I was feeling the effects and very drowsy. Green 2 [Pilot Officer Jack Ross] and myself chased the E/A south-east but Green 2 had to break away as some more Me 110s came onto his tail. I dived down through the clouds and came out about fifteen miles South of Manston aerodrome. I suddenly spotted a Do 215 [*sic*] flying at 5,000ft towards France. I carried out two head-on and beam attacks and the E/A's starboard engine went up in smoke and it dived down towards the sea, whereupon I lost sight of it owing to haze.

The lack of oxygen, however, forced Bird-Wilson, Green 1, to 'land at Southend [ORB]'. No.17 Squadron suffered no loss in the action.

For 10 Group's 238 Squadron, up from Middle Wallop and which encountered the enemy fifteen–twenty miles South of London at 15.00 hrs, the resulting action 'was the most successful the Squadron has yet had [ORB]'.

Pilot Officer Aubrey Covington:

> I was Green 3 and Squadron patrolled base and then Brooklands – Kenley where strong formations of E/A encountered. Blue 1 ordered sections line astern and I dived with Section. I fired short 1-second burst from under at 200 yards, closing and broke away, climbing. I attacked an Me 110 from above, full deflection, firing 2-second burst

> at 200 yards, closing, and E/A started going down and then burst into flames. I followed him right down and to the ground where he hit and continued on fire. Two people jumped by parachute.
>
> I climbed up again and saw Hurricanes attacking Me 109 but could not catch it. Went onto reserve and then had to forced-land at East Grinstead in a field. Broke tail wheel and there was a hole in the starboard petrol tank. Landed approx. 15.30 hrs. Came back to Middle Wallop by train.

Only three Me 110s were lost on this day, all from V(Z)/LG 1; it is likely that this was the machine down at Hothfield.

Five He 111s destroyed, a probable and two damaged were also claimed by 238 Squadron, along with two Me 110s destroyed and one damaged. This success, however, was tempered by the loss of a pilot: Sergeant Leslie Pidd was shot down over Kenley and baled out, 'his body being found some days later in a wood near Tonbridge' – according to Sergeant Eric Bann, he had seen Pidd machine-gunned by a German fighter during his descent. Flight Lieutenant Minden Blake's Hurricane being so badly damaged that he was forced to land at West Malling, the Hurricane being written-off; Pilot Officers Charles Davis and Vernon Simmonds both returned to base with damaged aircraft, but all of these pilots were unhurt.

At 15.00 hrs the withdrawing Germans approached Gravesend, and were sighted by Squadron Leader Ronald Kellett and the Poles of 303 Squadron. Kellett, flying Blue 1, led Blue Section:

> into a quarter frontal attack on bombers, which wheeled eastwards. Red and Yellow then attacked and simultaneously another squadron attacked the formation about five miles to starboard. The Me's were slow to fall upon the Hurricanes and the lateral guard of the Me 109s avoided them, but the Me 110s closed with them after the first rush and the Squadron was compelled to break up and use individual defensive tactics and escape in clouds. Whole enemy formation loosened, most turning eastwards and some due South. [ORB]

After the battle, Squadron Leader Kellett claimed an Me 110 destroyed and a 'Do 215 [*sic*]' probable; His Blue 2, Flying Officer Walerian Zak, also claimed a 'Do 215' destroyed, and Flying Officer Witold Urbanowicz, two. Me 110s destroyed were also claimed by Pilot Officer Miroslaw Feric and the Canadian Flight Lieutenant Johnny Kent, and Sergeant Miroslaw Wojciechowski an Me 109.

The Hurricanes of Kellett, Zak, Wojciechowski, Feric and Urbanowicz all returned to base with combat damage, although none of the pilots were wounded. Sergeant Tadeuz Andruszkow was shot down and baled out safely over Dartford, but Sergeant Michal Brzezowski was never seen again, it being assumed that he had been shot down and crashed into the Thames Estuary. There was good news back at Northolt, however – Squadron Leader Kellett had been awarded the DFC:

> By his excellent example and personality this officer has been largely responsible for the success of his Squadron which in one week destroyed thirty-three enemy aircraft, of which Squadron Leader Kellett has destroyed three. His leadership and determination in attacking superior numbers of enemy aircraft have instilled the greatest confidence in the other pilots of his Squadron.

Patrolling high over the Biggin Hill area, Squadron Leader Sandy Johnstone and his 602 Squadron Spitfires sighted the retreating Dorniers and Me 110s flying South at 14,000ft. The enemy was already under attack by Hurricanes, so 602 Squadron joined the queue, engaging in line astern over Beachy Head, out of the sun, from 2,000ft above the Germans. The bombers held their formation, however, and after this initial attack 602 was unable to re-form, and the typical individual combats followed. Green 1, Pilot Officer Andrew McDowell attacked the leader of a vic of Dorniers from above and head-on, closing from 400 to 50 yards. The bomber's Perspex canopy shattered and a red glow was seen inside the fuselage; this was credited as a probable. Green 2, Sergeant Cyril Babbage, attacked a straggling Dornier from astern, also shattering the bomber's canopy and silencing the rear-gunner. Return fire, however, damaged Babbage's engine, forcing him down at Shoreham, although he was unhurt.

Flying Officer Allen Edy, Red 2, a Canadian, shot a Do 17 down into the sea, which was seen to crash by Pilot Officer Osgood 'Pedro' Hanbury, who also claimed a bomber destroyed over the water. Yellow 1, Pilot Officer

Archibald Lyall, attacked a straggling Do 17 which was already being assailed by other Spitfires, the enemy aircraft, of 5/KG 2, crash-landing near Hastings; three of the crew were captured, but one had baled out over the sea, before the pilot turned back to forced-land, but remains missing. All of the Spitfires except Babbage returned safely to base.

At 15.30 hrs, the Spitfires of 10 Group's 609 Squadron were patrolling over Rye when the Do 17s and escort were seen flying south at the same height and vicinity. This was the same formation attacked by 602 Squadron. Flying Officer John Dundas, Yellow 1, reported:

> I was in line astern behind Red Section. Red Section attacked rear vic of Do's, and as they did so two Do's detached themselves from formation and tried to dive away. I selected one and went in after it had been attacked by a member of Red Section. I opened fire at 350 yards and closed to 150, attacking from dead astern and slightly above. At first, I experienced return fire and was twice hit. Then pieces started to fall off and flames came from starboard wing and engine. After breaking away I saw the E/A spin and members of the crew escaped by parachute. I also made a short attack on a second 215 [*sic*] which crashed inland.

The second bomber Dundas engaged, together with Squadron Leader 'Uncle' George Darley, and Pilot Officer Michael Staples, was the 5/KG 2 machine down near Hastings. Pilot Officers Michael Appleby, John Curchin and Michael Staples shared the destruction of a second Dorner, five miles south of Rye. According to the ORB,

> two stragglers of a large formation of Dorniers, returning from their bombing London, were sent into the 'Drink'. Subsequent scrutiny of films taken by two pilots reveals the fact that the approach of their cine-guns caused 'alarm and despondency' to one of the Dornier pilots, who had baled out and was descending by parachute. The Squadron received the signal 'Well done once more' from the Chief of Air Staff.

Apart from the minor damage to Dundas's Spitfire, 609, still smarting from the loss of Pilot Officer Gaunt earlier in the day, suffered no other casualties.

These combats over the East Sussex coast signalled the end of day's second attack on London. This vast German armada, however, had been subjected to ferocious attacks by a great number of RAF fighters, assisted by 11 Group again having ample time to deploy squadrons, the position of the afternoon sun and because the Me 109s, clearly conscious of the desperate need to conserve fuel, were not as aggressive as usual. Moreover, although damage had been caused, cloud over London's docklands had thwarted the Dorniers' attack. The operation's end result, therefore, was hardly the required 'knock-out blow' – and the surviving enemy aircrews returned to France knowing full-well that Fighter Command was far from a spent force. Twenty-one bombers had been lost, and twelve or more fighters. Fifteen RAF fighters had been lost and over twenty damaged; three pilots had been killed, ten wounded (including one who later died of his injuries), and one captured.

Having watched the action from the vantage point and perspective of 11 Group's underground Operations Room, the Prime Minister watched with concern as the lights on the tote board indicated that all of Park's squadrons were either in the process of returning to earth or already landed and being rearmed and refuelled. Twenty-eight squadrons had been scrambled, and all had engaged. At airfields all over southern England, groundcrews worked feverishly to get the fighters back on 'top line'.

This was, perhaps, the day's tensest moment – because had another raid come in at this time, none of Air Vice-Marshal Park's squadrons were available. At 15.05 hrs, RDF indicated '6+' was plotted over Cherbourg; this was a concern, especially with 10 Group's 238 and 609 Squadrons airborne over 11 Group – nonetheless, the Spitfires of 152 Squadron remained at Warmwell and were well-able to deal with such a small incursion.

Then, at 15.25 hrs, 213 Squadron at Tangmere reported that it was replenished. One by one, the 'At Readiness' bulbs glowed, indicating that 11 Group was again ready for action. What was a critical moment had passed, and the Prime Minister took his leave. Churchill climbed the stairs and returned to the surface, just as the 'All Clear' sirens wailed over London: '"We are very glad you have seen this", said Park. "Of course, during the last twenty minutes we were so choked with information that we couldn't handle it. This shows you the limitation of our present resources. They have been strained beyond their limits today."'

The raid plotted at 15.05 hrs, however, was not '6+' – this was the start of Luftflotte 3's attacks on Portland and Southampton. As an insurance policy when the raid was first detected, 152 Squadron had scrambled to patrol the Dorset coast – and just before 15.30 hrs sighted the twenty-seven unescorted He 111s of KG 55, seven miles south-west of Portland, flying north-west at 15,000ft. The Spitfires passed the bombers, travelling in the opposite direction in order to get into position for an astern attack.

This, however, enabled the enemy to bomb Portland unopposed. Fortunately, comparatively little damage was caused: houses were hit near the imposing Verne Citadel, UXBs causing the evacuation of several streets, telephone communications were disrupted, but the Royal Navy reported incidents within the naval base as 'insignificant'. As the Germans turned about and headed back to France, 152 Squadron engaged, five miles south-west of Portland Bill.

Green Section attacked a straggling He 111, Green 3, Sergeant Kenneth Holland's fire causing black smoke to pour from the bomber's starboard engine. As the Heinkel lost height, Green 2, Pilot Officer Arthur Watson, attacked, leaving smoke billowing from both engines as the aircraft's undercarriage dropped. Holland attacked again, causing further smoke to emit, while Watson fired a long burst at another straggler which fell into the sea some fifteen miles off Swanage. Blue 1, Pilot Officer Eric 'Boy' Marrs, who was leading the squadron, attacked a He 111 of the rearmost section from astern, but being by then dangerously far out to sea, the pilot sensibly broke off the combat and returned to base.

All of 152's pilots landed safely back at Warmwell. The Heinkel seen to crash into the sea by Watson belonged to 9/KG 55, three of the crew being killed and one captured. Two other enemy aircraft would crash-land in France, badly damaged and carrying dead or wounded crewmen.

The next threat by Luftflotte 3, however, was potentially much more serious, given that this raid was directed at the Vickers Supermarine Aviation Works at Woolston.

At 17.40 hrs, RDF indicated another raid assembling over Cherbourg, which by 17.50 hrs was three miles south of St Catherine's Point on the Isle of Wight. Nos. 213 and 602 Squadrons were airborne again, covering Tangmere, and 607 Squadron was sent from there towards Southampton, and 609 Squadron was ordered from Middle Wallop to Portsmouth –

because clearly either Southampton or Portsmouth – perhaps both – was the likely target.

The raid comprised ten Me 110s and three Me 109s of *Erprobungsgruppe* 210, led by *Hauptmann* Martin Lutz, who used cloud cover to approach Southampton stealthily before diving at a shallow angle from 7,000ft, approaching Woolston from the east. Bofors and other anti-aircraft guns banged away but failed to prevent the Me 110s, from dropping twenty-three bombs on Woolston at 17.55 hrs – and Lutz reached his target unopposed by RAF fighters.

Again, though, the Supermarine Works escaped any serious damage, just one skylight being smashed by flying debris. The adjacent residential area suffered, however: terraced housing near the Spitfire factory and east of the railway line was devastated; six people were killed, nineteen seriously injured, and twenty-three more were treated for comparatively minor injuries at Royal South Hampshire Hospital. In total, thirty-four houses were destroyed; eighty-one so badly damaged that they were consequently demolished; 351 were badly damaged but repairable, while 755 sustained minor damage.

As *Erprobungsgruppe* 210 withdrew, the Hurricanes of 607 Squadron, led by Flight Lieutenant Francis Blackadder, apparently intercepted the raid between Poole and the Needles – although reports arising make no sense. The ORB states that 'between 30 and 40 Me 109s and Me 110s' were seen to the south:

> Immediately after some Do 17s were seen in small groups, in vic formation, emerging from clouds below and to the South. These groups began joining into larger formations after having apparently completed their bombing. Squadron made a stern attack but the Me 109s hampered the attack by diving down on the Hurricanes.

Flight Lieutenant Charles 'Chatty' Bowen and Pilot Officer John Sulman shared the destruction of a 'Do 17', Bowen reporting that 'the starboard engine caught fire, the aircraft then dived down and crashed into the sea'. The Polish Pilot Officer Boleslaw Wlasnowolski also claimed a Do 17 shot down into the sea – but no Do 17s were lost in this area, and nor did *Erprobungsgruppe* 210's Me 110s suffer any casualties. Nor can the reference to so many German aircraft be reconciled with the available facts, the only logical conclusion being that 607 Squadron's recording of this action went seriously awry.

Whatever happened with 607 Squadron, Supermarine had once more survived – and the enemy's objective of overwhelming Britain's aerial defences had failed.

That evening, Fighter Command's squadrons flew standing patrols, but only the odd reconnaissance raider was apparent. Between 19.30–19.45 hrs, Flight Lieutenant Ken Gillies was leading 'B' Flight of 66 Squadron on patrol over Biggin Hill when a lone He 111 was sighted at 8,000ft, just above cloud. The Spitfires attacked, damaging the Heinkel, which eventually disappeared into thick cloud some ten miles east of Dungeness. The enemy aircraft, of KG 1, made it back to France but crash-landed at Valery-sur-Somme with three wounded crewmen aboard and was written-off.

So closed the day-fighting.

The following day, *The Times* newspaper trumpeted that Fighter Command had destroyed a total of 175 German aircraft on 15 September 1940, for the loss of only thirty RAF fighters and ten pilots.

A day later, the British victory claim had risen to 185 (178 by fighters, seven by AA guns). In fact, the enemy had lost fifty-six machines in total, less than on 15 and 18 August 1940 (seventy-five and sixty-nine respectively), with three damaged beyond repair and twenty-three less-so; eighty-one Luftwaffe aircrew were killed, sixty-three captured and thirty-one wounded.

The RAF's casualties were more accurately reported by *The Times*, as twenty-nine aircraft and twelve pilots had actually been lost – fewer pilots than on 8 August (fourteen), 11 August (twenty-five), 15 August (thirteen) and 7 September 1940 (thirteen).

The weather had compromised both German attacks on London, a strong headwind increasing flying times from France to London, thereby providing greater opportunities for interceptions, this wind also contributing to the Me 109s running short of fuel and turning about. Moreover, during the afternoon, cloud covered London, thus preventing accurate bombing. Consequently, the Luftwaffe failed to repeat the hammer-blow of 7 September 1940, or, indeed, deliver the required 'knockout blow'.

The enemy had been met over London by an unprecedented number of RAF fighters – twice. According to Cajus Bekker in *The Luftwaffe War Diaries*, on 14 September 1940, Luftwaffe Intelligence firmly believed that

Fighter Command had been knocked out, and this is what the German aircrews had been led to believe. The effect on the Germans' morale, when met by hundreds of RAF fighters, therefore, was shattering. Furthermore, it was now abundantly clear to Hitler and the OKW that the Luftwaffe was unable to defeat the RAF or inflict such damage on the British economy and morale as to cause a state of chaos – both being objectives crucial to the launch of Operation *Seelöwe* – the future of which now clearly being in doubt.

As we have seen, Luftwaffe after-action reports marvelled at the size of RAF fighter formations engaged over London, albeit exaggerating the number as being up to eighty per formation. Nonetheless, there is no doubt that the Duxford Wing's arrival during both London actions was a significant sight for both sides – but for very different reasons.

That day, Pilot Officer Richard Jones was flying with 19 Squadron:

> Early in September 1940, I was transferred from 64 Squadron at Kenley in 11 Group to 19 Squadron at Fowlmere in 12 Group ... My immediate impression of flying with a wing comprising five squadrons of Spitfires and Hurricanes, instead of anything between five to ten aircraft taking off from Kenley to intercept large numbers of enemy aircraft, was one of security in numbers. This gave me great confidence, looking around and seeing anything from upwards of fifty fighters keeping me company!

In this, Jones is surely right – and the arrival of the pirate-like, swashbuckling, fearless Bader over London with his five squadrons must have surely inspired and given hope to even the hardest-pressed RAF fighter pilot in action over the capital – but was a crushing blow to the enemy's morale. Duxford's squadrons had undoubtedly played a big part in the day's outcome; the 310 Squadron ORB recording that 'the day's "bag" for the Station' was 'fairly conclusive proof of the efficiency of the wing formation'.

Arguably that was not so, however. The Duxford Wing had been requested to patrol 11 Group airfields north of London. Instead, Squadron Leader Bader had led the wing off on another free-range fighter sweep, heading straight for the action over London, where enemy formations were already being hacked down by 11 Group squadrons, operating in strength. Certainly Bader's arrival over London was impressive, but it was not the full story – and the Luftwaffe bomber crews were already hard at it fending off the large numbers of 11 Group fighters. KG 26 He 111 pilot *Leutnant* Roderich Cescotti remembered that he and his *Kameraden* were 'shaken by the numbers of fighters the RAF was able to put up that day, and by the determination of the pilots'.

Nonetheless, as Bekker commented, across the Channel 'the battle was regarded as far from lost'. That may be so, but it was obvious that against such ongoing defensive strength, the German bomber force could not continue to absorb such losses indefinitely. Indeed, again as Bekker also said, 'If things went on like this the Luftwaffe would bleed to death over England.

The time was fast approaching when Hitler would have to make his final decision regarding Operation *Seelöwe* – which would be heavily influenced by the events of 15 September 1940.

On the wider stage, throughout the day, Coastal Command had flown the usual round of anti-invasion patrols, convoy escorts, mine-laying and reconnaissance sorties, in addition to searching for U-boats. At 17.25 hrs, two Me 109s of 7/JG 53 were scrambled from Etaples to intercept Blenheims, *Feldwebel* Hermann Neuhoff claiming a Blenheim destroyed 20km off the French coast – although, as no Blenheims were lost, more likely this was a 500 Squadron Anson escorting a convoy, the air gunner of which was wounded when attacked by Me 109s; the Anson was damaged but returned safely to Detling.

As ever, the PRU was actively monitoring the invasion ports, and at night 53 and 59 Squadrons of Coastal Command successfully attacked enemy shipping at Le Havre, and Flight Lieutenant Francis of 22 Squadron, flying a Bristol Beaufort, undertook the first nocturnal torpedo attack when he reportedly hit a 3,000-ton ship off Ijmuiden. Because of the lack of suitable cloud cover, however, Bomber Command's daylight operations were scrubbed, excepting an uneventful North Sea sweep by a flight of Blenheims. By night, though, Bomber Command 'Ops' were very much on: maximum effort.

A large force of nearly fifty Blenheims attacked invasion barges at Flushing, Dunkirk and Boulogne, and the heavy artillery battery at Cap Gris-Nez. The Whitley force successfully attacked various industrial targets in Germany, Wellingtons bombed marshalling yards in Germany and Belgium, and enemy shipping at Calais, and Battles hit Boulogne. The laurels, however, went to the Hampden force, and specifically 18-year-old Sergeant John Hannah, a Wireless Operator/Air Gunner on 83 Squadron.

While making a low-level attack on enemy shipping at Antwerp, the Hampden of Pilot Officer C.A. Connor was hit by flak in the bomb-bay, the resulting fire in the wireless operator's compartment and rear gun turret was so fierce that the belly gun turret began disintegrating. Immediately, the navigator and rear gunner baled out, but, with both fuel tanks holed and in great danger of the fire spreading, Hannah fought his way through the flames to reach two extinguishers with which he fought the blaze. When both were expended, he used his gloved hands and W/T book to continue beating the flames, ammunition exploding around him all the while.

Almost blinded by the intense heat and in danger of being overcome by fumes, Hannah, burnt about the face, succeeded in putting the fire out. Then, he crawled forward, passing his pilot the navigator's maps, thereby enabling Pilot Officer Connor to return the badly damaged aircraft to base. For this incredible act of bravery, a 'signal act of valour' indeed, Sergeant Hannah received the Victoria Cross – becoming the second airman of Bomber Command to receive the highest award for gallantry during the Second World War, and the youngest. Pilot Officer Connor's efforts that night were recognised with a DFC.

By night, German bombers were also active, nearly 200 returning to London and stating large fires.

Monday, 16 September 1940

As Britain awoke and went about its daily business, the morning newspapers were full of reports concerning the previous day's fighting, *The Times*' headline being: '175 Raiders Shot Down … RAF Batter Invasion Machine'. Still deeply moved, the events involved remained very much on the Prime Minister's mind:

> Yesterday eclipses all previous records of Fighter Command. Aided by squadrons of their Czech and Polish comrades, using only a small proportion of their total strength, and under cloud conditions of some difficulty, they cut to rags and tatters three separate waves of murderous assault upon the civil population of their native land, inflicting a certain loss of 125 bombers and 53 fighters upon the enemy, to say nothing of probables and damaged, while themselves sustaining only a loss of twelve

> pilots and twenty-five machines. These results exceed all expectations and give just and sober confidence in the approaching struggle.

The Daily Home Intelligence Report:

> Yesterday's aerial successes have produced enthusiastic praise for the RAF... Most people anticipate an invasion in a few days, and are very confident that it will be a failure.

After the massive effort of 15 September 1940, both sides were no doubt relieved that the 16th was overcast and stormy, with much low cloud and strong winds. At 07.30 hrs, 100 German aircraft crossed the coast of Kent, possibly fighters because no attack arose; single raiders, flew *Störflug* operations, although little damage was caused. The only interception concerned 616 Squadron, based at Kirton-in-Lindsey, up in 12 Group:

> Blue Section scrambled at 09.22 hrs. They were vectored over convoy 'Pilot' at 10,000ft. A Ju 88 was then sighted and chased. Blue 1 [Flight Lieutenant Colin MacFie] and Blue 2 [the American Pilot Officer Phillip 'Uncle Sam' Leckrone] fired at enemy, but no effect noticed. Blue 3 [Sergeant Tony Iveson] did not catch up and owing to lack of petrol landed on sea next to a minesweeper. Suffered slight cut on nose, otherwise alright. Brought into Yarmouth and then by transport to Kirton. Blue 1 and 2 landed at Bircham Newton. [ORB]

That morning, the usual 12 Group fighter squadrons had gathered in the Duxford Sector, but as there was so little aerial activity no assistance call came from 11 Group. There was, however, one wing patrol, as the 310 Squadron ORB reports:

> The Squadron, led by the CO, took off at 07.40 hrs to patrol London at 27,000 feet. This again was a wing formation, the squadrons involved being the same as yesterday. They landed at 08.45 hrs without having made contact with the enemy. The weather deteriorated about 10.00 hrs and there was some rain and considerable mist. This provided a respite which did not come altogether amiss.

Squadron Leader Douglas Bader's log book records that he led the Duxford Wing on this patrol, in his words, of 'North Weald'. Given that enemy air activity was minimal, and 12 Group had not been requested to reinforce 11 Group, why was the Duxford Wing patrolling over 'North Weald', or, indeed, according to the Czechs, 'London'? This is firm evidence that the wing was suiting itself, with Squadron Leader Bader confident in the support and protection of both Air Vice-Marshal Leigh-Mallory and Wing Commander Woodhall.

The poor weather also reduced the extent of Coastal and Bomber Command operations, by both day and night, although Blenheims bombed Dunkirk, Calais, Ostend and Zeebrugge, two convoys and Hamstede aerodrome. Night operations, however, were completely scrubbed.

For the Luftwaffe, it was a day of reflection and recriminations. According to a report by *Major* von Falkenstein, a Luftwaffe staff officer at OKW, 15 September 1940 had seen 'large air battles and great losses ... due to a lack of fighter protection'. The OKL noted that the 'heavy losses ... are due to British fighters attacking bombers returning in small groups without fighter escort'. It was clear, then, that the German bomber force could not sustain the current rate of attrition – and would break before the RAF. *Reichsmarschall* Göring was furious and held a conference at Boulogne with his *Luftflotten* and *Fliegerkorps* commanders.

Naturally, it was *Generalmajor* 'Oncle' Theo Osterkamp, the *Jagdfliegerführer*, who was the object of Göring's rage. The *Reichsmarschall* blamed the fighters, the weather, his belief that Fighter Command was so strong over London because the bulk of Dowding's force was now concentrated to defend the capital – what the Luftwaffe chief could not see was that Fighter Command was, in fact, as strong now as it had been in July 1940.

Hitler, embarrassed at the Luftwaffe's failure, summoned the *Reichsmarschall* to Berchtesgaden.

Tuesday, 17 September 1940

Unable to delay any further, owing to moon and tide predictions, Hitler made his decision on the future of Operation *Seelöwe* in the early hours of 17 September 1940. This simple OKW communication was sent to all commands: 'Wird Bis Auf Weiteres Verschoben', Operation *Seelöwe* was postponed until further notice.

The effect across the Channel was immediate: the *Kriegsmarine* command ordering that the assembly of invasion barges must cease forthwith, and the fleet assembled dispersed.

The reason *Seelöwe* never sailed was entirely because the Luftwaffe had failed to win aerial supremacy over southern England – which had always been perceived as the essential prerequisite. During his interview with Hitler, however, Göring had remained insistent that the RAF would be destroyed in 'four or five days'. The *Reichsmarschall*, who was never particularly enthusiastic regarding *Seelöwe*, still believed the Luftwaffe capable of defeating the RAF – if left to his own devices. The invasion was off – but the air battle would continue.

The British had sensed that 15 September 1940 had been a turning point, and indeed it was. On this day, Churchill said:

> Sunday's action was the most brilliant and fruitful of any fought upon a large scale up to that date by the fighters of the RAF. The figures have already been made public. To the best of my belief – and I have made searching inquiries and taken several cross-checks – those figures are not in any way exaggerated …
>
> The German attacks upon the civilian population have been concentrated mainly upon London, in the hope of terrorizing its citizens into submission, or to throw them into confusion, and also in the silly idea that they will put pressure on the Government to make peace.
>
> The deliberate and repeated attacks upon Buckingham Palace and upon the persons of our beloved King and Queen are also intended, apart from their general barbarity, to have an unsettling effect upon public opinion. They have, of course, the opposite effect. They unite the King and Queen to their people by new and sacred bonds if common danger, and they steel [*sic*] the hearts of all to the stern and unrelenting prosecution of the war against so foul a foe.

The people were also more confident, as evidenced by the Daily Home Intelligence Reports on 17 September 1940:

> While many continue to anticipate invasion, and indeed hope that it will come within the next few days, reports show that some people are suggesting that its likelihood has diminished. Rumours that it has already been attempted and failed has been reported.

In London:

> Morale steady; public on whole settling down to new air-raid life cheerfully, and show fewer signs of tiredness ... Stoke Newington contact states bombed people in district very philosophical: majority set to work to clean up mess at once and say 'it might have been worse'.

So far as the day's air operations were concerned, things began slowly, with just the usual reconnaissance raiders prowling around, although even these sorties were of a reduced scale, which was unsurprising given that according to 41 Squadron, the weather was 'Wind WSW 20/30 mph, gusty, veering towards WSW, mainly cloudy, visibility poor, becoming good, then very poor [ORB]'. One of these lone raiders penetrated as far as Merseyside, where the Rootes aircraft factory was unsuccessfully attacked, and only two of these aircraft, both Ju 88s, were intercepted.

The first was caught at 10.45 hrs by Red Section of Westhampnett's 602 Squadron, but the bomber was lost in cloud off Brighton. The second, of *Stab* II/LG 1, on a sortie to attack Speke airfield, was intercepted by Blue Section of 152 Squadron, which was patrolling over Portland Bill. Sighting the raider a mile away, inland and flying north over Shepton Mallett, the Spitfires carried out a No.1 Attack before attacking individually. Blue 1, Pilot Officer Eric 'Boy' Marrs' Spitfire was hit in the oil cooler by return fire, seizing up his engine and forcing him to land at Colerne airfield. Blue 2, Sergeant Kenneth Holland, an Australian, and Flying Officer Peter O'Brian, a Canadian, continued attacking the Ju 88, damaging both engines but then losing the bomber in cloud. The 'engine of Blue 2 became hot so he landed at Yatesbury aerodrome and found that his aircraft had been hit by machine-gun fire in three places [ORB]'.

The enemy had not escaped back to France however, but had crashed at Warminster; it was an expensive loss: *Major* Heinz Cramer, a Knight's Cross holder and the Gruppenkommandeur who was captured along with two of his crew, both of whom were killed, and *Leutnant* Otto Heinrich was killed.

The main German effort of the day involved a huge fighter sweep during the afternoon weather window. When RDF, unable to differentiate between fighters and bombers, indicated a large raid building up, Air Vice-Marshal Park again reacted in strength, scrambling twenty squadrons in addition to 12 Group's Duxford Wing and 10 Group units. Only six of these squadrons, all from 11 Group, intercepted the enemy in running battles between Maidstone and Rochester.

Eleven Spitfires of 41 Squadron scrambled from Hornchurch at 14.50 hrs with orders to patrol Manston.

At 15.30 hrs, the Spitfire pilots sighted up to forty Me 109s, individual dogfights ensuing. Sergeant John Norwell [whose combat report is incorrectly timed at 13.30 hrs] reported seeing 'three Me 109s in line astern, racing for the French coast', ten miles west of Manston, '[he] did a vertical attack on the last aircraft, hitting it between the pilot's cockpit and the tail unit'. This was claimed as damaged. Pilot Officer George 'Ben' Bennions engaged at 15.35 hrs, over Ashford:

> After the commencement of the engagement I found myself 2,000ft below a section of five Me 109s. Two of the Me 109s dived down onto me and I evaded by turning sharply right; then one dived away and as I turned to follow, three more came down on me.
>
> After turning and twisting violently, I spun out and on pulling out, I found that one only had followed me down. I turned to engage and he disappeared in the clouds. I climbed back to 15,000ft and sighted a loose formation of four Me 109s circling. I attacked the rear one from the inside of a left-hand turn and after a short burst, I saw pieces fly off the aircraft, which then rolled over and spun inverted at about 8,000ft, then dived straight into the ground midway between Canterbury and Herne Bay, near a very large wood.

The Me 109 pilot, *Unteroffizier* Manfred Langer of 9/JG 53, was killed when he crashed near Bishopden Wood, Dunkirk, Kent.

Flying Officer John Boyle, a Canadian, reported the following:

I was Blue 1 acting as lookout for 'Mitor' Squadron. The Squadron was proceeding in a south-easterly direction when Vector 270° was given by Control. As we were turning around to the right, I noticed two formations above and five to ten miles SE of Dover. I warned the Squadron and started to climb up to the left of the first formation, which was composed of seven Me 109s.

I turned towards them and closed range to fire. As I gave the first burst, the formation wheeled around, back towards France. I did not see the effect of my fire. One of the Me 109s collided with another and they both spun down. I then approached the second formation and as I moved into position to attack, I was attacked myself and did violent evasion to get away.

Two 9/JG 53 Me 109 pilots, *Oberleutnant* Jakob Stoll, the *Staffelkapitän*, and *Oberleutnant* Herbert Seliger, were reported missing, having crashed into the sea – although exactly what or who caused their demise is impossible to say. Two other Me 109E-4s of *Stab* II/JG 53 returned to France damaged, making forced-landings at Wissant, on the French coast. No.41 Squadron, however, did not escape unscathed. Flying Officer Boyle returned to base with a damaged Spitfire, as did Pilot Officer John MacKenzie, whose machine was written-off, and Pilot Officer Harry Chalder; Pilot Officer Henry Baker was also shot-up, crash-landing at Stelling Minnis. Fortunately, none of these pilots were wounded. Spitfires were claimed destroyed by *Leutnant* Erich Schmidt and *Feldwebel* Eduard Koslowski, both of 9/JG 53.

Squadron Leader Harry Hogan had led eight 501 Squadron Hurricanes off from Kenley at 15.03 hrs to patrol with 253 Squadron, and were also engaged by JG 53 over Ashford at 15.30 hrs. The Hurricanes were attacked from above by twenty Me 109s, Squadron Leader Hogan hitting an Me 109 which was 'seen to turn inland [ORB]'. Sergeant James 'Ginger' Lacey DFM, however, was shot down and baled out, unhurt – but Sergeant Eddie Egan was missing.

Sergeant Tony Pickering:

I was flying with Sergeant Eddie Egan when he was killed. I didn't know Eddie terribly well, but I suppose I could count him as a friend. We were flying along, just the two of us, looking out all the time for trouble, and I saw four Spitfires, or what we thought were Spitfires, behind us. We were talking to each other on the R/T, monitoring the movements of these fighters. Suddenly one of them zoomed forward, just left the others standing, shooting Eddie down. I turned towards Eddie's assailant but the old Hurricane was just too slow. The Hun just shot Eddie down and flew off with the others, they just climbed high and left us.

I looked over the side and saw Eddie going down, the aircraft in flames. Eddie crashed in a wood outside Ashford in Kent. After landing I filed a report on the location, and six months later had to see the Air Ministry and pin-point the site as Eddie had not been found. The next I ever heard of Eddie Egan was when I happened to read a newspaper article about his bones having been found by an aviation archaeology group – at the very spot I had told the authorities about in 1940. I got in touch but was not called as a witness by the resulting inquest, which was rather surprising given that I had actually seen Eddie go in.

Sergeant Egan's remains were recovered by aviation archaeology enthusiasts of the London Air Museum on 11 September 1976; the 19-year-old pilot was buried at Brookwood with full military honours. Without doubt, Egan had been shot down by *Hauptmann* Wolf-Dietrich Wilcke of *Stab* III/JG 53, who claimed a Hurricane destroyed over Ashford in this action.

'A' Flight of 607 Squadron was already on patrol when Flight Lieutenant Jim Bazin led his 'B' Flight up from Tangmere with 213 Squadron to patrol from Biggin Hill to Gravesend at 17,000ft. With the latter squadron providing a rearguard, the Hurricanes were 'attacked almost simultaneously from above and behind [607 ORB]'.

Pilot Officer Harry Welford, Blue 2:

When attacked we were warned to break formation. I broke and took evasive action as a result of which I lost the Squadron. As we had instructions to reform rather than fly alone, I saw a group of fighters ahead and intended joining up with them when I saw that they were Me 109s! I took a quick burst but then an unseen 109 fired a cannon shell which hit my air intake. I did a quick flick roll which dropped me below cloud. Again no 109s about and just a lone Hurricane which

> guarded my tail as I forced landed. The engine had seized and looking down I saw a field into which I thought I could land.
>
> As I made the approach glycol and smoke streamed from the engine and when I opened the hood the fumes were sucked through the cockpit and impaired my vision. The field was smaller than I thought but there was a wattle fence which acted like an arrester wire and the plane skidded across the second field, and was brought to an abrupt stop by a tree at the far end, making me crack my head on the reflector sight and blood poured from my face. Thinking that the plane might catch fire, I undid my belt and jumped out only to fall flat on my face because my leg, which had been injured by shrapnel, collapsed on me.
>
> Two farm workers rushed over and picked me up and put me on a wattle fence telling me that there was a German plane down in the next field with the pilot in it, very dead. I regret now that I declined their offer to show me, but at the time I felt pretty dicky. I gave my report to Flight Lieutenant Jim Bazin in hospital and he acknowledged that I had shot down the German aircraft in the field next to mine.

Pilot Officer Welford had been shot down by *Hauptmann* Edu Neumann, the *Kommandeur* of I/JG 27. Welford did not return to his squadron until 20 October 1940.

Green 2, the Polish Pilot Officer Franek Surma, saw Blue 3, Sergeant John Lansdell, also being attacked by *Hauptmann* Neumann and rushed to his aid, firing short bursts at the 109 which disappeared into cloud. The damage, however, had been done: Lansdell was killed, his Hurricane crashing at Beltring; the 23-year-old, who was an Associate Fellow of the Royal Aeronautical Society with a First in aeronautics, was taken home and buried at Hempnall, Norfolk. Neither 213 or 607 squadrons filed any combat claims after this unsuccessful action.

At 15.15 hrs, 1(RCAF) Squadron had scrambled from Northolt, to patrol north of Biggin Hill, encountering 'some Me 109s which were already being engaged by Spitfires. It was impossible to engage under these circumstances [ORB].' Flying Officer Briese, however, was picked off by *Leutnant* Gustav 'Mickey' Sprick, *Staffelkapitän* of 8/JG 26; he forced-landed, unhurt, near Stoke, on the north bank of the Thames Estuary. After the action JG 26 headed for home, but the engine of *Unteroffizier* Heinz Bock's Me 109 failed, forcing the pilot down at Rye, where he was captured.

The Poles of 303 Squadron were also up from Northolt and in company with the Canadians. The formation had first investigated a distant formation of aircraft which proved to be friendly Hurricanes, but the Poles were 'split up owing to large numbers of British fighters over the Estuary. Large numbers of Me 109s were seen up to 27,000ft and it was impossible for the Hurricanes to overtake them [ORB].' Sergeant Miroslaw Wojciechowski saw Me 109s attacking the Canadian Flying Officer Briese and immediately went to assist, claiming to have hit one enemy fighter which,

> shook and dived towards the earth. The burst was accurate but I could not follow the E/A down as I was engaged with the others. I fired again at another Me and after the-second burst his right wing caught fire; I also saw flames inside the cockpit as he fell away from me, but I could not follow him down as I had another one of them on my tail. I evaded this one in cloud and afterwards could not find him.

It is typical of this unit that although the 109 had not been seen to crash it was credited as destroyed; whether this was one of the two missing 9/JG 53 pilots or one of the two damaged 109s which made it back to Wissant it is impossible to be certain. No.303 Squadron suffered no casualties, returning to base to celebrate the DFM awarded this day to their Czechoslovak ace, Sergeant Josef Frantisek.

The Spitfires seen by 1(RCAF) Squadron were those of 603 Squadron, Flight Lieutenant John Boulter claimed an Me 109 probable south-east of Ramsgate:

> Blue 2 asked me to cover him in an attack. I did so and he attacked an Me 109, causing white and brown-black smoke to come from the Me, which dived steeply from 20,000ft to approx. 10,000ft. The Me entered cloud with Blue 2 in pursuit. I went below cloud and waited for it, attacking when it appeared from the cloud, as Blue 2 did not appear to be following. I caused further smoke to come from it, and when I broke away in accordance with R/T instructions, when approx., 10–15 miles out to sea, the Me 109 was 1,000ft above sea-level and flying at approx. 150 mph, still smoking.

Pilot Officers Basil 'Stapme' Stapleton, Ronald 'Raz' Berry and John Soden also claimed probables, 603 Squadron suffering no loss.

At 15.10 hrs, a three-squadron-strong wing comprising 17, 73 and 257 Squadrons had left the Debden Sector with orders to patrol Hendon at Angels 20, the former squadron leading. The Me 109s were sighted but flying too high for the Hurricanes to engage, the Hawker fighter lacking the Spitfire's superior high-altitude performance. No.73 Squadron reported that 'All machines returned safely, though Sergeant Marshall reported having had a 2-second burst fired at him by a Hurricane at 16.10 hrs near Hornchurch at 16,000ft and 300 yards range. An unpleasant experience which one hopes will not befall any member of the Squadron again [ORB].'

As we have seen, such incidents of so-called 'friendly fire' were understandably not uncommon – although fortunately this occasion had not resulted in tragedy. Sadly, this was not the case for Sergeant Denis Helcke of 504 Squadron:

> One flap during the afternoon over Kent but no interception made. Sergeant Helcke got into difficulties when his Section was attacked by our own aircraft. Baled out but did not open his parachute and was killed at Faversham. No explanation could be given unless he got into a spin. He baled out, not being able to correct the spin, and was hit by the machine. [ORB]

Elsewhere, it is written that Helcke had been engaged on a practice flight and was subject to a dummy attack by friendly fighters; clearly, however, this was not the case: 504 Squadron was attacked by friendly fighters, which indirectly caused Helcke's death on what was an operational flight.

After the Germans retired, both sides counted the cost. Four RAF fighters had been destroyed, with eight damaged, plus 73 Squadron's Sergeant Alfred Marshall, shot down by a friendly fighter and who forced-landed at Wick with a holed petrol tank; three RAF pilots were killed and one wounded. Three Me 109s had been destroyed in addition to JG 26's 7/ JG 26's *Unteroffizier* Heinz Bock who was forced to land near Rye and captured owing to engine failure, and two damaged; three German pilots were killed.

The final action of the day involved 151 Squadron, which had been withdrawn to Digby in 12 Group, when Flight Lieutenant Rod Smith and Sergeant John Winstanley intercepted a He 111 at 17.30 hrs which escaped into cloud. Owing to low cloud, however, the wing of Winstanley's Hurricane struck a hillside causing him to crash, although fortunately the pilot was not seriously injured.

During the day, Coastal Command had once more flown the usual round of routine patrols, and PRU aircraft maintained a watch over the invasion ports and enemy coast. A lack of cloud cover over France, however, led to six of 2 Group's Blenheims aborting raids on the Channel ports, although nine pressed on and attacked the barges successfully. By night, Coastal Command's Blenheim-equipped 53 Squadron hit German shipping at Cherbourg with 22 Squadron's Beauforts and FAA Albacores of 826 Squadron. Bomber Command also deployed more aircraft than ever before to attack the invasion barges: twenty Battles attacked Boulogne, forty Blenheims bombed Dunkirk and Boulogne, while thirty-nine Hampdens reported successful raids on shipping at Flushing, Terneuzen and Antwerp. Moreover, forty-two Wellingtons also reported successful attacks on Calais and Ostend, and targets in Germany.

The Whitley force was sent to attack the much-feared battleship Bismarck at Hamburg, which was bombed in the face of heavy flak, and also struck at shipping at Zeebrugge. A 22 Squadron Beaufort, engaged on the Cherbourg raid, crashed at Tourville, killing the crew, and a 44 Squadron Hampden was hit by flak attacking Antwerp, that crew also being lost.

That night, the German bombers returned to London, South Wales, Liverpool and East Anglia, and mines were sowed in the Thames Estuary. The night-bombing remained a problem, and having been withdrawn as a day-fighter, the Boulton-Paul Defiant turret fighter was starting to be used in the night-fighting role – a role it had actually been designed for by the manufacturer. Having been withdrawn north to Turnhouse, on 13 September 1940 'B' Flight of 141 Squadron flew south to Biggin Hill, and began nocturnal patrols in the defence of London.

The night of 15/16 September 1940 was brightly lit by the moon, visibility being 20–25 miles, enabling Pilot Officer John Waddingham and his air-gunner, Sergeant Alfred Cumbers to intercept two He 111s, between 23.59 and 01.16 hrs over the Kent and Sussex coast, claiming one destroyed and a probable, no German aircraft were actually brought down. The honour of achieving the Defiant's first confirmed nocturnal victory, therefore, would go to Sergeant George Laurence and his gunner, Sergeant Wilfred Chard, on the night of 17/18 September 1940; the former reported:

> I was ordered on patrol line Maidstone to Tonbridge at 15,000ft but before reaching my position I was vectored by the Controller over Bexley. I came across a E/A which although not illuminated by searchlights, shone in the brilliant moonlight about 150 yards away. He was coming on converging courses at the same height as myself. I quickly turned and gave chase, and managed to keep him in sight until I overtook him to about 50–60 yards away.
>
> My gunner gave him a short burst, which caused him to make a complete turn right over my own craft and at the same time he dropped, or rather jettisoned, two large bombs. He then proceeded SE and speeded off. I again turned and gave chase and managed to keep him in sight, until I overtook him in about three minutes and took up my position under the starboard mainplane.
>
> My gunner then again proceeded to let him have another short burst which again caused him to turn over my aircraft, but during this evasive manoeuvre my air gunner let him have another short burst from underneath, and as the enemy began to dive he let go one last burst right into his cockpit, which sent him crashing to earth. In all, only 35 rounds were used from each gun.
>
> Although we had a certain amount of difficulty, as the E/A was not illuminated by searchlights, my gunner and I felt pretty convinced that the E/A was a Ju 88. This turned out to be correct, as the Police confirmed later on finding the E/A together with four dead gunners at Bsarming R1775, at 23.40 hrs.

The Ju 88 involved belonged to 3/KG 54 and on a mission to bomb London's docklands. The bomber broke up over Maidstone, and as the Police confirmed, the crew were all killed. Together with the Blenheim, from this point on the Defiant would provide sterling service defending Britain's night skies until the arrival of new and superior aircraft equipped with airborne radar. This, however, was progress – although the night Blitz remained a vexing issue for Air Chief Marshal Dowding.

Another developing issue for Fighter Command's Commander-in-Chief behind the scenes was the growing confidence of the 'Big Wing' supporters. On 17 September 1940, Air Vice-Marshal Leigh-Mallory reported to Fighter Command HQ on the actions fought by his Duxford-based 12 Group wing on 7, 9, 11 and 15 September 1940:

(I) During the first three wing formations, the following main difficulties were experienced:
  (a) The fighters attacking the bombers were unduly interfered with by enemy fighters. This would appear due to the fact that there was not sufficient fighters both to neutralise the enemy fighters and to attack the enemy bombers successfully.
  (b) It was also found that after the wing attack had been delivered, there were many enemy bombers which had become detached and were easy targets, but which could not be attacked because there were no fighters left with sufficient ammunition to carry on the engagement.

(II) As a result, the following conclusions were arrived at:
  (a) For an operation of this type to be really successful, three objects have got to be achieved:
    (i) To neutralise the enemy fighters while the attack on bombers is being made;
    (ii) To break up the bomber formation;
    (iii) To shoot down the bombers after (ii) has been achieved.
  (b) From the size of enemy formations we have met up to the present, it was considered that at least two Spitfire squadrons are required to neutralise the enemy fighters.
  (c) In addition to the two squadrons required to neutralise the fighters, at least three squadrons are required to break up the enemy bomber formations and carry on the main attack on them.
  (d) It was hoped that when the bomber formations had been disintegrated, one of the two squadrons neutralising the fighters might be able to detach itself and shoot down isolated bombers.

In his report on the afternoon action fought on 15 September 1940, Leigh-Mallory stated that the Duxford Wing had been caught at a tactical disadvantage owing to not having been scrambled until 14.30 hrs. This was untrue, the wing's squadrons had actually become airborne from 14.05 hrs onwards.

Nonetheless, on paper the wing had destroyed 105 enemy aircraft, plus forty probables and eighteen damaged, against a balance sheet of six pilots killed or missing, five wounded, and fourteen fighters destroyed. Apparently, therefore, the 12 Group Duxford Wing was performing excellently.

Air Vice-Marshal Strath Evill, Fighter Command's SASO, however, was unconvinced, writing in his covering letter to Dowding:

> The figures of enemy losses claimed … can, in my opinion, be regarded only as approximate.
>
> It will be shown from these figures that the loses inflicted upon the enemy were not increased in relation to the number of fighters engaged on the latter patrols when a large number of squadrons took part. Nevertheless, the losses incurred by the wing were reduced and I am, in any case, of the opinion that the AOC 12 Group is working along the right lines in organising his operations in strength.

The AOC-in-C responded:

> I am sure that L-Mallory is thinking along the right lines, but his figures do not support his theory. More aircraft per squadron were brought down by the entire strength of three squadrons (though few bombers).
>
> Little check is put on the estimate of 310 Squadron, who are exuberant in their claims.
>
> One can generally tell from reading the combat reports what degree of reliability to attach to claims – some of which are more thoughtful wishing.

It is here that Dowding undoubtedly made a grave error of judgement. Leigh-Mallory was not 'thinking along the right lines', but confounding the system by encouraging Squadron Leader Bader to fly free-booting fighter sweeps over 11 Group. If Evill should have acted upon Air Vice-Marshal

Park's previous complaint regarding Leigh-Mallory, then Dowding should have been much more astute at this juncture and taken his errant 12 Group AOC in hand.

Indeed, he would one day say as much. It is unfair, though, that Dowding charged 310 Squadron with exuberant combat claims – when 242 Squadron was by far the worst offender, so much so that this must surely have been obvious – even to a blind man – at the time.

At the Air Ministry, Air Vice-Marshal Douglas, the powerful DCAS, accepted the Big Wing's claims without question, however, and agreed with Leigh-Mallory that the defence of targets should be left to AA fire, while fighters made a concentrated attack, in strength, upon the enemy – if necessary after targets had been bombed. This, now, really was completely contrary to the system and how the battle was being fought – or should have been.

Despite all, Fighter Command had won the Battle for London, by day at least, although much air fighting still lay ahead, and the immediate threat of invasion had now passed. Nonetheless, in the corridors of Whitehall dark political forces were starting to gather – with far-reaching ramifications for both architects of victory, namely Air Chief Marshal Dowding and Air Vice-Marshal Park. It was a sad end and postscript to such a significant phase of the Battle of Britain.

Reflections

At the time, the events of 15 September 1940 were seen by the British as the major turning point in the Battle of Britain, the decisive day forevermore commemorated as 'Battle of Britain Day'. In more recent times, some have argued that other days were harder fought – and as we have seen, on certain previous days more sorties had been flown, more aircraft destroyed or lost, and more pilots killed; indeed, 15 August 1940 had witnessed the defeat of an entire Luftflotte in a single day.

All of that is true, and those days were undoubtedly significant. Then, though, earlier in the Battle, the Luftwaffe was stronger and more able to sustain losses and continue the assault on Britain, victory – owing to woefully inaccurate and inadequate intelligence – only being expected to take a few days of good weather to achieve. The events of 15 September 1940, when hundreds of RAF fighters had twice intercepted the raids on London, however, crushing Luftwaffe aircrews' morale, confirmed that the RAF was far from the defeated force Luftwaffe intelligence believed it to be – and it was then clear to Hitler that the Luftwaffe could neither achieve a decision in short order, or bomb the British into submission any time soon.

Always mindful of what a hazardous undertaking a seaborne invasion was, ultimately 15 September 1940 convinced Hitler that the circumstances necessary for Operation *Seelöwe* had not and would not be achieved. Time had run out. With the advancing autumn weather, unsuitable for such a seaborne operation, and unfavourable future moon and tides, on 17 September 1940 Hitler postponed *Seelöwe* indefinitely. There can be no doubt, then, that 15 September 1940 was indeed a significant day – a significance going far beyond statistics. In summary, 15 September 1940 is fully deserving of its place in history as 'Battle of Britain Day' – and, having failed to eliminate Britain as a base in Western Europe from which war could be waged against Germany, it could even be legitimately argued that on that day, Hitler lost the Second World War.

We have previously considered the relevance of the official start-date of the Battle of Britain – 10 July 1940 – and concluded that if we are to accept that the battle was fought in order for the Germans to achieve the aerial superiority prerequisite for Operation *Seelöwe*, then 2 July 1940, when Hitler agreed to the possibility of invading Britain, must surely be a more appropriate date. We must also consider whether the official end-date of 31 October 1940 is appropriate.

Accepting the reason why the Battle of Britain was fought, because *Seelöwe* was postponed indefinitely on 17 September 1940, thereby eliminating the threat of invasion, it could be robustly argued that the Battle of Britain actually ended on that day. Certainly, the daytime air-fighting continued, and the bombing by night, but those operations were not directly appended to achieving the conditions necessary for an invasion – and that is what the Battle of Britain was really all about.

The Luftwaffe's failure meant that Hitler was denied what had been an unexpected but unique opportunity to invade Britain – although the *Führer*'s indecision over Operation *Seelöwe* and the conduct of the air war in July 1940 had wasted much time and was a contributory factor. For the first time, the Luftwaffe – and Hitler – had suffered a reversal, a loss of face, and Goring's prestige suffered accordingly. Nonetheless, the *Reichsmarschall* still believed that his Luftwaffe alone could defeat Britain, and so now the Battle of Britain entered yet another phase: a return to attacks on Fighter Command installations and aircraft factories.

And so, as the autumn leaves fell, the killing continued …

Acknowledgements

This unique series of books has arisen from over forty years of research and study of the subject, throughout which time I led a privileged relationship with survivors, and the relatives of casualties – too many to thank individually, but all have my appreciation.

In relation to this special project, I must thank Charles Hewitt, Martin Mace and Matthew Potts of Pen & Sword, and the production and marketing teams, who are always a pleasure to work with and collectively do a first-class job. Martin, of course, deserves a special mention for his sterling work on my behalf at The National Archives, and for being a very good friend and kindred spirit.

Suffice it to say, it has been an absolute privilege to produce this work for the Battle of Britain Memorial Trust and National Memorial to The Few, and I must thank our Chairman, Richard Hunting CBE, Honorary Secretary, Group Captain Patrick Tootal OBE DL RAF, Trustee Wing Commander Andrew Simpson RAFVR(T), *Major* (Ret'd) Jules Gomez, Site Manager, National Memorial to The Few, and both Malcolm Triggs and Becca Collier-Cook for their help in promoting 'Battle of Britain: The People's Project'.

As ever, my old friend Andy Long was ever-helpful, and I would also acknowledge kind assistance from Edward McManus of the London Monument; Tony and Trish Osmand; Kate Ashby; Glenn Gelder, Neil Wallington and Dinah Winch, Curator, London Fire Brigade Museum, and Joseph Hill, Curator of The Battle of Britain Bunker, Uxbridge.

Finally, I must reserve a special thanks to my wife, Sue, and all our supportive family and friends.

Bibliography

The National Archives

The National Archives at Kew is the main repository for primary source documents; the following documents were consulted during the course of research for this book.

Operations Record Books

AIR 27/2018: 'A' Flight, 1 Photographic Reconnaissance Unit
AIR 27/2015: 'B' Flight, 1 Photographic Reconnaissance Unit
AIR 27/589: 1 Squadron
AIR 27/528: 1(RCAF) Squadron (Listed as 401 Squadron by TNA)
AIR 27/32: 3 Squadron
AIR 27/164: 12 Squadron
AIR 27/202: 15 Squadron
AIR 27/252: 19 Squadron
AIR 27/287: 23 Squadron
AIR 27: 305: 25 Squadron
AIR 27/317: 26 Squadron
AIR 27/341: 29 Squadron
AIR 27/360: 32 Squadron
AIR 27/441: 43 Squadron
AIR 27/447: 44 Squadron
AIR 27/460: 46 Squadron
AIR 27/554: 50 Squadron
AIR 27/503: 53 Squadron
AIR 27/511: 54 Squadron
AIR 27/528: 56 Squadron
AIR 27/554: 59 Squadron
AIR 27/598: 66 Squadron
AIR 27/624: 72 Squadron
AIR 27/629: 73 Squadron
AIR 27/640: 74 Squadron
AIR 27/655: 77 Squadron
AIR 27/664: 79 Squadron
AIR 27/681: 82 Squadron
AIR 27/712: 87 Squadron
AIR 27/776: 97 Squadron

AIR 27/801: 101 Squadron
AIR 27/807: 102 Squadron
AIR 27/813: 103 Squadron
AIR 27/826: 105 Squadron
AIR 27/841: 107 Squadron
AIR 27/857: 110 Squadron
AIR 27/866: 111 Squadron
AIR 27/882: 114 Squadron
AIR 27/969: 141 Squadron
AIR 27/984: 145 Squadron
AIR 27/1008: 150 Squadron
AIR 27/1025: 152 Squadron
AIR 27/1298: 210 Squadron
AIR 27/1315: 213 Squadron
AIR 27/1340: 217 Squadron
AIR 27/1360: 219 Squadron
AIR 27/1365: 220 Squadron
AIR 27/1371: 222 Squadron
AIR 27/1385: 224 Squadron
AIR 27/1428: 232 Squadron
AIR 27/1442: 235 Squadron
AIR 27/1445: 236 Squadron
AIR 27/1453: 238 Squadron
AIR 27/1471: 242 Squadron
AIR 27/1495: 248 Squadron
AIR 27/1498: 249 Squadron
AIR 27/1511: 253 Squadron
AIR 27/1526: 257 Squadron
AIR 27/1553: 264 Squadron
AIR 27/1558: 266 Squadron
AIR 27/1661: 302 Squadron
AIR 27/1663: 303 Squadron
AIR 27/1680: 310 Squadron
AIR 27/1941: 500 Squadron
AIR 27/1949: 501 Squadron
AIR 27/1964: 504 Squadron
AIR 27/2059: 600 Squadron
AIR 27/2068: 601 Squadron
AIR 27/2028: 604 Squadron
AIR 27/2088: 605 Squadron
AIR 27/2093: 607 Squadron
AIR 27/2102: 609 Squadron
AIR 27/2106: 610 Squadron
AIR 27/2112: 612 Squadron

AIR 27/2123: 615 Squadron
AIR 27/2126: 616 Squadron
AIR 27/2263: 928 Squadron

Pilots' Combat Reports
AIR 50/1: 1 Squadron
AIR 50/4: 3 Squadron
AIR 50/9: 17 Squadron
AIR 50/10: 19 Squadron
AIR 50: 29 Squadron
AIR 50/16: 32 Squadron
AIR 50/18: 41 Squadron
AIR 50/19: 43 Squadron
AIR 50/20: 46 Squadron
AIR 50/21: 54 Squadron
AIR 50/22: 56 Squadron
AIR 50/24: 64 Squadron
AIR 50/25: 65 Squadron
AIR 50/26: 66 Squadron
AIR 50/31: 73 Squadron
AIR 50/32: 74 Squadron
AIR50/33: 79 Squadron
AIR 50/36: 85 Squadron
AIR 50/37: 87 Squadron
AIR 50/40: 92 Squadron
AIR 50/43: 111 Squadron
AIR 50/62: 145 Squadron
AIR 50/63: 151 Squadron
AIR 50/64: 152 Squadron
AIR 50/83: 213 Squadron
AIR 50/84: 219 Squadron
AIR 50/85: 222 Squadron
AIR 50/88: 232 Squadron
AIR 50/89: 234 Squadron
AIR 50/91: 238 Squadron
AIR 50/92: 242 Squadron
AIR 50/96: 249 Squadron
AIR 50/100: 257 Squadron
AIR 50/104: 264 Squadron
AIR 50/105: 266 Squadron
AIR 50/116: 302 Squadron
AIR 50/177: 303 Squadron
AIR 50/122: 310 Squadron
AIR 50/163: 504 Squadron

AIR 50/165: 601 Squadron
AIR 50/166: 602 Squadron
AIR 50/167: 603 Squadron
AIR 50/171: 609 Squadron
AIR 50/173: 611 Squadron
AIR 50/172: 610 Squadron
AIR 50/175: 615 Squadron
AIR 50/176: 616 Squadron

Casualty Files
AIR 81/3230: Wing Commander JS Dewar

Miscellaneous documents
AIR 22/296: Personnel: Casualties, Strength and Establishment of the RAF.

RAF Station Operations Record Books
AIR 28/64: RAF Biggin Hill
AIR 28/178: RAF Croydon
AIR 28/345: RAF Hawkinge
AIR 28/384: RAF Hornchurch
AIR 28/512: RAF Manston
AIR 28/526: RAF Martlesham Heath
AIR 28/419: RAF Kenley
AIR 28/509: RAF Lympne
AIR 28/601: RAF Northolt
AIR 28/815: RAF Tangmere
AIR 28/907: RAF West Malling
AIR 28/603: RAF North Weald

Pilot's Flying Log Books (ranks as at time consulted)
Air Vice-Marshal Sir Keith Park (courtesy RNZAF Museum)
Squadron Leader D.R.S. Bader, 242 Squadron (courtesy RAF Museum)
Squadron Leader R.G. Kellett, 303 Squadron
Flight Lieutenant H.C. Burton, 66 and 616 squadrons
Flight Lieutenant B.J.E. Lane DFC, 19 Squadron (AIR 4/58)
Pilot Officer D. Crowley-Milling, 242 Squadron
Pilot Officer H.S.L. Dundas, 616 Squadron
Pilot Officer D.M.C. Crook DFC, 609 Squadron (AIR 4/21)
Pilot Officer R.L. Jones, 19 and 64 squadrons
Pilot Officer A.G. Osmand, 213 Squadron
Pilot Officer A.F. Vokes, 19 Squadron
Flight Sergeant G.C. Unwin, 19 Squadron
Sergeant B.J. Jennings, 19 Squadron

German Documents

OKW Directives for Invasion of the UK, Operation *Seelöwe*, Summer and Autumn 1940, Bundesarchiv

Luftflotte 2 and 3 records, available via Digital History Archive (see website detailed below)

German fighter combat claims can be found in the OKL records of the *Chef für Ausz. und Dizsiplin Luftwaffe-Personalamt LP(A)V* (available via various online sources)

German loss records can be found in the *Oberfehlsaber der Luftwaffe Genst. Gen. Qu/6 Abteilung/40.g. Kdos.I.C.*, records, preserved by the Imperial War Museum.

Miscellaneous Sources

Interview of Air Chief Marshal Sir Keith Park: BBC Archive/British Library 1 January 1961 http://www.bbc.co.uk/archive/battleofbritain/11422.shtml

Battle of Britain Bunker Oral History Recording, 2 November 2010, Joan Fanshawe (nee Moxon), Ops 'B' WAAF Plotter, 11 Group Operations Room.

Death certificate, *Leutnant* Robert Zhebe.

Unpublished Sources

Correspondence, papers and interviews, Dilip Sarkar Archive.

Original and uncensored manuscript of *Spitfire Pilot*, Flight Lieutenant D.M. Crook DFC.

The Memories and Thoughts of the Late Reverend J.H.K. Dagger, Battle of Britain Padre: RAF Exeter 1940–41. (Courtesy of his son Christopher Dagger).

Unpublished memoir of Group Captain R.G. Kellett.

Published Sources

Ackroyd, P., *London: The Biography*, Chatto & Windus, London, 2000

Adams, P., *Hurricane Squadron: 87 Squadron at War 1939–1941*, Air Research Publications, New Malden, 1988

Aders, G. and Held, W., *Chronik: Jagdgeschwader 51 'Mölders'*, Motor Buch Verlag, Stuttgart, 2009

Addison, P., and Crang, J.A. (eds.), *The Burning Blue: A New History of the Battle of Britain*, Pimlico, London, 2000

Addison, P. and Crang, J.A. (eds.), *Listening to Britain: Home Intelligence Reports on Britain's Finest Hour – May to September 1940*, Vintage Books, London, 2011

Alexander, K., *Australia's Few and the Battle of Britain*, Pen & Sword, Barnsley, 2015

Allen, Wing Commander H.R., *Fighter Squadron: A Memoir 1940–42*, Granada, London, 1982

Anon., *The Battle of Britain: August-October 1940*, Ministry of Information on behalf of the Air Ministry, London, 1941

Anon., *The Battle of Britain*, Air Ministry Pamphlet 156, Issued by the Department of the Air Member for Training, August 1943

Anon., (MoI), *Roof Over Britain: The Official Story of The AA Defences 1939–1942,* HMSO, London, 1943

Anon., *Air/Sea Rescue: The Second World War 1939–1945, Royal Air Force*, Air Publication 3232, Air Ministry (AHB), London, 1952

Anon., *The Rise & Fall of the German Air Force 1939–45*, Air Ministry Pamphlet 248, Public Record Office, London, 2001

Ashworth, C., *RAF Coastal Command: 1936–1969*, PSL, Sparkford, 1992

Bekker, C., *The* Luftwaffe *War Diaries*, Corgi Books, London, 1972

Bekker, C., *Hitler's Naval War*, Corgi, London, 1976

Bialer, U., *The Shadow of the Bomber: The Fear of Air Attack and British Politics 1932–39*, Royal Historical Society, London, 1980

Bishop, E., *The Battle of Britain*, George Allen & Unwin Ltd, London, 1960

Bowyer, M.J.F., *2 Group RAF: A Complete History, 1936–1945*, Faber & Faber, London, 1974

Calder, A., *The People's War: Britain 1939–45*, Pimlico, London, 2008

Caldwell, D., JG26: *Top Guns of the Luftwaffe*, Orion Books, New York, 1991

Caldwell, D., *The JG26 War Diary: Volume One, 1939–42*, Grub Street, London, 1996

Campion, G., *The Good Fight: Battle of Britain Propaganda and The Few*, Palgrave-Macmillan, London, 2010

Cannandine, D. (ed.), *The Speeches of Winston Churchill*, Penguin, London, 1990

Churchill, W.S., *The Second World War, Vol II, Their Finest Hour*, Cassell & Co, London, 1949

Clapson, M., *Britain in the Twentieth Century*, Routledge, Abingdon, 2009

Clausewitz, Carl von, *Principles of War*, Dover Publications Inc, New York, 2003

Collier, B., *The Defence of the United Kingdom*, HMSO, London, 1957

Cox, S. and Probert, H., (eds.), *The Battle Re-Thought: A Symposium on the Battle of Britain*, Airlife, Shrewsbury, 1991

Cox, S., 'RAF & Luftwaffe Intelligence Compared' in Handel, MI (ed.), *Intelligence & Military Operations*, Frank Cass, Abingdon, 1990

Dean, Sir Maurice, *The Royal Air Force in Two World Wars*, Cassell, London, 1979

Deere, Air Commodore A.C., *Nine Lives*, Hodder Paperback Ltd, London, 1959

Deighton, L., *Fighter: The True Story of the Battle of Britain*, Triad/Panther Books, St Albans, 1979

Dierich, W., *Kampfgeschwader 'Edelweiss': The History of a German Bomber Unit, 1939–45*, Purnell Book Services Ltd, London, 1975

Dierich, W., *Chronik: Kampfgeschwader 55 'Greif'*, Motorbuch Verlag, Stuttgart, 2012

Deighton, L., *Fighter: The True Story of the Battle of Britain*, Triad/Panther Books Ltd, St Albans, 1979

Donnelly, M., *Britain in the Second World War*, Routledge, London, 1999

Donnelly, L., *The Other Few: The Contribution Made by Bomber and Coastal Aircrew to the Winning of the Battle of Britain*, Red Kite, Walton-on-Thames, 2004

Dowding, ACM Lord H.C.T., *Dispatch: The Battle of Britain, The London Gazette*, London, 1946

Ellan, Squadron Leader B.J., *Spitfire! The Experiences of a Fighter Pilot*, John Murray, London, 1942

Fleming, P., *Invasion 1940*, Rupert Hard-Davis, London, 1957

Foreman, J., *RAF Fighter Command Victory Claims of World War Two, Volume One*, Air Research Publications, Red Kite, Walton-on-Thames, 2003
Forrester, L., *Fly For Your Life: The Story of R.R. Stanford Tuck DSO, DFC and Two Bars*, The Companion Book Club, London, 1956
Galland, A., *The First and the Last: Germany's Fighter Force* in the Second World War, Fontana, London, 1954
Gleave, Group Captain T.P. (writing as 'RAF Casualty'), *I Had a Row with a German*, MacMillan & Co., London, 1941
Gleed, Wing Commander I.R., *Arise to Conquer*, Victor Gollanz Ltd, London, 1942
Green, W., *Aircraft of the Battle of Britain*, MacDonald & Co. (Publishers) Ltd and Pan Books Ltd, London, 1969
Hallam, I.N., *One of The Few: Ian Lewis McGregor Hallam*, privately published, 2020
Handel, M.I. (ed.), *Intelligence and Military Operations*, Frank Cass, Abingdon, 1990
Hough, R., and Richards, D., *The Battle of Britain: The Jubilee History*, Hodder & Stoughton Ltd, London, 1990
Humphreys, R., *Dover at War 1939–1945*, Alan Sutton, Stroud, 1993
James, T.C.G., *The Battle of Britain*, Frank Cass, London, 1990
Jenkins, R., *Churchill*, MacMillan, London 2001
Johnson, AVM J.E., *Wing Leader*, Chatto & Windus Ltd, London, 1956
Johnstone, AVM A.V.R., *Spitfire into War*, William Kimber & Co Ltd, London, 1986
Jones, Wing Commander I., *Tiger Squadron*, Award Books, New York, 1966
Kesselring, Field-Marshal A., *The Memoirs of Field-Marshal Kesselring*, Greenhill Books, London, 1997
Kershaw, I., *Hitler: 1936–1945, Nemesis*, Penguin, London, 2001
King, R., *303 Squadron: Battle of Britain Diary*, Red Kite, Walton-on-Thames, 2010
Kingcome, Group Captain B.F., *A Willingness to Die: Memories from Fighter Command*, Tempus Publishing, Stroud, 1996
Legg, R., *Battle of Britain Dorset*, Dorset Publishing Company, Wincanton, 1995
Lisiewicz, Squadron Leader M. (ed.), *Destiny Can Wait: The Polish Air Force in the Second World War*, William Heinemann Ltd, London, 1949
MacDonell, Air Commodore A.R.D. (MacDonell, L. and MacKay, A., eds.), *From Dogfight to Diplomacy: A Spitfire Pilot's Log 1932–1958*, Pen & Sword, Barnsley, 2005
MacMillan wrote in his 1967 memoir *The Blast of War 1939–1945*, MacMillan, London, 1967
Mason, F.K., *Battle Over Britain*, Aston Publications, Bourne End, 1990
Middlebrook, M. and Everitt, C., *The Bomber Command War Diaries: An Operational Reference Book 1939–1945*, Midland Counties Publications, Hinckley, 1996
Morgan, E. and Shacklady, E., *Spitfire: The History*, Key Publishing, Stamford, 1987
Moyes, P.J.R., *Bomber Squadrons of the RAF And Their Aircraft*, MacDonald, London, 1964
Muggeridge, M. (ed.), *Ciano's Diary 1939–1943*, William Heinemann Ltd, London, 1947
Orange, V., *Park: The Biography of Air Chief Marshal Sir Keith Park*, Grub Street, London, 2001

Orange, V., *Dowding of Fighter Command: Victor of the Battle of Britain*, Grubb Street, London, 2008

Overy, R., *The Air War 1939–1945*, first edition, Europa Publications Ltd, London, 1980

Overy, R., *The Battle of Britain*, Penguin, London, 2004

Overy, R., *Goering: The Iron Man*, Bloomsbury Revelations, London, 2021

Pope, R., *War & Society in Britain 1899–1948*, Longman, Harlow, 1991

Price, A., *Battle of Britain Day: 15 September 1940*, Sidgwick & Jackson, London, 1990

Prien, J., *Jagdgeschwader 53: A History of the 'Pik As' Geschwader, March 1937-May 1942*, Schiffer Publishing Ltd, Sedona, Arizona, USA, 1997

Priestley, J.B., *Postscripts*, William Heinemann Ltd, London, 1940

Quill, J.K., *Spitfire*, Arrow Books, London 1985

Ramsay, W. (ed.), *The Battle of Britain: Then & Now, Mk V Edition*, Battle of Britain Prints International Ltd, London, 1986

Ramsay, W. (ed.), *The Blitz Then & Now, Volume I*, Battle of Britain Prints International Ltd, London, 1989

Rayner, G.H., *One Hurricane: One Raid*, Airlife Publishing Ltd, Shrewsbury, 1990

Richards, D., *RAF Bomber Command in the Second World War: The Hardest Victory*, Penguin, London, 2001

R.A.F.H.S., *Air Intelligence: A Symposium*, RAFHS, London, 1997

Rootes, A., *Front Line County: Kent at War, 1939–45*, Robert Hale Ltd, London, 1980

Roskill, Captain S.W., *The War at Sea 1939–45, Volume 1*, HMSO, London, 1954

Rohwer, J. and G. Hunnelchen, *Chronology of the War at Sea*, Ian Allen Ltd, London, 1972

Russell, B,. *Which Way to Peace?*, M Joseph Ltd, London, 1936

Sarkar, D., *Missing in Action: Resting in Peace?*, Ramrod Publications, Worcester, 1998

Sarkar, D., *The Final Few*, Amberley Publishing, Stroud, 2015

Sarkar, D., *Letters from The Few: Unique Memories From the Battle of Britain*, Pen & Sword Ltd, Barnsley, 2020

Sarkar, D., *Battle of Britain 1940: The Finest Hour's Human Cost*, Pen & Sword Ltd, Barnsley, 2020

Sarkar, D., *Sailor Malan: Freedom Fighter*, Pen & Sword Ltd, Barnsley, 2021

Sarkar, D., *Forgotten Heroes of the Battle of Britain*, Pen & Sword Ltd, Barnsley, 2022

Schenk, P., *Operation Sealion: The Invasion of England*, Greenhill Books, Barnsley, 2019

Shirer, W.L., *The Rise and Fall of the Third Reich*, Simon & Schuster, New York, 1960

Shores, C. and Williams, C., *Aces High: A Tribute to the Most Notable Fighter Pilots of the British & Commonwealth Forces in WWII*, Grub Street, London, 1994

Smith, M., The RAF. In Addison, J. and Crang, J.A. (eds.), *The Burning Blue: A New History of the Battle of Britain*, Pimlico, London, 2000

Spurdle, B., *The Blue Arena*, William Kimber & Co., London, 1986

Steinhilper, U. and Osborne, P., *Spitfire on my Tail: A View From the Other Side*, Independent Books, Bromley, 1989

Taylor, A.J.P., *English History 1914–1945*, Oxford University Press, Oxford, 1965

Titmuss, Professor R.M., *Problems of Social Policy*, HMSO, London, 1950

Toliver, Colonel R.F. and Constable, T.J., *Fighter Aces of the* Luftwaffe, Schiffer Publishing Ltd, Atglen, PA, 1996

Townsend, Group Captain P., *Time & Chance: An Autobiography*, Collins, London, 1978

Townsend, Group Captain P., *Duel of Eagles: The Classic Account of the Battle of Britain*, Weidenfeld & Nicolson, London, 1990

Trevor-Roper, H.R. (ed.), *Hitler's War Directives 1939–45*, Pan Books, London, 1966

Vasco, J.J. and Cornwell, P.D., Zerstörer: *The* Messerschmitt *110 and its Units in 1940*, JAC Publications, Norwich, 1995

Vasco, J., *Bombsights Over England: The History of* Erprobungsgruppe *210* Luftwaffe *Fighter-Bomber Unit in the Battle of Britain*, JAC Publications, Norwich, 1990

Wakefield, K., *The First Pathfinders: The Operational History of* Kampfgruppe *100, 1939–1941*, Crécy Books, Somerton, 1992

Wallington, N., *Firemen at War: The Work of London's Fire-Fighters in the Second World War*, David & Charles, London, 1981

Warner, G., *RAF Biggin Hill: The immortal story of one of the Battle of Britain's most famous fighter stations*, Putnam & Co Ltd, London, 1969

Wellum, Squadron Leader G.H.A., *First Light*, Penguin, London, 2003

Wicks, B., *Waiting For The All Clear: True Stories From Survivors of The Blitz*, Bloombury, London, 1990

Willis, J., *Churchill's Few: The Battle of Britain Remembered*, Guild Publishing, London, 1985

Wheatley, R., *Operation Sealion*, Oxford University Press, Oxford, 1958

Wright, R., *Dowding and the Battle of Britain*, Corgi, London, 1970

Ziegler, F.H., *The Story of 609 Squadron: Under the White Rose*, MacDonald, London, 1971

Ziegler, P., *London at War 1939–1945*, Pimlico, London, 1995

Websites

The National Archives: www.nationalarchives.gov.uk
Commonwealth War Graves Commission: www.cwgc.org
Battle of Britain Memorial Trust: www.battleofbritainmemorial.org
Battle of Britain: The People's Project: www.battleofbritainthepeoplesproject.com
Dilip Sarkar: www.dilipsarkarauthor.com
Digital History Archive: www.digitalhistoryarchive.com
Kenley Revival Project: www.kenleyrevival.org
Battle of Britain London Monument: www.bbm.org.uk

Films

Battle of Britain, directed by Guy Hamilton (Spitfire Productions, 1969).

Television

The World at War, directed by David Elstein (ITV, 1973).
First Light, directed by Matthew Whiteman (Lion Television, 2010).

Other Books by Dilip Sarkar

Spitfire Squadron: No.19 Squadron at War, 1939–41
The Invisible Thread: A Spitfire's Tale
Through Peril to the Stars: RAF Fighter Pilots Who Failed to Return, 1939–45
Angriff *Westland: Three Battle of Britain Air Raids Through the Looking Glass*
A Few of the Many: Air War 1939–45, A Kaleidoscope of Memories
Bader's Tangmere Spitfires: The Untold Story, 1941
Bader's Duxford Fighters: The Big Wing Controversy
Missing in Action: Resting in Peace?
Guards VC: Blitzkrieg 1940
Battle of Britain: The Photographic Kaleidoscope, Volumes I–IV
Fighter Pilot: The Photographic Kaleidoscope
Group Captain Sir Douglas Bader: An Inspiration in Photographs
Johnnie Johnson: Spitfire Top Gun, Part I
Johnnie Johnson: Spitfire Top Gun, Part II
Battle of Britain: Last Look Back
Spitfire! Courage & Sacrifice
Spitfire Voices: Heroes Remember
The Battle of Powick Bridge: Ambush a Fore-thought
Duxford 1940: A Battle of Britain Base at War
The Few: The Battle of Britain in the Words of the Pilots
Spitfire Manual 1940
The Sinking of HMS Royal Oak *in the Words of the Survivors* (re-print of Hearts of Oak)
The Last of the Few: Eighteen Battle of Britain Pilots Tell Their Extraordinary Stories
Hearts of Oak: The Human Tragedy of HMS Royal Oak
Spitfire Voices: Life as a Spitfire Pilot in the Words of the Veterans
How the Spitfire Won the Battle of Britain
Spitfire Ace of Aces: The True Wartime Story of Johnnie Johnson
Douglas Bader
Fighter Ace: The Extraordinary Life of Douglas Bader, Battle of Britain Hero (re-print of above)
Spitfire: The Photographic Biography
Hurricane Manual 1940
River Pike
The Final Few: The Last Surviving Pilots of the Battle of Britain Tell Their Stories
Arnhem 1944: The Human Tragedy of the Bridge Too Far

Spitfire! The Full Story of a Unique Battle of Britain Fighter Squadron
Battle of Britain 1940: The Finest Hour's Human Cost
Letters from The Few: Unique Memories of the Battle of Britain
Johnnie Johnson's 1942 Diary: The War Diary of the Spitfire Ace of Aces
Johnnie Johnson's Great Adventure: The Spitfire Ace of Ace's Last Look Back
Sailor Malan – Freedom Fighter: The Inspirational Story of a Spitfire Ace
Spitfire Ace of Aces – The Album: The Photographs of Johnnie Johnson
The Real Spitfire Pilot, being the previously unpublished original manuscript of *Spitfire Pilot,* by Flight Lieutenant David Crook, with introduction, commentary and photographs by Dilip Sarkar
Bader's Big Wing Controversy: Duxford 1940
Bader's Spitfire Wing: Tangmere 1941
Spitfire Down: Fighter Boys Who Failed to Return
Forgotten Heroes of The Battle of Britain
Faces of The Few
Spitfire Faces
Arise to Conquer: The Real Hurricane Pilot by Wing Commander Ian Gleed, introduction, commentary and photographs by Dilip Sarkar
Free French Spitfire Hero: The Diaries of and Search for René Mouchotte (with Jan Leeming)
I Had A Row with a German by Group Captain Tom Gleave, introduction by Dilip Sarkar
Battle of Britain: The Finest Hour in Cinema
Battle of Britain: The Movie (contributor to and publisher of the now late Robert Rudhall's original edition (2000), and editor and substantial contributor to 2022 revised edition)
Faces of HMS Royal Oak: *The 'Mighty Oak' Disaster at Scapa Flow*
Battle of Britain Volume 1: The Gathering Storm – Prelude to the Spitfire Summer of 1940
Battle of Britain Volume 2: The Breaking Storm – 10 July 1940–12 August 1940
Battle of Britain Volume 3: Attack of the Eagles – 13 August 1940–18 August 1940
Battle of Britain Volume 4: Airfields Under Attack – 19 August 1940–6 September 1940

Index